MBA PREFERRED™

MBA PREFERRED™

Celebrating 50 Years

PROFILES OF DISTINGUISHED MBA ALUMNI

Oklahoma State University

JERETTA HORN NORD
LAWRENCE A. CROSBY

Additional copies of this book may be ordered online:

www.amazon.com or
www.barnesandnoble.com

Jeretta Horn Nord
Professor of Management Science and Information Systems
Oklahoma State University
jeretta.nord@okstate.edu
405-744-5091
Founder and CEO, Entrepreneur Enterprises LLC
jeretta@acupofcappuccino.com
405-747-0320

CONTENTS

CHAPTER TEN: THE LEADER WITHIN

To all Oklahoma State University MBA Alumni
and Future MBA Alumni

PREFACE

It was 1966 and I was a junior in high school in Michigan when I first heard about the MBA degree. My father was an automobile industry executive who had never attended college himself but wanted the best for his son. He was very impressed by Robert McNamara, one of 10 former World War II officers who joined Ford and were known as the "Whiz Kids." McNamara became the first non-family member president of Ford in 1960, and is credited with turning the company around by implementing modern management systems (he went on to be Secretary of Defense under both Kennedy and Johnson). McNamara held an MBA from the Harvard Business School (1939), which my father believed was the key to his success.

The other part of the "equation for success" at the time, especially in Detroit, was to have an undergraduate degree in engineering and a few years of technical work experience, before going back to school for the MBA. This combination was believed to provide a sure-fire path to the top and the keys to the corner office.

While I eventually found my way to the MBA (and a PhD), it was not by the linear route my father had prescribed . . . actually it was psychology and marketing that got me there! Nevertheless, the MBA degree remained a potent tool for my generation of "baby boomers" as we struggled to differentiate ourselves amid the hordes of like-minded, upwardly mobile young people.

My rationale for relaying this background is to suggest three pillars that have sustained the popularity of the MBA over the 100+ years of its existence. One is the opportunity these programs offer to gain insight regarding state-of-the-art management principles and practices that would be difficult (albeit not impossible) to obtain via the "school of hard knocks." It's about the acceleration of learning. Another pillar is the chance the MBA provides to turn any prior degree or work experience into a more valuable asset. It has enabled engineers to become managers of engineers (and in some cases CEO's), doctors to become health system administrators, musicians to own record companies, and so forth. And finally, the MBA has served as a point of distinction for those seeking to manage their own "personal brand."

As we celebrate the 50th Anniversary of the MBA at Oklahoma State University, we see among our alumni the career-transforming impact of the degree in these and other ways.

From an artist to a freelance graphic designer to an MBA alumnus to CEO of The Charles Machine Works, Inc., Tiffany Sewell-Howard is the top executive of the manufacturer of Ditch Witch underground construction equipment and will serve as the first woman chair of the Association of Equipment Manufacturers.

From small town farm boy to an MBA alumnus to co-founder and CEO of Cerner, Neal Patterson has nurtured his company's growth to what is now the largest stand-alone supplier of healthcare information technology in the world with healthcare clients in 25 countries on six continents and nearly 8,000 associates worldwide. Also co-owner of FiveStar Lifestyles, a real estate development and country club management group of enterprises, Neal and a partner had the opportunity to purchase the Kansas City Wizards Major League Soccer team in 2006.

From living next door to aspiring gang members to an undergraduate degree in engineering and an inventor to an MBA alumnus, Paul De La Cerda owns a firm, De La Cerda & Associates that focuses on public and government relations, marketing and business development, and access to capital for small to medium-sized businesses.

From a member of the Marine Corps to an MBA alumnus to Exxon USA to a unique sailing circumnavigation excursion, Roger Cagle has recently co-founded SOCO International PLC, a London based company currently trading at a market cap of around $1.9 billion.

From MBA to PhD to Professor to CIO and VP for IT, Brad Wheeler took the helm of Indiana University's $125M IT budget and 1,000-person staff.

From Ethiopia to a mechanical engineer in the aviation industry to MBA alumnus, Dag Yemenu is now a director on the management team of ISNetworld, and has recently moved to Europe to oversee their London operations.

From a civil engineering undergraduate major to an MBA alumnus to Senior Vice-President of Integrated Marketing at MTV, Angela Courtin has been recognized as one of the most amazing women in showbiz and has been a guest lecturer at Harvard Business School and the USC School of Media Studies.

From being told that economic trade was selected as her field by the Albanian government to receiving a Fulbright scholarship to earning an MBA, Monica Mamica Mezezi-Pino co-founded genX International IVFonline, LLC and LifeGlobal. Her primary focus is to bring the most advanced technologies, products, and services to the market to help improve embryo and cell culture.

Against many examples of success, the MBA degree (in general) is not without its critics. They point to how ambitious MBA's seem to have undermined the core of Arthur Andersen and Enron. Fingers are pointed at MBA's for unethical behavior and the recent Wall Street meltdown. Others belittle the degree for its graduates being "a dime a dozen" due to its proliferation and the inroads of heavily marketed for-profit programs. Still others contend that, with fewer opportunities in big business today, training in entrepreneurship provides a better way to leverage one's passions into a career or a start-up company.

While these criticisms of the MBA degree probably contain at least a kernel of truth, reports of its imminent demise are greatly exaggerated (as they say). In fact, the MBA has proven remarkably adaptable and resilient through the years, and I'm happy to say that the OSU MBA has kept pace with many of these changes! For example, we complement education in the analytical aspects of business with development of those "soft skills" (like communication, leadership, and judgment) that are so important in highly dynamic environments. This is aided by a shift toward more experiential learning. Business ethics is a theme throughout the students' coursework, and we endeavor to help them identify ethical choice situations. We've worked to ensure that our programs retain the highest level of academic accreditation (since 1958, fully accredited by the Association to Advance Collegiate Schools of Business or AACSB). For MBA's who see themselves more in entrepreneurial roles and creating new businesses, the opportunity exists to take anywhere from a single course to a specialization in entrepreneurship. And I could go on. My point is that the MBA isn't static but continues to evolve, and by doing so, continues to provide a positive ROI for those who invest in this form of graduate management education.

When we look out over the pool of nearly 3,000 OSU MBA alumni, a number that is dramatically accelerating, we see many examples of that positive ROI. Contained in this book are just 50 of those many examples of success, but they typify what our graduates have been able to achieve. Through their hard work and adept application of what they learned in the classroom, they've created value for their families, local communities, Oklahoma, the United States, and people around the world. They've made a difference.

Of course, the administration, faculty, and staff that have shepherded this program through its first 50 years deserve considerable credit. The stories of some of those who also hold an OSU MBA are also contained in the pages that follow. Still, there are countless others who also provided the content, advice, mentoring, inspiration, and support that helped enable the types of success we read about in this book.

As a relatively new dean (starting in the spring, 2010), I can take credit for none of this! But what I can do is try to ensure that the forward momentum of the OSU MBA degree is maintained while not neglecting those roots which account for the past and current achievements. If we think about the MBA from a systems perspective (input-process-output-feedback), it is easy to grasp the "process" and "output" elements. In terms of process, we might think about the curriculum, quality and methods of instruction, growth opportunities outside the classroom, etc. In terms of output, we might think about the skills of our graduates, their starting salaries, their career and life accomplishments, etc. Clearly, if we want to improve our output metrics, we need to be creative and innovative around process.

We already have innovations for the MBA "in the oven" as it were, with more entering the pipeline soon. The areas of focus tend to follow the school's strategic plan with a heavy emphasis on student engagement (with student organizations, community not-for-profits, real companies with real opportunities and challenges, nascent start-ups, societal issues such as sustainability and healthcare, economies in the developing world, etc.). Through these experiences, MBA students will feel increasingly challenged, inspired, driven to explore, supported, and transformed. Programmatically, we foresee greater use of graduate certificates as a stepping stone to the MBA or as additional credentialing on top of the MBA. Through MBA updates, we'll provide a way to keep the degree current and we'll open the door to a new degree option beyond the MBA, the executive PhD.

While the process elements of graduate education are no doubt key drivers of future success, they only provide a partial explanation. Equally important are the "input" and "feedback" elements. Some would argue that the hallmark of the top-rated MBA programs in the country/world is neither their faculty nor their money; it's the quality of their input, i.e., the applicants and entering students, typically measured by admission rates, undergraduate GPA's, and test scores. And these are the factors which the rating services pay attention to! While I don't totally discount these metrics, and we do pay some attention to them, I believe they miss the mark in one very important way . . . they say nothing about the incoming students' values and integrity. We are very fortunate at Oklahoma State that our input comes to us already programmed with "the right stuff". I believe this explains, to a large extent, the OSU MBA success stories documented here and yet to be reported. Based on research we've conducted over the past year as part of our visioning effort, we've identified a set of shared values among students, alumni, faculty, and staff. In a nutshell:

We at the Spears School dream big and pursue our passions. We expand our horizons, stretch, and reach our potential. We work hard and expect our hard work to pay off. We strive to always do the right thing. We know that success depends on working together and the support of our community. We explore and constantly move forward through creativity and innovation. We use our resources efficiently and effectively. We transform the environment and the lives we touch. We make a difference.

It is important that we continue to select for these values even as we cast a much wider net for MBA applicants, well past the borders of Oklahoma. It is likewise important that we endeavor to live these values every day and recognize shining examples, as this book attempts to do. These values are part of our DNA, what defines us, what makes us unique. MBA's who practice this code will not bring down an Enron or trigger the collapse of the financial markets.

The other element that is frequently overlooked is the notion of feed-back. This is an area where I think we could do much better, particularly as we plot a future course for the MBA at OSU. To this end, we are using the occasion of the 50th Anniversary of the MBA to establish much closer relationships with our alumni base by practicing what we preach, i.e., customer relationship management. This effort will involve more effective use of databases, social networking, events, an alumni speakers' bureau, and electronic newsletters, as well as more effective use of an MBA advisory board. That said, it's also the case that relationships are a two-way-street. So we will be encouraging our MBA alumni to become more deeply engaged with the School and to keep their contact information up-to-date so that we can maintain a dialogue.

These are exciting and dynamic times at OSU, in the Spears School, and in the MBA program. We have a lot to be proud of, and we are particularly proud of the 50 MBA graduates profiled in this book and the other 2,950 or so who have passed through our halls in the last fifty years. We will continue to strive for excellence, respect, and recognition as we pursue our noble purpose.

Through our values, we inspire and engage the student in everyone to dream big, stretch their leadership potential, transform organizations, and make a difference in the world.

Go Pokes!

Larry Crosby
Dean, Spears School of Business
April, 2011

INTRODUCTION

The Master of Business Administration (MBA) is among the most coveted of graduate degrees and one that signifies management and leadership training. Oklahoma State University's MBA program graduated its first student in 1961, and 2011 marks the 50th anniversary. As a part of this celebration, we decided to publish stories of 50 top graduates since the inception of the MBA program at OSU ('50 of 50'). The publication of these stories is intended to honor and recognize the successful MBA alumni featured and to inspire, educate, and empower future MBA graduates and others for years to come.

Stories are *powerful* and touch us both emotionally and intellectually having a much greater impact than when ideas are explained only through logic and analysis. Those who fail to understand and embrace the high correlation between motivation and success *and* the power of stories risk failure. Research has shown that we learn more from stories and remember what we have been told longer than through other methods of knowledge transfer because the narrative structure of stories mirrors our thought patterns. We are inspired, educated, and empowered not only from reading about others successes but also their adversities and challenges. The stories included in this book are filled with wisdom based on life experiences of passion, perseverance, integrity, networking, and hard work.

The title of the book, *MBA Preferred*, is representative of job ads for desirable positions indicating the preference for an individual with an MBA degree (*MBA preferred*). Over 125 MBA alumni were nominated for consideration as one of these 50. Each of the nominees was interviewed by a current MBA student as part of a class assignment. For consistency, students were provided with specific questions to ask during the interviews. Following the interviews, the MBA students wrote the stories of these distinguished alumni including life experiences, successes and words of advice. Many of the alumni disclosed adversities they experienced during their lives and careers, and those were included as well. (Names of all nominated MBA alumni and MBA student interviewers are listed at the end of this book.)

Each of the stories was read with interest and edited before beginning the difficult process of narrowing this incredible group of more than 125 successful alumni down to 50. Following much discussion, the final 50 were named. Each story includes the alumnus' name and a *contributed by* notation with the name of the MBA student who conducted the interview. Stories selected for publication include the first male and female graduates of the MBA program, extraordinary entrepreneurs, athletes, bankers, administrators, professors, individuals in the corporate world, young alumni who are on the fast track to success, and others. Separate chapters divide the stories into groups and inspirational quotes separate each story. In many cases, the quotes were taken directly from the stories and credited to the alumnus.

Chapter Three—*Forever Orange* recognizes OSU MBA graduates who either stayed or returned to OSU, making an impact on the program and a difference in the lives of our students. This brings the total to 58 MBA graduates who are being honored and whose stories are published in this book. The individuals from OSU who were nominated and interviewed include Spears School of Business faculty and staff and the Vice-President for Administration and Finance for the Oklahoma State University—Tulsa campus.

Student responses were very positive to this project, which allowed them to reach out to those in the real world and connect with successful graduates with the same degree they are pursuing. Knowing the potential for publication of their stories added additional incentive. Although the alumni were extremely busy, they were gracious enough to take time to be interviewed and to interact with the students, and many were excited to give back by sharing their experiences and offering advice to OSU's future MBA alumni.

Students quickly noticed the benefits of their interviews, which included learning from the alumni, networking, and establishing new relationships. From this experience, students gained knowledge, mentors, referrals, and even job offers. Following are a few of the students' comments regarding this initiative:

This was a great learning and networking opportunity.

I loved every moment of our interview, so the primary benefit was the smile it put on my face. However, talking to her also showed me the importance of being open to change and following what you want.

He was extremely professional, courteous, and experienced. He had some amazing stories and was a successful and qualified professional.

I believe talking to the MBA alumnus was a priceless experience. My interviewee had several life experiences that I learned from and will use as I begin my career. He taught me three keys to success and how I can improve through self-determination and mentors.

This was a wonderful assignment and I look forward to a long-lasting relationship with the person I interviewed.

She has tenacity and a drive about her. She truly believes she can accomplish anything. She was very fun to talk to, and I've learned so much just from talking to her about her experiences.

After this interview, I know that someone from OSU who works hard and fights for every inch can truly make a difference in the world and accomplish anything.

I learned many life and work lessons. It was one of the most incredibly worthwhile assignments of all my time in school.

His fortitude and perseverance, as well as work ethic and dedication, make him a role model to many.

She made the point that even when odds are against you, as they were when she entered the male-dominated industry of finance, confidence and determination will enable you to come out on top.

I will remember this interview for the rest of my life.

I continue to be inspired, educated, and empowered by the stories of successful individuals such as those who are featured in this book. I trust that each of you who read this book will gain as much as the students and I have from the knowledge transferred through these stories.

Jeretta Horn Nord, Professor
Management Science and Information Systems

ACKNOWLEDGMENTS

Sincere appreciation is extended to the following:

Oklahoma State University MBA alumni for sharing their stories which will inspire, educate, and empower others.

Oklahoma State University MBA students enrolled in MSIS 5623 who interviewed MBA alumni and were truly engaged in the process.

Dr. Larry Crosby, Dean of the Spears School of Business, for providing leadership that incorporates expertise from experience in both academics and business, and for adding value to all through encouraging relationships with our alumni and other external constituents.

Dr. Rick Wilson, Department Head of Management Science and Information Systems, for leading the department in a positive manner and for encouraging faculty to follow their passion and excel in their own way.

Dr. Robert Dooley, Associate Dean for Graduate Programs and MBA Director, and Dr. Julie Weathers, Director of the Center for Executive and Professional Development, for their support, guidance, and advice as steering committee chairs for the MBA 50th Anniversary Celebration.

Dr. Bob Hamm, Professor Emeritus, who had the vision of featuring distinguished MBA alumni in a book.

The following members of the MBA Steering and Alumni Committees who have worked diligently in the planning and execution of the MBA 50th Anniversary Celebration.

Steering Committee Chairs:
    Robert Dooley
    Julie Weathers

Steering Committee Members:
- Jan Analla
- Kevin Cates
- Shelby Clanahan
- Larry Crosby
- Shona Gambrell
- Bob Hamm
- Joe Haney
- James Hromas
- Ruth Inman
- José Sagarnaga

Alumni Committee:
- Danielle Hollingsworth
- Dan Howard
- Joe Kreger
- Roger Lumley
- Julie Polk
- Andrew Solheim
- Nichole Bostian Trantham
- Bruce Yee

MBA Graduate Assistant:
- Sarah Summers

Frances Griffin, Bev Dunham, and Deborah Cooper for their excellence in editing and proofing and for working hard to meet demanding deadlines.

Alison Hargis and Erin Marcom, MBA students and graduate assistants, for their assistance throughout the process of creating this book.

Jan Analla, Assistant Director of the MBA Program, Lori O'Malley, Deborah Cooper, and Pam Moore who are responsible for the MBA program implementation and strive for excellence as they interact with the MBA students and faculty on a daily basis.

Julie Weathers, Shona Gambrell, Alvina Shearer, Jami Spiva, Debi Gaddy, and Simon Ringsmuth for making it possible for students around the world to earn an OSU MBA online through the distance learning program.

Deans, program directors, faculty, and staff over the past 50 years who have been instrumental in making the MBA program what it is today.

Families and friends who have provided their support, for without them, life would not be complete.

CHAPTER ONE
SETTING THE STANDARDS

The first male and female OSU MBA graduates are featured in this chapter. When you read their stories, you will agree that they set the bar high for future graduates.

Throughout the centuries there were men who took first steps, down new roads, armed with nothing but their own vision.

—Ayn Rand

PLAY TO YOUR STRENGTHS

Larry Ferree— "So, Larry, how would you like to be the first graduate of Oklahoma State's MBA program?" The question seemed so big, life-changing, and full of promise. How could I refuse?!

In actuality, it was so surprising to me that I could scarcely believe it. You see, I came from a modest background, born and raised in Oklahoma City in a family in which I was the first college student. Of course, we did see the necessity of education in light of the continually expanding economy of the 1950s. Following my graduation from Classen High School, I decided to attend college at Oklahoma State for my undergraduate degree. While I was there, my life went through many transitions as I considered my career path.

"What direction should I take?" was a recurring question. During those undergrad years, I became acquainted with the field of human resources; it was actually called personnel management at the time. Edward Burris, the Vice Dean of the business school was hugely influential in my developing a passion for this field. Under his advisement, I began expanding my coursework in this topic and was even offered opportunities to lecture in classes.

Yet, how was I to put this interest to use? Well, my progress through that decision took a number of directions. The first was the military. After completing the two-year compulsory ROTC, I volunteered for the advanced ROTC program with the Air Force. I failed an eye exam for pilot training, during my junior year, which was a big disappointment to me, and for that reason I dropped out of school and the ROTC to join the Air Force Reserves for a six-month tour of duty. My eyesight had eliminated aviation as a career choice, but the six-month reserve tour enabled me to satisfy my military obligation and return to finish my degree.

In January, 1958, I returned to school and in August I married my college sweetheart, Suzy. Oh, what a great time that was! One of my favorite things about my time at OSU was being a married student. There were many other young couples to build relationships with. I continued with class and working part-time at the library, while Suzy taught kindergarten at the local First Christian Church. Many of the friendships made during that time have lasted to this day.

Then my undergraduate program approached its close and I was again confronted with the question of what to do. Fortunately I was surrounded by wise counselors. It was actually Dr. Romans, Head of the Management Department, who posed that huge question to me: "Why not get an MBA?" Pursuing that venture seemed like a good choice. The interviews that I'd had with companies during my senior year seemed bleak and unpromising, making it clear to me that gaining an MBA would provide more opportunities for placement and advancement. OSU had just begun such a program, and if accepted, I would actually be the first to graduate from it. As I had grown to love the city, campus, and people, the direction I should take seemed obvious.

So, in the fall of 1959, I began my study in Oklahoma State's MBA program. The same aspects that I loved from my undergrad years continued into that year and a half. Suzy continued teaching while I spent my days in study and research. Surprisingly, I actually had my best grades while in the MBA program. This may have been partly due to the new structure of the coursework. No longer was I just reading texts and listening to lectures. The curriculum was more driven by projects and research. This was a great change as it gave me more opportunities to see the practical application of my studies.

My coursework came to a close in December of 1960, and that decision about career direction was again posed to me. I had continued a concentration in human relations while in the MBA program, but at the time of graduation I was presented with more opportunities outside that sphere. I eventually decided to take a position in data management, a seemingly progressive field, with the McDonnell Aircraft Company in St. Louis, Missouri. I had planned to use this position as a skill-building endeavor but was overall dissatisfied. In comparison to my passion in human relations, this position in data management fit neither my skill set nor my interests.

In an interesting turn of events, the transition away from this career was forced upon me. In 1962, my Reserve unit with the Air Force was activated, and I shipped out to France for ten months. Suzy and I decided that it would be best that she return to Oklahoma to be closer to family during the time, and fortunately, she found a teaching position again.

During my time in these two positions, I really began to see that I was best fit to work in a career in human relations. Data management was a good field, showing much promise, but it was not the skill-set that I had developed during my undergrad and MBA. I decided during those months overseas that once I returned home, I should really play to my strengths. I was good at human relations; it was a career in which I could thrive.

So, at the end of the ten months, I did return home and began a career in my field of interest with a company called Sandia in Albuquerque, New Mexico. Wow, what a great transition! My career took off with this company, as I got to employ all my interests in the field, ranging from recruiting to health benefits to union relations. Overall, this broad experience was rewarding as well as challenging.

From that point, my career continued through a number of company transitions and I gained more responsibility all the while. Following six years in Albuquerque, I was contacted by my good mentor and friend, Edward Burris from OSU, who was looking to refer me to the Oklahoma City-based company, Macklanburg-Duncan. Suzy and I were more than excited to come home again to be closer to friends and family, so we jumped at the opportunity. While with that company, I moved up through the ranks to achieve positions as Human Resource Manager and eventually Vice President of HR. But these positions did not come without their challenges. During my first year at Macklanburg-Duncan, we had two campaigns by a union attempting to organize our employees. Two elections were held, both of which we won handily, and we stayed union-free. The strategic management concepts acquired at OSU played an important part in establishing a professional HR function within M-D, which is still union-free to this day. I continued with that company for twelve years.

I was recruited away from M-D for an executive HR position by a major manufacturer in the oil industry. However, the "bust" in the oil industry followed shortly after this move, and my next three employers were either purchased or dissolved after I had been there just a short time. Even though these events were not according to my plan, obviously, I found valuable experience in them. Job searching and exit-counseling were added to my resume, and characteristics such as these proved advantageous in gaining a great position with Express Personnel in Oklahoma City. As a company with 400 franchises, I again moved up through the positions of HR manager and eventually Vice President again. Again, challenges were always present, as can be expected. The main ones dealt with ever-changing federal labor regulations. But human resources was my passion, and through these challenges, I thrived. Overall, it was quite a rewarding career.

I retired from Express in 2005, but still maintain an active life. Currently, I assist my son-in-law, on a part-time basis, with his construction business, *Evans Building Concepts*. Life now provides more freedom for me to pursue and develop other interests. I have taken up photography and formed a business, *JEWELS Photo Art*, which has been rewarding and award-winning. Yet, still I like to play to my strengths so I am currently working as a human resource management coach for businesses in the Oklahoma City Area. I truly believe that the success in my career life has its root in my gaining an MBA from Oklahoma State so many years ago. What a worthwhile investment it was!

If I had the opportunity to voice some words of wisdom to students at the onset of a career, I would be sure to include a number of things. First, maintaining integrity in career and life is essential to success. This character-reliability will bear rewards both from sources of employment and from inter-personal networks. Second, proving one's work ethic and maintaining networks is crucial to placement and advancement. I was so motivated by the fact that Edward Burris called me after those many years to refer me for a job. This would not have been possible had I not proved myself to him and kept a positive relationship.   Third, and last, as I have stated before, play to your strengths. Many times a new and more glamorous career may come across your path, but that is no guarantee that it will be a rewarding one to you. So my advice is to do what you are passionate about and what you are good at. With that outlook, you will find happiness and motivation through life's challenges.

Larry Ferree
Contributed by Danny Hunget

KEY SUCCESS FACTORS: Maintain Integrity, Prove Your Work Ethic, Maintain Networks, Play to Your Strengths

EDITOR'S NOTES: Throughout his career time in human resources, Larry Ferree held positions as president of local chapters of the HR Society and National Management Association. He was awarded the certification of Senior Professional in Human Resources in 1996 by the Society for Human Resource Management. Beyond the realm of his career, Larry serves as director of the Hearts for Hearing non-profit organization and is on the board of directors for the Oklahoma Medical Research Foundation. During retirement, he has had the opportunity to pursue his love for the outdoors through photography, hiking, and bike-riding. Among his favorite activities, Larry loves to travel with his wife, Suzy, and attend the activities of his four grandchildren.

The future belongs to those who believe in the beauty of their dreams.

—Eleanor Roosevelt

DON'T TELL ME I CAN'T!

Betty Murrell Hove—I was 21 in the summer of 1964 when I became the first woman to receive an MBA from Oklahoma State University. My husband, Larry, who had just turned 25, received his engineering PhD from OSU on the same day. We were a young couple with sky high expectations. Watch out world, here we come! As I ironed my graduation gown that August day, I remember having a strong feeling that my life was about to change in an earth shattering way.

A small town girl, I was born in Sentinel, Oklahoma, and raised in Altus, Oklahoma. My mother and father treated me as if I were the smartest, most capable, most talented person and could literally do anything. Significant teachers and adult mentors reinforced these positive feelings. Is there a more precious gift one can give a young person? Therefore, I have believed and suppose always will believe the world is there just for the taking. I began career planning early on and knew in the first grade when *all* the other girls in my class wanted to be a nurse or a teacher that I just *did not*. At some point I decided instead to be President of General Motors. Of course, in the 50s and 60s the so-called corporate glass ceiling for women wasn't so much glass as concrete. Never mind. Batten down the hatches and full speed ahead! I was determined to make it in the "Mad Men" world of business.

I chose Oklahoma State for undergraduate, and graduate work as well, simply because . . . well, where else would a dyed-in-the-wool "Aggie" coming from a long line of Aggies go to school? Besides that, OSU just happened to have the degree I wanted and just in the nick of time (the MBA program was instituted in 1960). Also, my husband was finishing his PhD at, where else—OSU.

I was the only woman in a class of 32. It never occurred to me that this would be a problem, and it was not, not ever. My teachers, advisor, and fellow students treated me like "one of the guys." I received a graduate assistantship to teach statistics lab, which was a fantastic blessing and further proof, as I look back on it, that I was not discriminated against in any way. At the time, I did not even pause to question whether I would be given equal opportunity. Both then and now, my hat is off to the many people at OSU who looked past my skirt and saw just another MBA student.

Once in a management class I chose the topic: "Would it be better to have a man or a woman boss?" After I gave my presentation, the discussion that followed was so lengthy and animated, evoking an opinion from just about everyone in the class, that the teacher suggested we take two class periods to discuss it fully instead of the one that was allotted. The give and take that followed was stimulating and provocative, never combative, bitter, or prejudicial. I did not know enough then to fully appreciate what a marvelous gift this was from my professor and fellow students. My MBA guys and I became very, very close. We went to class together, studied together, drank cups and cups of coffee together, cried and moaned some, and laughed and debated a lot. I still have friends among those great guys.

Towards the end of my course work, I began to check the boards for companies visiting the campus for interviews. In those days, when listing the requirements of persons they wanted/needed to hire, employers could *and did* stipulate "Male Applicants Only." So day after day I would look through the lists and find that every one of the companies looking for MBA types would only consider "male applicants." Out of all those trips to peruse the employment boards, I found only one company with which to interview on campus and later at their facility in Albuquerque. That was Sandia, which was a government-funded company and as such was paying a bit more attention to equal opportunity employment. There was no employment opportunity of interest to my husband in Albuquerque, however, so we decided on Fort Worth, where he accepted an offer from General Dynamics. After graduation we would relocate, and I would begin my job hunting in the land "where the West begins," where men are men and women . . . well, *aren't*. I got really good at interviewing, and at last landed my first job with Arbrook, a manufacturing company that was a division of Johnson and Johnson. I worked in accounting.

Most of my work has been accounting related. (Certainly had I had any idea that would be the path my career would take, I might have paid more urgent attention in my graduate level accounting classes!) After Arbrook, I worked in Public Works for the City of Fort Worth, at Bell Helicopter, at American Commercial Colleges, as CFO in a defense-engineering business owned by my husband, and was self employed as a provider of accounting services for small businesses that did not require a full-time accountant.

Now that I am retired, I can look back with satisfaction and appreciation for the diversity of my many-faceted career working in private, governmental, and educational areas, including being a business owner. I feel that my MBA from OSU helped me achieve many goals and was the stepping stone and leverage to a satisfying working life. Other accomplishments I am proud of involve developing a business for myself that allowed me to work from my home after our two supremely brilliant and talented children were born; filing and winning an Equal Employment Opportunity Commission complaint; a 50-year marriage to Mr. Wonderful; chairing the first walk/run for The Women's Center (non-profit), which has become a major fund raiser; doing a double pirouette; and climbing Hen Egg Mountain in the Big Bend area just last month.

My future plans are to LIVE until I die and not have my years outlast my quality of life; I want to wear out, not rust out.

Betty Murrell Hove
Contributed by Jay Dobson

KEY SUCCESS FACTORS: Follow your Dream, Have a Sense of Humor, Read, Look at the Stars, Take Deep Breaths, Put Family First, Keep Eye Contact, Find the Good in People

EDITOR'S NOTES: Betty lives in Fort Worth, Texas with her husband Larry or, as she would call him, Mr. Wonderful. Betty and Larry have two children, Jennifer and Eric. Jennifer graduated from OSU in 1993 and Eric graduated from OSU in 1995. She has five grandchildren: Conor, Devon, Riley, Cole, and Jack. Though none of them are old enough to be in college, she is quite confident that they are all OSU bound.

Betty may be retired but that does not mean her life has slowed down. Betty's hobby is people, pure and simple. She loves building bridges and cementing bonds. She also enjoys helping others, which is quite evident by her community involvement. She serves on multiple boards, including the board of The Women's Center and the board of the Texas Ballet Theatre. Betty takes pride in being a Planned Parenthood volunteer. She is also involved in various organizations, including the National Organization of Women, the Ballet Guild of Fort Worth, and the Tarrant County Historical Society.

CHAPTER TWO
EXTRAORDINARY ENTREPRENEURS

The MBA Alumni featured in this chapter have found their passion and created empires and are truly living the dream.

We all have "extraordinary" coded within us, waiting to be released.

—*Jean Houston*

IT'S NOT SUNSET YET

Neal L. Patterson—I was born in Anthony, Kansas, a small town near the Oklahoma-Kansas border, at the dawn of a new decade—1950 to be precise. The middle of three brothers, I grew up on a farm near Manchester, Oklahoma. My beginnings were pretty humble, but full of lessons. My father and mother were tenant farmers. My family's water was hand-pumped out of a cistern designed to catch the rainwater off the roof. Our "bathroom" was located on a path outside the house—a real issue in winter. The only source of heat was a propane furnace in the living room, which was a popular place when you returned from the outhouse. Our household phone line was a party line with our neighbors on the west side of town. We were a long and a short (ring); if you needed to call the other side of the highway, our neighbor Mabel had to connect you through the operator console "patch panel" in her home. I remember going to our uncle's house to see my first color TV. Each time a new technology was acquired that created value in our lives, it was exciting and noteworthy. I was impatient to see more. Perhaps that was the genesis of my interest in technology. I am still a fan of the "next new."

The geographic area where I grew up was so sparsely populated that at age five I was asked to join school a year early in order to be a playmate for Joe McCray, who would otherwise have been the only boy in the first grade class that year—something that the school board felt could harm his social development. This might have been all right if I had been judged mature for my age, but as I understand it, I spoke a language only my older brother, Kent, could interpret. It wasn't long before my mother was making the 100-mile round trip to a speech pathologist in Enid, Oklahoma, so that I could learn to speak. To this day I have language deficits.

As I mentioned, my father and mother were farmers. They belonged to what has been called the "Greatest Generation," the one that was hardened by the Great Depression and braved World War II. Like many of their generation, they were common sense, proud, hardworking people who cherished their family and friends and who pursued their modest dreams without the luxury of a safety net. Looking back, it is now clear that risk was a huge part of their life and, by extension, a huge part of my early life as well. I remember one year sitting on the porch with my father, both of us helpless to stop the hailstorm that was destroying our entire wheat crop and the year's only source of income for our family. The wheat had taken all of our focused efforts and most of our resources to plant and grow, and it was gone in a few minutes. I also recall standing in my front yard at age eight or nine and watching my dad attempt to buy our family home and farm being sold at auction, with the local neighbors not bidding against dad, but a total stranger driving the bidding past dad's prearranged bank financing. As our family was absorbing the profound nature of our circumstances, I had my first real experience with a true Good Samaritan. Sheriff Burchfield, one of the wealthiest persons in the county, stepped in and bought the farm, offering it to us and financing it for dad. It was the first farm Dad owned. It was not his last.

In my parents' rural Oklahoma world, hard work was a given, but it wasn't the only thing. Success was something that happened when you had the right plan, worked very hard, *and* the conditions cooperated. Risk, the part you did not control, was always there. You did your part, which my dad always said included "one more round after sundown," and you prayed and hoped that the conditions would be right to yield a good harvest. If and when things didn't go well . . . well, you adapted, rebuilt the plan, and planted another crop.

Looking back, nothing has had a greater impact on my entrepreneurial outlook than my years on the farm and my time with my parents. Not all entrepreneurs have Oklahoma farming in their background, but most share an uncommon tolerance for risk and the courage to go forward after what seems like a failure. The difference between entrepreneurs and those who don't launch businesses isn't the quality of the ideas. Most people have good ideas, I've noticed, good enough to start a successful business. Entrepreneurs just seem to have a mutation that allows them to risk everything and still sleep soundly at night. If the hail (drought, insects, and flood) doesn't come … your hard work is rewarded. You can afford the new tractor, and if you have three good years in a row, you might buy another quarter section of land, growing your operation.

My mother is still a major source of wisdom. My father passed away a few years back, but his lessons are indelible. Thanks in part to my father's handed-down work ethic and my mother's belief that education was the path for her sons to have a better life, all three Patterson boys went to Oklahoma State University. My first business was Patterson Brothers, where we raised hogs to finance our college education. My older brother, Kent Patterson, received his B.S. in Civil Engineering and M.S. in Bio-environmental Engineering from OSU, was a successful entrepreneur and one of the founders of a successful environmental consulting and engineering firm on the east coast; he was inducted into the OSU Engineering Hall of Fame in 2006. My younger brother, Bryan Patterson, received his B.S. in Business Administration and became my father's trusted partner and successor, continuing to grow the family farm.

I received my undergraduate Finance degree from Oklahoma State University in 1971. While an undergrad, I served as chapter treasurer of Pi Kappa Alpha fraternity, where I met my close friend John Williams. To my mother's surprise, I became a good student and loved everything about school. But the Vietnam War was at its peak, and on December 1, 1969, I watched on a TV in a Stillwater laundromat how external events shape our lives. The draft was reinstated using a lottery system, awarding me with a very low draft number. My service was through the National Guard, where I did my basic training, then came back for an MBA before starting my career.

I have wonderful memories of my days at OSU. Through the experience I grew confident in my intelligence and my ability to navigate new challenges. Those years went by in a blink. I thoroughly enjoyed the entire experience; I loved every course and almost every professor. One of my fellow students at the time was Mike Holder, the OSU All-American golfer. He was getting an MBA while waiting for the legendary Labron Harris to retire as the OSU golf coach. Mike, as it turned out, was a good choice and coached OSU golf for 32 years, winning 25 conference championships and eight national championships before becoming the University's athletic director, where he is at the center of moving OSU to even higher levels of competition and recognition.

After completing my MBA in 1972, I took a job in Kansas City with Arthur Andersen as an information systems consultant. This was in the Administrative Services division, which later became Andersen Consulting and then Accenture, the global management consulting, technology services, and outsourcing company. I can't remember my 1973 salary, but I do remember that I received a premium because I had my MBA. That was the first but not the last time my OSU education paid me back.

At Andersen, I met Paul Gorup and Cliff Illig, fellow twenty-somethings who would later become my business partners. In the summer of 1979, Paul, Cliff, and I would spend our Saturday mornings at a park in Kansas City, half studying for the CPA exam and half discussing and planning the idea of what would later become Cerner. At the time, we had no idea that Cerner would be a healthcare IT company. Our initial concept was for it to be an application software company that "automated the mission-critical processes of an information-driven industry." In September of that year, I made the leap and left Andersen. A week later, I convinced Paul and Cliff to join me after I had sold more business than I could fulfill alone. Our first client in the healthcare industry—a clinical laboratory—opened our eyes to an industry where information played not just a big role but *the biggest role* imaginable. In healthcare, information is not just critical to its operations; in many circumstances it is a matter of life or death. The systemic problems were there. The complexity was high. We could provide both vision and value. We were hooked.

Our first hospital development partner was St. John Medical Center in Tulsa, Oklahoma, followed by North Kansas City Hospital. Today about 30% of hospitals in the United States have Cerner solutions installed, and Cerner is the largest stand-alone supplier of healthcare information technology in the world. We have healthcare clients in 25 countries on six continents, ranging from single physician offices to healthcare systems to national governments. Cerner has nearly 8,000 associates worldwide, including 4,500 in the Kansas City metropolitan area where our world headquarters is located. What's really interesting is that Cliff Illig, Paul Gorup and I are still actively involved in the company rather than out golfing. The job isn't done. Somewhere in the 1990s, we began to articulate our desire to eliminate all avoidable errors, variance, waste, delay, and friction from healthcare. Healthcare is challenging, and ultimately it becomes personal, affecting the lives of people you love. When you're doing something challenging and meaningful, it's hard to step away.

They say entrepreneurs get itchy. Unlike many "serial" entrepreneurs who hop from business to business, Cerner has remained the consuming professional endeavor of my life. Over the past decade, though, business partner Cliff Illig and I have made some moderate investments in non-healthcare enterprises. In 2002, we formed FiveStar Lifestyles, a real estate development and country club management group of enterprises with properties in Missouri and Oklahoma. FiveStar employs 90 people year-round and about 350 in the summer. In 2006, Cliff and I had the opportunity to purchase the Kansas City Wizards Major League Soccer team from sports visionary Lamar Hunt. It was important to the legendary and ailing sports entrepreneur that the team have local Kansas City owners who would keep the team in the community and build a soccer-specific stadium. We decided to go for it. Although I am not involved in the daily management of the team, it has been a good decision and the right thing for our community. We are on schedule to complete construction in 2011 of a soccer-specific stadium for the team, recently rechristened Sporting KC. OnGoal LLC is the name of the partnership between Cliff and me, three minority owners of the soccer team, and the stadium real estate development group. OnGoal employs about 70 people. My wife, Jeanne, and I also own Southpoint Farms, a small group of farms in Missouri, Kansas, and Oklahoma.

Part of being interviewed for something like this book is that you are asked a lot of questions that are bound to make you sound a little self-important if you choose to answer them, questions like, "What are your success factors?" I think the ingredients, journey, and definition of success are bound to be different for different people. As I mentioned before, I think risk tolerance and impatience are self-selecting preconditions for entrepreneurs. But there *are* some general factors I think make for success, whether you're a risk-it-all entrepreneur or a leader inside an existing enterprise. Here are some things I have shared with my own children and aspiring leaders who work for Cerner.

1. Have a vision. If you want people to follow you, it is imperative that you be able to articulate a compelling description of a future state (vision) that creates purpose for others to pursue. The same vision that guides you and your internal team provides significant transformational value for your external clients—try to communicate that vision often, both internally and externally.

2. Create value. I have a saying I live by: Create real value and good things will happen. If you are an entrepreneur or working for one, the only source of cash flow must come from creating, selling, and delivering value to your clients using a valid business model.

3. Think. Schedule time to think—alone and with others. Ultimately it is your ability to think clearly and insightfully that enables you to lead.

4. Hire attitudes and intelligence—attributes that don't tend to change. I always want to hire people who are smarter than I am and who are willing to work inside the team. The more brilliant your hires are, the more creative you must be in defining the team. Never define any one person as more important than the broader team. Be quick to eliminate people who are divisive and abusive to others. Maybe it's a bias, but I do like to hire MBAs . . . .

5. Lead. Remember that nearly all people want to follow, but this requires a leader they can follow. Most of us will only voluntarily follow someone we believe and trust will lead us down the right path—usually because they possess not only vision, but also competence and integrity.

6. Have a life. Some people don't struggle with this. The hard-driving types will. Put it on your schedule as "HAL" if you have to. Make time for connecting with family, for keeping traditions, and for

going somewhere new, following your need for adventure.

Overall, trial and error will be the greatest teacher in your career. The least painful path is to learn from the trials and errors of others. Reading is one way to do this. I have enjoyed some very good mentors over my career; some I have actually met and others I have only read about or observed. You can study a person's attributes and techniques from afar even if you do not have the opportunity to form a close personal relationship. Use mentors when they are available, but recognize that they will not carry you to success. A note: Beware the assigned mentor. My experience tells me that successful mentoring relationships are seldom created by a third party.

If I could give any advice to future MBA grads regarding how to advance in your first career, I would say three things: First, become so good at your job that management does not want to ever lose you. Second, do your boss's job; think through what your boss needs to do and have it so well prepared and thought through that his/her role becomes much easier. Third, create your replacement—build a team of A-players. This is necessary to keep you from getting trapped because you are too good to be moved. If you do these three things, a star will be born. You will become very visible, and when the tougher, failure-is-not-an-option projects come up, your name will be on the list. Repeat the process and you will have a good shot at the corner office.

Being a business leader can be a hollow accomplishment if you are not also giving back to your community and world. It is important to create a culture of giving in your organization and to encourage others to give as well. I encourage you to take part, but with a thoughtful approach. Beware organizations that exist to convene meetings, not to deliver value. I carefully choose my broader civic involvements, giving time to only a few organizations whose strong missions I believe in. On a corporate level, I support Cerner's unique First Hand Foundation, which directly gives to individual children with unmet healthcare needs. I am also a lifetime director of American Royal, a more-than-century-old organization that bridges agricultural lifestyles and values into our urban society—something with a great deal of meaning for me. Within my immediate family, we have established the Patterson Foundation, which supports other organizations in the community and country that foster important causes. Apart from that, I make an occasional invest-ment of time in cultivating an environment that is conducive to young entrepreneurs in the Kansas City region. Be careful with your time. At the end of the day, your greatest contribution may be growing your company, fulfilling its vision, and creating jobs in the community.

After all these years, some things haven't changed. I am still a hard-working, risk-taking farm boy enthralled by technology. Family is still important and a source of strength. I still believe in learning something new every day, though I often lack patience. Other things have changed dramatically. I found a calling I could never have imagined when I was a child or even a student at OSU. By some standards, I have found "success," but by my own measures, my work isn't finished. I can almost hear my dad say, "It's not sunset yet."

Neal L. Patterson
Contributed by Blaine Rider

KEY SUCCESS FACTORS: Risk-taking, Vision, Value, Thinking and Leadership

WEBSITE: www.cerner.com

EDITOR'S NOTES: Widely respected for his vision and strategic thinking, Patterson has the unique ability to articulate how informa-tion technology will transform healthcare. His commitment to this vision creates value for health systems, providers, and their commu-nities by reducing healthcare costs, increasing efficiencies, and enabling improvements in healthcare quality and safety. Cerner associates extol Patterson for his passion and foresight, his ability to drive change within organizations, his entrepreneurial spirit, and his candid, uninhibited conversational style. In the 1990s, it was Patterson's clear vision and entrepreneurial instincts that led him to bet Cerner's future on the $400 million initial investment needed to develop its person-centric information architecture, *Cerner Millennium*. Patterson has five times been named one of *Modern Healthcare's* "100 Most Powerful People in Healthcare," and he is in demand as a speaker on healthcare topics and trends. In 2010, *Forbes* ranked Neal fourth in their list of "America's Best-Performing Bosses." He serves as a trustee of the Midwest Research Institute and is active in healthcare leadership networks and local entrepreneurial organizations. Patterson is co-founder and serves on the executive board of the First Hand Foundation, Cerner's nonprofit foundation that provides assistance to children with critical healthcare needs. Outside of healthcare, Patterson is co-owner of the Sporting KC Major League Soccer team and serves as a lifetime director for the 111-year-old American Royal livestock, horse show, and rodeo. When time allows, Patterson can be found working in his woodshop or reading a history book. A life-long OSU Cowboy fan, Patterson and his wife, Jeanne, live in Loch Lloyd, Missouri. They have reclaimed the original Oklahoma family farm and enjoy spending time there. They have four adult children and two grandchildren.

No amount of ability is of the slightest avail without honor.

—Andrew Carnegie

APPRECIATING LIFE THROUGH HARD WORK AND INTEGRITY

James Don Carreker—I was born and raised just 65 miles from Stillwater in Oklahoma City, the great state of Oklahoma's capital city. When I was growing up, my dad was a truck driver; and from him, I learned early what it means to work hard. I watched him start at the bottom and work his way up to become the operating manager of his company. He was a great example and the ideal first mentor. Dad showed me that with hard work and perseverance, goals are achievable.

Growing up, working was normal and my work ethic came natural for me. I started working odds-and-ends jobs at twelve, was projecting movies at a small theater by fourteen, and was unloading trucks by eighteen at the same company where my dad worked. I went to high school at Northwest Classen High in Oklahoma City. In high school, I started playing a number of sports. I loved football the most. Football required a lot of passion and willingness to work hard, and playing with the team taught me a lot about both. Dad always told me when I was a kid that it was his job to put me through high school and my job to find my way from there. Dad kept his word. I realized football could be a way to pay for college if I worked hard enough for it. That hard work paid off quick when I found out I got a scholarship to play college football at Oklahoma State University. I have always been so grateful that a strong work ethic was instilled in me at such a young age. There is something about getting there on your own, paying your own way, or earning your own keep that makes you appreciate things more in life.

I started my college career at Oklahoma State University in the late 1960s. My older brother had already started school at OSU and was studying industrial engineering. I was really good at math, so I decided to give industrial engineering a try as well. Come to find out, mixing an engineering student's workload with an athlete's workload is like mixing oil and water; it just does not work. By that time, I had decided anyway that with my outgoing personality and love for people, engineering might not provide the social setting I was looking for. I wanted to work more with people. Marketing seemed to be a great fit for me, so I switched my major my junior year and decided to minor in mathematics. That has proven to be a great decision. Marketing has always just made sense to me. I understood what they were trying to accomplish and why; I understood the laws, etc. It just seemed to grab hold of me. I graduated in 1970 as the Marketing Student of the Year.

During undergraduate school, I interned for Sanger-Harris, a department store, and found that I loved retailing. I was really motivated to go places and wanted to prepare myself as much as possible for what lay ahead. An MBA seemed like a good fit, so I went on to graduate school, where I focused on finance, and graduated Beta Gamma Sigma in 1972.

After graduating, I did not feel comfortable starting my own business right away, and I knew there was still so much I wanted to learn. I interviewed with three large companies in a variety of industries. Because I loved my internship and had found my passion for retailing at Sanger-Harris, I decided to accept a position with them for my first full-time job as a management trainee. Back then, not very many people went on to earn an MBA; in fact, I was the first MBA graduate ever hired to work for Sanger-Harris. The company had a great learning environment as well, which played a big part in my decision to work there.

Sanger-Harris also paid me a little more than other companies would have, but more importantly, I was on a different track than I might have been elsewhere. My MBA placed me as a fast-tracked employee, and I rotated through many jobs in the department store, learning about all the levels. They placed me in areas where I could perform my job and be recognized. It was a succeed or fail track . . . luckily I succeeded.

I found that as an undergraduate student, you learn critical skills such as accounting, marketing, and other disciplines. The higher you go in your education, the more encompassing everything you learn is and it challenges you to think and to see the whole picture. This was perfect for me because I loved the challenge. My education in the MBA program at OSU taught me how to think better. In my first role at the department store I was in charge of back-of-house operations. I really did not need a degree to do this, but I was there to learn the business. Having an MBA made me view things differently and analyze how to make the most of the situation. I learned so much about the company as a whole, and the MBA provided me with the critical skills to do this.

I was promoted at Sanger-Harris to eventually become the Senior Vice-President of Operations and Finance by 1982. When I was 37, I became the President of Burdines Department Stores.

I left retailing in 1988 when I got an offer to work in the hotel business. I was the President of Wyndham Hotels, a company started by Trammel Crow Company. At the time, Wyndham only had 18 properties. Most would think the transition from retail to hospitality may be a tough switch, but it really was not. When you reach the higher levels in the retail business, it is just as much about real estate, location of stores, building, etc., as it is about merchandising. The property aspect made it really easy to switch to hotels. I can remember having problems proving myself to the people I worked with though. I'm sure they thought, "What in the world is this retail guy doing trying to run a hotel chain?" One of my biggest challenges has been to prove to people that I could learn the business and add value. I believe the biggest challenge with any company is earning your right to lead, especially in changing environments. They just weren't believers. Once I showed them I could do it, they jumped on board. When I left the company in 1999, Wyndham had become a fully-integrated branded hotel company with 450 properties. In 1994, I had also taken on the role of CEO of Trammel Crow, a real estate development and services company.

In 2000, I began my own company, JDC Holdings, a private equity investment firm. We focus primarily on restaurants, technology, and oil and gas. It is so much fun doing what I do now. I am able to help out those people who have helped me in the past. Several of the owners of the companies I currently invest in are people I worked with in the past. The way I see it, I am investing in people, and it is such a blessing to help them live their passion.

One of the biggest blessings in my life was having some great mentors take interest in me. Sometimes it is important to take initiative and ask for a mentor; other times they will approach you. When I was in charge of companies, I would insist that my employees try to find a mentor. It is invaluable and something that has always meant a lot to me. Finding a mentor who believes in you and that you can learn from is so critical. Sometimes they can be extremely critical and say hard things to you that you may not want to hear, but it is important that you listen. You will learn and be inspired in the end. Trammell Crow, one of the greatest real estate developers this country has ever seen, became my mentor when he was 82 and recruited me from the department store to work for Wyndham. I could not have done the things we did there without his guidance.

If I could give a word of advice to others regarding their careers, I would tell them, "Always feel good about what you have learned so far, but enter the rest of your life with the mindset that you have just begun your learning. Carry that attitude with you the rest of your life. The biggest mistake you can make is to think you already know it all. Secondly, know that the most important aspect of a business is not the business plan; it is the values and integrity of the people who build it. You need both, but integrity is the most important thing you have. It is your reputation and your livelihood. Always be true to who you are. For those who are just beginning your careers, find a company that values learning. That is the best way to get started. It's not always how much you get paid, it's how much you learn."

James Don Carreker
Contributed by Alison E. Hargis

KEY SUCCESS FACTORS: Integrity, Values, Responsibility, Commitment, Teamwork, Networking, Passion to Learn, Perseverance

EDITOR'S NOTES: Mr. Carreker serves on the boards of Crow Holdings, the investment arm of the Trammell Crow family; The Minto Group of Canada; Westec Intelligent Surveillance; Aimbridge Hospitality; and the UT Southwestern Board of Visitors.

Jim has also led many active roles in his community. He served as the director of Junior Achievement of Dallas in the early 1980s and has also served as a member of the Dallas Citizen's Council, chairman of the Dallas Housing Authority, Vice-chairman for the United Way in Dallas, Texas, and Miami, Florida, and is a member of the advisory committee of Southern Methodist University's business school gradu-ate program.

He has been a member of the Board of Governors for the Miami Chamber of Commerce and an appointee by the Governor of Florida to the Florida Council of 100, member of the Orange Bowl Committee, and trustee for the University of Miami.

Jim Carreker remains active with his alma mater. He was recently inducted into the Oklahoma State University's Alumni Hall of Fame, has served on the Hotel and Restaurant Administration School's Advisory Committee, and has been a guest speaker in the Spears School of Business.

Mr. Carreker is married to Robin Carreker and resides in Dallas. He has two sons by his late wife, Jane. Court Carreker is married to Megan and is pursuing his MBA in Finance at Southern Methodist University. He has two children, Dylan, age four, and Holland, age one. Chris Carreker is married to Lindsay and works as a brand manager at The Richards Group in Dallas. He also has two children: Cohen, age two and Rett, a newborn. Jim and Robin attend Park Cities Presbyterian Church.

Jim is currently semi-retired. He enjoys traveling abroad and spending time on his yacht. He says his goals and plans for the future are now to experience life as much as possible while still staying active in busi-ness, to be more of a mentor and less of a doer, and to spend as much time with his family as possible. He says he is at a point in his life where he is more willing than ever to give back to those people and institutions that have helped him throughout his life. He is very proud to be an OSU Cowboy and MBA Alumnus. He is proud of what the University has achieved through scholarship development programs and other improvements. One thing that he is most proud of is the students who come from humble backgrounds and who have faith. In his words, "They will make huge differences in the world."

The world is round, and the place which may seem like the end may also be only the beginning.

—Ivy Baker Priest

GLOBAL SUCCESS

Roger Cagle—While growing up, I always envied those people who seemed to know at an early age exactly what they wanted to do in life. As a young man in rural southeastern Oklahoma, I hadn't a clue. However, I knew that if I had my way, I would be doing it far away from there! Where would it be and how would I get there? More importantly how would I know when I arrived?

I was born in the small town of Heavener into a large family in which I was the youngest of eight siblings (four boys and four girls, seven surviving). The house I grew up in was built largely by volunteer laborers and with contributions from the community after the previous home had burned to the ground during the middle of the night; our family was lucky to escape without injury. The building was distinguished by the pock-marked, uncovered front porch, the sole remnant of the former house. Financially, we were comfortably below the poverty level. But we were no more disadvantaged than many of our neighbors.

My parents' education did not extend beyond the elementary school level. My mother lost her own mother as a pre-teen, and at a very early age she began working to care for her siblings and doing the cooking and cleaning for boarders. My father was a skilled stone mason, but his work was project based and seasonal rather than steady. They both worked very hard in a variety of jobs, trying to make ends meet.

There is a wide age spread among the siblings; the eldest is 23 years my senior. The older siblings left home early, all striving to improve their own stations in life. They, along with my parents, provided a strong combination of nurturing, grounding, and influence that endures today. Externally, the major influences were my teachers. In the town where I grew up—and I suspect in many small towns across America at the time—the educators were generally venerated. It was particularly meaningful to me that they did not achieve their status through their financial standing, and that fact began to instill in me a strong interest in education. Scholarships were not difficult for me to obtain, and I received a great deal of encouragement from my teachers to make the most of my ability.

My father died while I was in high school. As the only sibling living at home, I went to work on a large ranch. As a teenager, I was happy to have the work, but the experience also made me realize that I wanted more out of life and reinforced my yearning for education. In my situation it was not simply a matter of choosing to attend university—there was no money for education. With the help of teachers and others, my tuition would depend on scholarships, student loans, and work. Perhaps even more daunting was the fact that the student population in most colleges would be several multiples of the population of the community in which I grew up. From another perspective, the curriculum provided by rural schools lacked the preparatory courses that helped students translate success at that level to success at the next level. There were few opportunities for classes that bolstered self confidence—speech, debate, foreign language—as the limited budgets had to focus on core secondary school curriculum requirements. While the transition to university was somewhat intimidating, over time I realized the need to push myself to cultivate the skills required to work through an impediment, particularly if these skills did not come easily or naturally.

So it was not without some trepidation that I enrolled in the College of Engineering at Oklahoma State University immediately after graduating from high school in 1965. I had not given a lot of thought to an engineering career, but I received a great deal of encouragement because of my grades and because it seemed at the time to be a sure-fire ticket to a better life.

Like a lot of kids, it was my first time to be away from home. I thoroughly enjoyed college life, in fact to excess, as I was foolish enough to treat it like teenage fantasy land. It was a challenge to maintain the grades to retain the scholarships, work part-time, and keep up an active social life. Ultimately, in the second semester of my sophomore year, I withdrew from the university and joined the Marine Corps. I worked a number of pipeline construction, oil field, and refinery jobs and got married, all before reporting for basic training.

There is a strong sense of duty in my family. Both of my brothers were in the military, and two of my uncles had military careers. I threw myself into this phase of life and graduated from basic training at the top of my company, earning a meritorious promotion. As this was at the height of the Vietnam conflict, most Marines were destined to see duty there. Surprisingly, and I believe largely due to having much more education than most of my enlisted peers, I was instead assigned to advanced Marine Corps finance schooling at Camp Lejeune, North Carolina. Again graduating at the top of my class, I received another meritorious promotion and was assigned a supervisory role at the Marine Corps Finance Center in Kansas City. After the military and with a growing family (I now had a son to support), I moved through a number of jobs. Looking for steady work and with my military background, I was recruited by the Oklahoma Highway Patrol and decided to interview. I drove to their headquarters for the scheduled interview, but the officer never showed up for the appointment. On the drive back home, I realized this was not what I wanted to do and made the decision to apply for the GI bill and renew my pursuit of an education.

Being a student the second time around was a very different experience. Confident that finding gainful employment was not going to be that difficult, I focused on a variety of subjects of interest rather than a course leading to a degree. I wanted to maximize the opportunity. I continued to work in college, and I strongly considered an academic career. As I was older than most of my peers, it was easy for me to make friends and interact with the faculty members at different levels. I received strong encouragement from the faculty to consider graduate school. After some interviewing during my senior year and not really being too excited about the various job offers, I decided to apply for the MBA program—one of the best decisions of my life. It was a fantastic experience.

After being accepted into the MBA program, I decided to stay in school year round. I particularly enjoyed summer school because the interaction in the smaller classes, with more focused and perhaps more relaxed students and teachers, provided a richer experience. There were fewer campus distractions as well. Many of my fondest memories of that time were not event driven, just the interaction. In retrospect, one of the things I really regret about that time was not spending more time networking with international students, many of whom also attended class year round. OSU had a large, diverse group of international students. Traveling was an early dream of mine, and one of the great experiences in my life has been the ability to spend a great deal of time interacting with different cultures.

One of my favorite classes, an entrepreneurship course, was a great influence on my professional career. The course was in association with the Small Business Administration and included providing on-site consulting advice for small businesses in the region that were usually facing financial or marketing challenges. This was my first introduction to the concept of entrepreneurship on a large scale. Previously, I had thought of entrepreneurs primarily as shop owners or small service providers. I knew that I didn't want to own a shop, but when I experienced that entrepreneurship course, I realized that I wanted an entrepreneur model, not necessarily of a sole proprietorship but having involvement with a large degree of control and influence over the success or failure of the business. The course really focused me on trying to find the model that best suited me.

I received my MBA in 1975 and went to work for Exxon USA. The on-campus recruiter was an OSU MBA graduate. (Later, I recruited on campus at OSU and several other campuses for Exxon.) Fortunate enough to have several job offers upon obtaining my MBA degree, my initial inclination was to choose based on the highest starting salary if the opportunities seemed comparable. However, when I wrote my "thanks, but no thanks" letter to Exxon, the senior guy that interviewed me during my on-site recruiting trip called to say, "You are making a big mistake." That guy's enthusiasm and conviction convinced me on the spot that he was right. I changed my mind and accepted a job at Exxon.

Oklahoma has always been a hot bed for the oil and gas industry and I had worked a number of nonprofessional jobs in the industry. Four family members eventually retired from Phillips Petroleum, so I knew a lot about the oil and gas business. It was always interesting to me and the founding characters, the old wildcatters who originally took the business from very entrepreneurial beginnings into creating the mega companies like Exxon Mobil and BP, were heroes of sorts. (Later Boone Pickens became one of those heroes as well.) So, I was thinking, "Of course you can't be one of those old wildcatters creating the initial wave that started this industry, but it is still fundamentally an industry of opportunity." I have never regretted my career choice.

Throughout my professional career I have held a number of jobs with increasing responsibility in major oil companies, entering the management level in the1970s. However, although the jobs were well paid and provided security with good retirement programs, the direct equity link did not exist. In the early 1980s, I joined with several colleagues in a start-up energy company focused on the "upstream" (exploration) business. The oil business is very cyclical, and we persevered through several cycles before selling the business in the early 1990s.

I have had yearnings to travel from an early age, so after the sale of this initial start-up venture, my wife and I decided to "retire" and take the opportunity for a unique travel experience at our relatively young ages rather than waiting for the typical retirement years. We joined my in-laws in Panama as they prepared their boat to embark on a circumnavigation. With never more than the four of us aboard, we sailed from the Panama Canal through many of the islands of the South Pacific and eventually on to Papua New Guinea. We had a number of non sailing-side excursions. During one hurricane season (a good time to not be on the boat) we took a side trip via a German-flagged freighter with a predominantly Tongan crew to Australia for several months. This was during the first anniversary of the reunification of Germany, so we were witness to a very special celebration. We also spent time in New Zealand and Asia. The excitement of the travel was the experience of interacting with such diverse peoples and cultures, particularly in the Islands and Southeast Asia. It made a significant impact on my view of life and made me realize the opportunity I'd missed by not interacting more with OSU's international students.

Several times during our sailing hiatus, I was offered opportunities to rejoin the industry; but I had either not exorcised the wanderlust or was not enthusiastic about the job. Eventually, as one exotic place began to blend with another, the timing and opportunity were right. I missed the challenges and stimulation of the industry and business world. I wanted to continue the entrepreneurial and equity focus, but this time concentrating on international projects. In 1993, I was contacted by my ex-Exxon colleague and took on the challenge of starting up a project based in Perm, Russia. After two years and a successful project start-up, the project management was handed off. My wife and I took a few months' sabbatical to sail the last leg of the boat's circumnavigation from South Africa across the Atlantic to the Caribbean before heading to London in 1997 to co-found SOCO International PLC with my former Exxon colleague.

SOCO, comprising several international projects including the Russian project, was IPO'ed on the London Stock Exchange. At the time, it was the largest industry IPO in over a decade on London's primary exchange. I am based in London as Deputy Chief Executive and CFO. Moving to London was another big shift in my life, but even though I grew up in rural Oklahoma, I have always loved big cities. London is one of the greatest cities in the world and a great place to live and conduct business. In my daily routine, I constantly interact with people from different cultures, generally interfacing in a seamless manner. I find this interaction invigorating.

SOCO's business model is to build shareholder value through the addition of new oil and gas reserves. The strategy is to identify or create opportunities with significant upside potential through exploration and selling projects at the right time to maximize value. It's a portfolio creaming exercise in other words. We have created value and sold projects in Mongolia, Russia, Yemen, Thailand, and Tunisia and currently have projects in Vietnam and Africa.

London was ideally suited for this business model for a variety of reasons: 1) the valuation of assets in the London market was based on net asset value, versus multiples of cash flow (being exploration driven, cash flow was immaterial at the time); 2) the London market had a better knowledge, appreciation, and appetite for our strictly international portfolio; and 3) through an earlier private placement in London, the investment bank had a very thorough knowledge of the company and its principals. We listed SOCO in mid-1997 with a market cap of around $200 million, just before the oil price slid down to around $10 a barrel. We survived, not easy as a newly-listed company, and today are trading at a market cap of around $1.9 billion.

I devote a great deal of time and passion to SOCO along with my other business interests (I hold non-executive directorships with two other companies). I don't really have hobbies, and the business pretty much consumes me. Our company philosophy: You should never be able to go home in the evening, on the weekend, or on holiday knowing that your work is complete because there is always something more to be done. In our company, everyone has an opportunity to do jobs that are beyond just their job descriptions. We were recently recognized as the most productive company on the London stock exchange, as valued by revenue per employee (Our London staff got a real kick out of this and I suspect will wish to revisit the fact during bonus time)!

Throughout my life, I've been inspired by a lot of people. My mother was an amazingly strong woman. Many high school teachers took an interest in me and gave me inspiration during difficult times in my life. My wife deserves mention for several reasons, but special recognition because when I was critically ill, she was at my side continuously and she has always been my soul mate. Several faculty members at OSU were really encouraging to me, particularly some in the MBA program. Dr. Fowler and Dr. Hamm come to mind. The guy who talked me into that first job at Exxon, of course, had a particular impact. He and I have worked together for the better part of the last 35 years. I do think mentors are important. I think it is helpful having someone with a road map, not only someone who traveled the path that you are hoping to travel, but also somebody who's taken a lot of detours along the way and can help you learn from their experiences.

When I look back, I realize the serendipitous nature of life. It was likely fortuitous that the Marine Corp did not send me to Vietnam. Many of my friends from the Corps never made it back. How different would my life have been if the officer had made it for my interview with the Highway Patrol? My life took direction from these events even though I was not making life choices. And that is the key. You do not make all the important choices that impact your life or career; however, you have the opportunity to make the most of any situation for yourself. On the other hand, when it comes time to make choices, choose wisely with the heart and the mind. I did not take what appeared to be the best (highest salary) job offer out of college. Salary at that time is obviously important, but not as important as the career choice. Finally, I only took the time a little later in life to appreciate diversity. Gen. Patton once said, "If everyone is thinking alike, then someone isn't thinking." I think I fully understand this now.

Some people never have an opportunity to get outside their comfort zone, and others make a choice not to. Being a student at OSU offers this opportunity through its large international student body. I encourage students to interact with many people of different backgrounds. Commerce is being conducted on a broad international—rather than national—playing field. Preparing oneself for this now could really be a key advantage to building a successful career in almost any industry.

There's no question in my mind that hard work is above all else a key factor for success. But hard work has several helpers. One is developing the ability to listen. Most people are busy sending rather than receiving. Inclusiveness is important as well. It is easy to join clubs and be associated with people who have similar lifestyles or backgrounds, likes and dislikes, but inclusiveness that involves diversity will ultimately separate you from others. Finally, I think that curiosity is important. If you are curious enough to view things from a different perspective, you can create an advantage.

In business, giving back to the community is a topic very near and dear to me. It's fundamental for our company to become good citizens and neighbors because we are always guests in someone else's country. We're in a very high-risk business of exploring internationally for oil and gas, often in third-world countries and most often in very inhospitable environments in emerging economies. So we should and do seek to have a positive impact on the people and places, knowing that our business activity at any single location may be relatively short-lived. We want the host country and in particular the local populace to be better off by our investment there, in a manner that is sustainable after we are gone. We build infrastructure to support our business such as roads and bridges, mindful of the opportunity for longer-term local use. We additionally build community centers, health facilities, and schools and seek to ensure that there are people or organizations in place to sustain these regardless of project success. So it is not just about providing funding; it is about a sustainable improvement to the overall quality of life.

I became a life member of the Alumni Association very early on after leaving OSU. OSU figures prominently in our estate plan. Both my wife and I are very interested in funding a scholarship program at OSU while we are around to participate in the process. Initial thoughts are to earmark the scholarships for international students and educational opportunities for OSU students abroad. We are hopeful that we can find the time to participate in the overall selection process. We strongly believe that international interaction is the key to a greater understanding of global issues and a key step in productively working in a united front to address many of the world's problems. At a minimum, such interaction will give insight as to the underlying motivation for the beliefs and actions of others.

Roger Cagle
Contributed by Phuong Pham

KEY SUCCESS FACTORS: Hard Work, Inclusiveness, Listening, Curiosity

EDITOR'S NOTES: Since re-entering the industry in 1993, Roger and his wife, Cindy, have lived and worked abroad. Travel is an integral part of their professional and personal lives. They return to the U.S. frequently to visit family, including a son and two granddaughters.

Roger likes many great quotes from Winston Churchill ("When you're going through hell, keep going" is a favorite) and George Patton ("If everybody is thinking alike then somebody isn't thinking"), both heroes of his, but, a quote attributable to John Lennon is most meaningful to him: "Life is what happens to you while you're busy making other plans."

Life is a succession of moments. To live each one is to succeed.

—*Corita Kent*

THE SECRET TO SUCCESS: FOLLOW YOUR HEART

Nita Bridwell—Like many Oklahomans, I was "born wearing orange," with a family lineage absent of other colors in its graduation tassels. Few, however, came into this world kicking and screaming at the exact same time as kickoff on Bedlam football day, on a year that Stillwater happened to be hosting the ongoing rivalry. This, along with my father's approval of any university—as long as it was OSU—was the beginning of an undying love for OSU. Though OSU didn't win on November 27, 1948, this fan has remained true to heart.

Being born and raised in Stillwater, Oklahoma, wasn't the only factor that shaped my path, however. Two of the greatest influences in my life have been my grandmothers. Their legacy includes a set of bold and unwavering principles to live by, including to always have a strong work ethic, to be proud of what I do, and that anything is possible as long as I put my mind to it. Such tenacious legacies were key drivers of my desire for success and to become more than a homemaker. Not attending a university was out of the question, as was going to a school other than OSU.

A creative at heart, I was initially drawn to a major in fine arts. However, scheduling time for creativity seemed contradictory; what was once a passion became an obligation. In an effort to maintain that love and move down a more promising path, I switched colleges after two years. An advisor's course recommendation immediately led to another love: photography. I was suddenly enraptured with taking pictures and began pursuing a photojournalism degree. Before long, this fascination with taking pictures led to positions as Editor, Managing Editor and Head of Photography at the *Daily O'Collegian*. It was at this time in my life that a sense of self-confidence and true self began to emerge. With success came the harsh reality of gender inequality, however, as women were not allowed on the football field and in many other places. Though this was a limitation, my reaction was not discouragement; rather, it inspired a will to work harder.

Following graduation I made a move to Texas for an editing position at the *Amarillo Globe News*. The move was short-lived, though, due partially to two straight weeks of tornados and a realization that the newsroom wasn't where I was happiest. Subsequently, I moved back to Oklahoma and became involved within the same industry as the family business: ladies ready-to-wear retail. Working with a women's sportswear line based out of Dallas spurred yet another move, this time to California. Four years in California enabled me to gain the essential skills needed to run a business, as well as the realization that I wanted to run my own business. With this realization came a fork in the road. The first option was to return home and run the family business; the second was to venture back to school for additional education. A deep desire to do things the correct way, not just the way that worked, was ultimately the determining factor when it came to making a decision. Though the family business had always been successful, the struggles we faced made it clear that we needed a better understanding of how to run a business. This ignited the flame, so to speak, for me to return to OSU and obtain an MBA.

Graduate school was the beginning of making my dream of helping people a reality. While a creative side had always been prominent, the MBA program led to the discovery of a new forte in finance. After completing my first finance course, I knew that was the direction I wanted to go with my career. Thus, instead of returning home to run the family business or open my own, I pursued finance. By becoming a Certified Financial Planner, I have been able to help people achieve their goals and determine their paths in life. After graduating and moving to Dallas, Texas in 1984, I spent 23 years with Merrill Lynch, followed by two years with Wells Fargo. Recently, I celebrated the successful launch of an independent financial services firm with two other partners. My love for helping people also carries over into the community. I have long been an advocate for the victims of muscular dystrophy and was formerly a chair within the Dallas association. Every day brings scientists and advocates one step closer to finding a cure for this heartbreaking disease.

A long and notable career within a male-dominated industry hasn't come without hardship, but the will to succeed overpowered the inclination to back away. Self-assuredness, along with strong-willed principles instilled by my grandmothers, and an MBA enabled me to gain respect and credibility within the industry. Additionally, working off commission generated the mindset that the only limitation I'd ever face was myself. Bold thinking was a key factor in breaking away from the mainstream financial industry and opening an independent financial consulting firm in 2010 alongside two colleagues. Bridwell Groschup Martin Wealth Management Group, LLC, is the result of three best friends living an intertwined dream. Small, independent firms are where I see the financial services industry going, as well as the rest of the world. Entrepreneurs are the lifeblood of communities, industries, and businesses everywhere. We could all take steps toward being more entrepreneurial in our thinking and actions.

Perhaps one of the most exciting aspects of my new venture is the freedom that comes along with being in charge. As partners, we have the ability to operate in ways that maximize benefits to clients, enabling us to form strong bonds and become part of their families. This personal interaction is what I thrive on and what makes a career in financial services so enjoyable. While running a business can be quite turbulent and scary, the joy it brings outweighs any adversity we face. Difficulties make it easy to back away or take a simpler but less satis-fying route. However, by following my heart and staying true to what I want to accomplish, they become irrelevant. My grandmothers always stressed that if you follow your head and heart, nothing can stop you.

Playing a large role in the productivity and efficiency of Bridwell Groschup Martin Wealth Management Group, LLC, is technology. Because the firm is so new, we are still in the process of establishing a Web presence. While a Web site is important, word of mouth is most important in the financial services industry. People trust other people, not computers. Thus, it is vital to find ways to connect with clients and potential clients through a combination of personal and digital commu-nications. The primary social network that Bridwell Groschup Martin uses is LinkedIn, as it provides an effective way to connect and communicate with business clients. Facebook is also useful for connecting with younger clients. Though Bridwell Groschup Martin doesn't engage in Internet monitoring, I experienced a good amount of such with Merrill Lynch and Wells Fargo. The primary reason behind monitoring is safeguarding against hackers, but loss in productivity due to Internet surfing was also a concern.

Some of the key uses of technology in the workplace are in operations. Several programs we use include ACT Software for client relationship management, IAS for private document exchange and storage online, and several programs for making reports. IAS is very exciting for us because it makes documents that were traditionally at risk of being destroyed or stolen (i.e. wills, birth certificates, stock certificates) 100% safe. The documents are stored in an online "vault," encrypted to ensure security, and can be accessed by the appropriate parties when needed.

It has been interesting to experience the effect that IT has had on my industry and the business world in general. Technology has made us five times, if not more, as efficient at everything we do. Sometimes it seems almost impossible to keep up with technological advances, so it is important to find what works for you and your business and follow through with it. We are also diligent to carefully balance the cost and relative benefits of the technologies we use.

The combination of strong family values, pursuit of a career that juxtaposes passion and skill, perseverance in adverse conditions, taking the initiative to follow my heart, and a vastly changing world have shaped my life into what it is today. Taking stock for the future, I see myself doing what puts a smile on my face every day: running Bridwell Groschup Martin Wealth Management Group, LLC. Helping people plan their paths gives me the "warm fuzzies" that everyone wants to experience in life; I get to meet new people every day, hearing their stories and successes as well as establishing a bond that runs deeper than the average professional relationship. My personal success stems from this passion for what I do and the people I help while doing it.

Nita Bridwell
Contributed by Sarah Summers

KEY SUCCESS FACTORS: Follow Through, Commitment, Work Ethic, Passion, Networking

SOCIAL MEDIA: Facebook—Nita Bridwell; LinkedIn—Nita Bridwell

EDITOR'S NOTES: Not only are Ms. Nita Bridwell's accomplishments impressive, but her path to discovering her true self is certainly inspiring. From lettering in bowling and graduating with honors from the OSU MBA program to gaining powerful positions in male-dominated fields, Ms. Bridwell has found success in whatever she does. Additionally, her ability to know what she wants in her heart and pursue it is reassuring in a world where few people live by such wise philosophies.   Ms. Bridwell is a great example of taking a chance to do what you love and making it lucrative in every aspect of life.

I know of no more encouraging act than the unquestionable ability of man to elevate his life by conscious endeavor.

—Henry David Thoreau

A SLOW START

Lee DeNoya—I was born and raised in Ponca City, 40 miles north of Stillwater. My mother went to Oklahoma A&M, the predecessor to OSU, in the 1940s but left after a year to marry my father. So I did not grow up immersed from an early age in the idea that I would go to college. Although I was one of five sons in my family, I spent most of my childhood alone. My three older brothers were sent to Vietnam, came back, married, had children young, and were not a daily part of my early life. When they were around, they were negative role models, with lots of anger and excuses and blame for others. My younger brother lived with my parents, while I lived with my paternal grandmother.

My mother had the idea for me to live with my grandmother across town when I was six. I always believed that she did that to help my grandmother. And while I certainly did help her, I learned the full story many years later. My grandmother had lived alone for years and had stopped eating during the day, ending up in the hospital for malnutrition every few months. My mother figured that if my grandmother had someone to cook for other than herself, she would eat. And sure enough, she did. Problem solved. I ended up living with my grandmother full time until my senior year in high school, running around with my mother on the weekends while my dad did shift work in the Medford Conoco plant. So with him busy with work and my brothers out of the picture, I was raised the son of my grandmother and mother.

Before I was born, my family had been amazingly wealthy. I am a member of the Osage Nation. Before the British developed the Saudi oil fields, the Osages were the wealthiest group of people on the planet, thanks to E. W. Marland and Frank Phillips, who developed the Burbank oil field on Osage land early in the 20th century. And the DeNoyas were the wealthiest of the Osage families. For example, throughout the 1920s, each share of Osage oil royalty was worth what today would be about $120,000 annually. My great grandparents each had a share, as did eight of their nine children. My great-grandfather had two brothers, each with comparably-sized families. So between the three DeNoya brothers, they had 30 royalty shares, generating what today would be just under $4,000,000 annual family income from their shares of tribal income distributions. On top of that, they had 23,000 acres of working ranch land, so they didn't need any of that income to live. And on top of that, they leased out their land to the oil companies and made what today would be an additional $2,000,000 annually from personal oil leases! My family's share of all that would have been about $1.6 million annual income in today's dollars and 7,000 acres of working ranch land. They earned that amount every single year throughout the 1920s. Some years, they made a good deal more than that. In the following decades royalties were lower, but they were still large enough to support an entire family. And that isn't even counting the income earned from the ranch. So they had plenty of opportunity to build wealth from their income.

Had they protected 20% of that money and tucked it away in a basic account, they still would have been able to live a very big life, and that account now would have, conservatively, $15,000,000 in it for the benefit of their grandchildren and future generations.

But that didn't happen.

They assumed the big money would always be there. By the time I came around, everything had changed. No wealth had been built. All the money had been spent. Most of the land had been sold. We were poor. The easy money that came from Osage oil was a blessing and a curse. It allowed my family to live well without consequences, without the need to build skills, without a value for education, without the foresight to build wealth from income.

After my father came home from World War II, his father gave him everything he needed to make a good living as a rancher. But in the short 16 years between 1945 and when I was born, he had misman-aged it all away. The oil money had been spent as fast as it had come in, so there was no accumulated wealth from prior generations to fall back on. All the thousands of acres of land had been sold. My father had to go to work for an hourly wage. My brothers were alcoholics and drug addicts who showed up at our rented derelict house on a regular basis to fight with each other and with my father. This was quite a steep socioeconomic fall from just a few years before. If it wasn't so personal, it would be a great study in the unintended negative consequences of fast, easy money.

Later on, I realized that the real reason my mother sent me to live with my grandmother was to remove me from a potentially harmful environment. She loved me and saw something in me that was different from my brothers. I didn't think about it in these terms as a child, but I think she thought that I could break the cycle. I can't yet say that she was right. To date, I am still the only member of my family to graduate from college. But my children are working on it, and I have confidence that they are finding their way. I am sure that the way I grew up and the things I later learned about my family's "no consequences" mindset are important to the lessons that I try to teach now about self-sufficiency and opportunity creation. Whatever success I have in life, I owe to my mother and grandmother for the launch they gave me. That was an act of grace that I did nothing to earn. No matter how highly we may value self-sufficiency in the USA, we can all use the occasional well-timed act of grace.

Although I grew up close to OSU, I had no desire to study there until my junior year in high school. I just didn't work very hard, made poor grades through middle and high school, and argued intensely for my own weaknesses. But by my junior year, I started to feel better about myself and turned my grades around. Once I decided to go to college, it was clear that I would go to OSU because it was close to home. Plus my first girlfriend—my future wife—was going there, so I had a compelling reason to go, too.

After I graduated with a Bachelor's of Science degree with a double major in Personnel Management and Marketing, I really had no idea what I wanted to do. I interviewed intensely and got invited back for second interviews with just about every company, but I received no offers. At the time, I blamed it on the poor economy. But later, while in the MBA program, I figured out that it was my fault. Like most things that have gone poorly in my life, I had nobody to blame but myself. I didn't receive job offers after my undergraduate degree because my boredom and disinterest were apparent during those second interviews. I didn't shine because I wasn't excited about those potential positions; I was just interviewing because that's what most students do after graduation.

So with the encouragement of my new wife, I started my MBA directly after graduation, during the summer semester of 1983. Having graduated early with her Bachelor's degree, she put her own potential career on hold and worked on campus so I could seek my MBA—another act of grace of which I was the beneficiary. During my last semester of the MBA program, along with about 40 of my fellow MBA candidates, I attended an evening with a couple of gentlemen from the consulting division of Arthur Andersen and Co. As they explained it, consulting in the Andersen model was a practical thing, not a purely thought leadership exercise. They actually worked on the projects and implemented the solutions with the clients, transforming every business process within an entire organization or across different organizations. The projects were challenging and had to be completed on a specific time schedule and budget. They never knew what they would be working on next. The work was constantly changing. And Andersen had an entire career path, education program, and methodology in place intended to support each consultant. At that moment, I thought this sounded like the job for me: constantly changing, project-oriented, tangible beginning and ending points, and team-based delivery. For the first time, I could picture myself in a role. I had never been able to picture myself as an investment banker, marketing executive, human resources director, or any other role that companies came to talk about during interviews. It was like a bolt of lightning, and it is really the only time I have ever had one of those "THAT'S IT!" moments in my life.

So I signed up for the on-campus interview. A few days later, I was very pleased to receive a letter in the mail inviting me to go to Tulsa for the all-day, in-office interview. While there, I spoke with a wide variety of interesting people and liked them all. Unlike every other interview I had experienced, they all had different things to ask me and different things to tell me. Or perhaps I just perceived it that way because I was more engaged and excited about the opportunity. Either way, I was confident that this was clearly the place for me. I felt that I had found my next step in life.

You can imagine my disappointment when I received the letter two weeks later and found that they had not extended an offer to me. I was so convinced that this was where I needed to be, I picked up the phone and called the Arthur Andersen office and asked for Steve Barnett, the Consulting Managing Partner with whom I had interviewed at the conclusion of my visit. I told Steve politely, but confidently, that there must have been some mistake. I was so confident that I could do the work and was passionate about having the chance. If Steve gave me the opportunity to come back over and have another visit, I was sure whatever impression was wrong could be made right. Steve politely, but hesitantly, said that he would see if he could arrange another interview and told me he would call back.

I later learned that the other Consulting partner, Neil Kidwell, thought that I was not aggressive enough to succeed in their sometimes-highly-charged work environment. After Steve hung up the phone with me, he walked into Neil's office and said, "Neil, you know that kid from OSU that you said wasn't aggressive enough? Well, he just called me to tell me that we made a mistake by not extending him an offer. Is that aggressive enough for you?"

In the end, I got the job. Sure, I had the courage to ask for another chance, but Steve didn't have to give it to me. Another act of grace. This one, perhaps, I had a hand in helping happen.

Having finished my MBA in 18 months, I graduated in December of 1984 and started my first job as a consultant in January of 1985. For 12 years with Andersen Consulting, I worked with a variety of consumer packaged-goods clients. I acquired significant leadership, facilitation, methodological, and business process knowledge. I was competent, and my competency, made me confident in a way that does not come easily to me.

Flash forward 12 years, and I found myself in a very challenging and highly visible role with a client in Atlanta. At this point I had not worked away from my family for several years. I knew I was going to have to go on the road again if I wanted to continue on the path toward Andersen Partner, but I had reached the point that I didn't want to be apart from my family. Also, the job of Partner no longer compelled me for a number of reasons. I loved what I was doing, and I had learned a lot from my consulting position. But I began to think about what I could do next to keep what I loved about my role with Andersen, yet create something different for my clients, my teams, my family, and me.

The particular role I was playing for my Atlanta client put me in a position to see an entrepreneurial niche that could be exploited if approached with a specific business model based on a few basic principles. My consulting experience to that point, combined with the commitment to these principles and a little courage to strike out on my own, allowed me to become an entrepreneur. With my partner, I launched a services firm founded upon a few core competencies and some guiding principles.

- I hired only deeply skilled people, treated them ethically, and paid them very well.

- I sought only "difference-making" roles with clients who recognized the value that could be added by such deeply skilled people.

- I stuck to a scope of operation that allowed us to have a crisply defined personality for both clients and employees, turning away perfectly good positions that didn't fit that scope.

- I was forthright with my clients, telling them "no" when I didn't have someone with the skills that they needed, so they would believe me when I told them "yes."

In this manner, I felt that I would help create value on a personal level and have more impact on our clients, employees, their families, and my own.

So in 1997, with zero capital investment, my partner and I launched IMPACT Technology Group, Inc. (www.impact-technology.com). I have been President and Chief Executive Officer of IMPACT ever since. Typically, there are 30-60 IMPACT Technology Group members, half employees and half contractors. Since 1998, the annual gross revenue has ranged from $10-$30 million. Since we have a near-zero overhead business model, almost all of that revenue has been translated into income for our employees and contractors, my partner, and myself.

IMPACT provides very deeply skilled personnel to companies who need help with SAP, EDI, integration, and supply chain projects in several industries across the U.S., Europe, and South America. I am currently helping to lead an ERP project in Salt Lake City. My client is using that "technology" project as the lever to merge the cultures of two $1.5 billion consumer packaged-goods companies into a single, cohesive $3 billion entity and to establish a solid process, systems, and reputation backbone for growth through merger.

For me, it's not having as many people working for me as possible or having as many clients as possible, it's having the number that I can care for effectively. I want to be able to understand where they want to go with their careers and help them have a better, more marketable story for themselves after each position they play for my clients. Whether they have their next role with my firm or another firm doesn't really matter to me. If I help them tell a better story for themselves, and we have collaborated to help our client, and IMPACT has made a little money, then we have done what we can do in the moment.

I have also been Chairman of VeLocs, (www.velocs.com) since 2009. VeLocs provides software for load optimization through collaborative planning across the customer order cycle. We weren't looking to develop a software product. VeLocs sprang for the technical and supply chain work that we had done with IMPACT's clients. We saw a better way to create a solution, so we created it and are currently in the process of introducing it to various industries. Perhaps this will be where I focus most of my energy for the next few years, but I will certainly never be far from our core business.

One of the things I remember hearing a lot when I was young in my career was "find a mentor." Through experience, I have adopted a different perspective. Sure, having a mentor can help, but I have seen people use the lack of a mentor as an excuse for not overcoming their own personal challenges. Instead of mentor-seeking, I encourage people to develop differentiating practical skills and excellent behaviors. With these, a person can make his/her own way, regardless of sponsorship.

I advise people to seek allies rather than mentors. Effective allies help reveal our personal inadequacies. None of us can be excellent at everything. The sooner we embrace that, the sooner we can get better at that at which we can indeed excel. If we open ourselves up to seeking allies, we automatically adopt a posture of openness to perspective. That is a valuable posture, both to ourselves and to those around us. There is always more than one successful path forward. Sure, there are guiding principles to which a person should stick, but within those principles, there is usually room for something other than a straight line from A to B, whether it be certain aspects of a business process or ethics. Staying open to those variations from the "one true path" makes us more effective team members and leaders. I think being attuned to finding allies helps us adopt that posture.

This posture also leads to each of us *becoming* mentors, because we are open to others. And if more of us *become* mentors, more of us will *have* mentors. So I feel that by seeking allies and being open to perspective, the whole mentorship thing takes care of itself.

As I look at what I've learned so far, I see seven guiding principles that have led to any success that I have had. I didn't recognize them when I started my career. I didn't recognize them all at once. And there are times when I stray from them and it costs me. Those times I stray are the most effective reminders to stick to these guidelines. So, if your reading this story is a sign that you are open to others' perspectives, if you are going to allow me to be your ally from afar, I hope that you will learn from my mistakes as well as my successes and adopt these principles much earlier in your career than I did.

1. Be principle-centered, not opinion-centered. Within whatever areas you operate, there are always principles from which you should not stray. I don't mean ethics: one can always stray from ethics. And people often do so in order to make a short-term gain. I choose to believe that ethical selfishness costs a person in the long run. But what I mean by "be principle-centered" has to do with principles of content, ways of doing business. There are very few problems that have not already been solved. Best practices and models of excellence have already been well-defined by people far smarter than me. People smarter than you. So before you try to create something from scratch, look first for the core principles that apply to your situation. This applies to just about every part of your life:

business, politics, relationships. If you are informed about the principles, you can act within the realm of fact, which is far easier to navigate than the realm of opinion.

2. Balance perfection with practicality. Life is not about being perfect. If people stick to principles in a zealous, rigid way, they risk getting the details but missing the point. For example, information systems projects should follow a methodology. Absolutely. You should freeze design before you begin development, finish development before testing, etc. But other facets of methodology, such as documentation methods, can be tailored to fit the scale and personality of a project. For example, if you apply the rigorous documentation requirement that fits a multinational pharmaceutical company to a $100 million dollar non- regulated manufacturing company, you will be true to your principle but drown what could be a highly impactful project team in documents that add no value in that situation.

3. Listen more than you speak, and...

4. Prepare longer than you perform. I think about these together because they help me to be patient. They help me inform myself before I try to inform others, remind myself that I have gathered expertise for years in order to get in front of clients and potential clients today and appear as though I am just speaking without a script. In fact, I am speaking from a prepared script in which I have invested years of conscious pursuit.

5. Hunt opportunities, but form relationships. In the "what have you done for me lately" world of business, it's easy to just skip from one opportunity to another without regard to the individuals involved. True, you should hunt down opportunities like you're going to starve without them. No matter how many mammoths you've killed and dragged back to the cave, you should get out there and hunt for more. (See Guiding Principle #7 to understand why!) However, at the same time, I find that you have to take care of others before you take care of yourself, regardless of whether they are making any money for you at that moment. Then that energy comes back to your benefit. Your well-nurtured relationships create opportunities for you.

Sure, some people will take advantage of you. But the positive far outweighs the negative if you take the time to stay in touch and take care of people when they aren't paying you to do so. If people only get calls from you when you have something to gain, they remember that—and not in a good way.

6. Never try to come across as the smartest person in the room. Even if you are, it creates ill will. Unless you are applying for MENSA, being smart is not the point. Being effective should be the point. If you are really the smartest person in the room, then surely you are smart enough to bring others to your proposed solution without making them feel inferior or bullied.

7. Never assume that it'll last forever. This applies to everything of value. I learned this lesson from my once-wealthy family and, more times than I would like to mention, from my own experiences. This one helps me focus on staying in the moment and protecting value for the future. As an entrepreneur, you will likely need some aggressive choices to launch your business. However, to sustain wealth, I encourage you to be aggressive at launch, then protective once in flight.

I will continue to work in my businesses. I didn't launch my services business to sell, but I would very much like to develop the logistics software business to a level that I could sell it. Comparable applications have been purchased by large software companies for tens of millions of dollars. I intend to work that part of my business intensely over the next two years. If I can make that kind of money happen, I will step out of my businesses and spend my time writing, helping my former employees with their careers, and working to create more personal liberty within my community by mentoring (being an ally!) to others to help them embrace an attitude of self-sufficiency. People have opportunities in the USA that are unparalleled in the history of mankind. I would like to encourage more people to develop an entrepreneurial skill set and mind set, so that they may enjoy the liberties that I have enjoyed.

My entire life was defined by that night in 1984 when my MBA class was visited by someone who introduced me to a career path with which I had previously been unfamiliar. I would love to have that same kind of impact on someone in the 2010-11 MBA class. Now you perhaps have a better idea of why I named my company IMPACT.

Lee DeNoya
Contributed by Jarasporn Sa-ngasoongsong

KEY SUCCESS FACTORS: Be Principle-Centered, not Opinion-Centered, Balance Perfection with Practicality, Listen More than you Speak, Prepare Longer than you Perform, Hunt Opportunities—but Farm Relationships, Never Assume It'll Last Forever

WEBSITE: www.impact-technology.com and www.velocs.com

SOCIAL MEDIA: LinkedIn—Lee DeNoya; PIPL Profile—Lee DeNoya

EDITOR'S NOTES: Mr. DeNoya currently resides in Atlanta, Georgia with his wife, who also attended Oklahoma State University, and children. Lee considers his family to be his dearest friends and loves spending time with them. He is also an active golfer and a member of a local golf association.

In the face of change, we always have two choices—be a victim or be a beneficiary. It's your call.

—Rick Darnaby

A DREAM AND A ROAD TRIP

Rick Darnaby—Everyone seems to ask what the defining moment in my life was and what I learned from it. I would love to have a clever and profound one-liner to tell them, but my life has been more of a journey with countless moments and experiences that have shaped me, delivering me to the place where I am today. In college I found myself knocking on doors trying to rent out mini refrigerators—and learning a lot about business. As a collections agent, I even knocked on the back doors of delinquent consumers, learning a great deal about people who are struggling to survive. Then the night of graduation in 1979, I hopped into my '72 Mercury on a mission to travel the country and knock on the doors of companies (some of whom had already turned me down) and ask them to hire me. These experiences led to a career where I have fortunately found myself holding the reins at companies like Monsanto, The NutraSweet Co., Motorola, Somera Communications, and now Darnaby & Associates LLC. But clearly the last 30 years cannot be summed up in a clever one-liner, so I will go back and start from the beginning.

I grew up predominantly in Tulsa, OK, but spent much of my childhood in Texas. My father was a great man, involved in the oil field equipment industry and, with help from my brothers and me, a part-time cattleman. I learned a lot about who I wanted to be by watching my father (the businessman) and my grandfather (the lawyer). They both had principles, integrity, and entrepreneurial spirit, and I watched closely as they interacted with others. My father was always meeting people and eager to serve the community through his leadership. The Union School District elected him president of the school board and actually named the James R. Darnaby elementary school after him in 1980, one of many proud events he provided for his family.

After I graduated from Tulsa Union High School in 1970, I headed for Oklahoma State University for several reasons, including the great sports programs. I played football, ran track, and wrestled in high school, so sports was a passion of mine. Stillwater was close to home and my sister Connie was there, so I already had a small network in place. Although my father had instilled an entrepreneurial spirit in me, I knew that oil and gas was not my preferred industry; this meant I arrived in Stillwater without knowing what my plan for my future was. I just knew that this was the first step towards that future. After two years of trying to find my footing as a student, I was introduced by my sister to T.O. Allan. My father was the man who gave me the curiosity for business, and Mr. Allan was the man who taught me business and ignited my passion for the world of business. He had his undergrad from Duke and his Master's from the Wharton School of Business. I thought that was pretty cool. Mr. Allan had a wealth of knowledge that I found incredibly intriguing, and I was more than eager to learn from him. His business, Collegiate Products, leased mini refrigerators to college students. I thought the service we provided was a great idea. I mean, students usually only need those fridges for one year, so why not rent? As a regional manager, I spent my time traveling for the company and assumed that I would finish my education at the campuses where I was based at the time. But my pockets were not deep enough for the out-of-state tuition, and I did have the urge to go back to school and finish my education. I found myself back at OSU, and it was as if a fire had ignited. I finally knew what the professors were talking about and how it related to real life applications. The theories that had flowed into the ears and then into oblivion before, I now understood and most of the time could actually think of ways that I had applied them or could in my future. This was the first series of stops and experiences on my journey, and I was now clear about what I wanted to do.

After earning my Bachelor of Science in Business Administration degree in 1978, I decided to stay at OSU for my Master's in Business Administration. I had found a new respect for OSU and knew the lessons I learned there were going to open many doors for me. But the greatest lesson I learned in Stillwater was not in the classroom. In my last year of my master's program, my father was diagnosed with cancer. There was little that we could do for him. He wanted me to graduate, but I wanted to be with him. While the nurses rearranged my father's hospital room to enable me to work on my thesis without having to lose a single moment with my father, my classmates made sure to fill in for me when I could not make it for class. The faculty showed an amazing level of tolerance and flexibility, toward not only my limited presence in class but my physical and emotional exhaustion, which allowed me to spend every last possible moment with my father. This is a lesson in life that cannot be found on the computer or in a book. It is a lesson that exemplifies that great professors are not dedicated to the black and white outline of their curricula; they are dedicated to enriching lives. And those are the types of professors I found during my time at OSU. It was a lesson in building loyalty through compassion and support for which I remain grateful.

A lesson that I learned repeatedly is that preparation and determination can open almost any door. I graduated with my MBA in August of 1979. My mother wanted to see me walk, so I participated in the symbolic ceremony of walking across the stage and receiving my diploma. But that night was much more than just the closing of the past two years. It was that night that I loaded up the '72 Mercury with most of my meager wardrobe and headed east. The only money I had was $200 in my bank account. I also had over $15,000 in debt from grad school expenses. But that didn't stop me from setting off on the road trip that would be just the beginning of a fulfilling career.

The first stop on this trip was determined by a chemical that I had heard about while at OSU named Glyphosate. It was the active ingredient in Roundup, an herbicide that was produced by a company named Monsanto. I knew I wanted to work for a company that was on the upswing. I felt that the opportunities would be plentiful in a company that was in the midst of innovation, and Monsanto seemed like the perfect fit. I had sent my resume to them twice, and they rejected me twice. Determined not to let them make the same mistake three times, I walked into their headquarters in St. Louis, Missouri. After a seven-hour wait in the lobby, I earned a handshake and introduction to a person in the HR department. After the handshake, I earned a dinner invite and after dinner, I got my first job offer. But that offer was not for the division that I wanted. I continued my road trip, visiting a total of ten businesses (three of which extended generous offers). But it was meant to be;

Monsanto made a second offer for the division that I had set out to work in, which I accepted, and I went to work in St. Louis.

Two years later, I got a big break. The president of Monsanto Ag Company called me into his office and asked me to take on a big challenge, taking agricultural technology into non- agricultural markets. I launched three businesses: consumer, greens and turf, and industrial. For the next decade I immersed myself into building this opportunity I had been given. Other people worked nine hour days; I worked twelve. Others worked six days a week; I worked seven. Others took 3-4 weeks of vacation; I took an occasional 3-day weekend. I learned how to identify, recruit, direct, and unleash high-impact people. It was a crash course in innovation, strategy, marketing, and leadership resulting in three huge and very profitable business units.

I was rewarded with a huge promotion—to president of Monsanto Canada Inc., where I over-saw their chemicals, biotech, pharmaceuticals, electronics, and food ingredients. After two years of performance improvements, I was offered the opportunity to lead the NutraSweet Company (a Monsanto subsidiary) as a division president. Here I led a successful global post-patent strategy. This became a business case study that is still used by many MBA programs. Throughout this time I was building a network, meeting people and learning who they were, what they did, and why they did it. Leading an organization is about leading each individual. Building and developing a network is a practice that has been a key to my success, and that network and my reputation as a leader provided an opportunity to interview for my next big opportunity.

I had no technology background, something that could have been a disadvantage in my previous two positions. Now I was sitting at an interview with Motorola's Chairman, Bob Gavin, for the position of corporate vice president. Every person who had held this job previously had had a technology background; I, on the other hand pulled from the skills I learned at Oklahoma State, Monsanto, and NutraSweet. I knew the basics about technology and could build on that. In addition to that foundation, I had studied marketing under Dr. Lee Manzer, who instilled in me the ability to understand who I was selling to and what products they would be interested in. After 28 subsequent interviews, I was offered and accepted the job of corporate vice president; before I left the company, I had also held the positions of senior vice president at GM, Consumer Solutions Group, as well as regional president of the European, Middle Eastern, and African division. After Motorola, I became chief executive officer at Somera Communications, where we helped the wireless phone companies build their extensive networks. I have learned to love technology and love to create it so that others can enjoy it.

My business life has seen its share of success, and I do not attribute this to luck. I believe that you need to drive yourself to meet more people and be the best you can at something. Shake as many hands as you can; you never know what door that hand can open or what lesson you may learn from that person. You must also be willing to work harder and smarter than others around you are willing to do. I never expected to keep a perfect balance in my life and there is nothing I would take back, but the long hours and extensive travel do take a toll.

The world has changed while I have been in the corporate world: the Information Age has given way to the Conceptual Age. It used to be enough to be decent at a few different things, but now it is better to be a master of one thing. I believe in the power of innovation and have made it a point of mine to teach others about the power of innovative practices. All of this can be summed up with a quote I shared at an OSU commencement: "Life is like business. Do something good— become a master of something. Get caught at it—meet more people."

So what is next for me? In 2004 I left Somera and started my own consulting company, Darnaby & Associates LLC, where we help companies with their global business and brand strategies. This year [2010] I am in the process of launching two new ventures. One is The Conceptual Edge, a company that is going to focus on innovative management techniques and strategies in industries that are struggling. Innovation will be the key to future success, and I hope to be able to teach innovation in a university setting. Future generations need to understand that they can either be the victims or determine their future successes. I want to instill in them that networking will be their biggest ally. A network that is created wisely will provide one with amazing friends, even better mentors, and unimaginable opportunities.

The BSBA and MBA degrees I earned from Oklahoma State University provided me practical lessons that were invaluable in the workplace. But the memories and connections I gained while in Stillwater will not become dated with time; they are experiences that I will carry with me for the rest of life. If it had not been for the education both in the classroom and in life, coupled with the encouragement and support that I gained during my years at OSU, my road trip the night of graduation might have simply ended in my accepting the rejection of a company and settling for a job instead of being just the beginning of a journey that has led to a career that has taken me all over the western world, including America, France, Belgium, England, and Canada, and filled my life with experiences and people I will never forget.

Rick Darnaby
Contributed by Misty Stutsman

KEY SUCCESS FACTORS: Be a High Impact Player, Master Something, Meet More People, Become a Student of Innovation, Have Great Mentors

SOCIAL MEDIA: Facebook—Rick Darnaby; LinkedIn–Rick Darnaby; Twitter—Rickdarnaby

EDITOR'S NOTES: During his career, Rick Darnaby, has served on a number of corporate boards of directors, as well as a number of government and academic boards and committees in the USA and abroad. In addition to his BS and MBA from Oklahoma State University, he holds an Advanced Management Degree from INSEAD in Fountainebleau, France.

Rick is currently concentrating on the launch of two new business ventures, including The Conceptual Edge. In addition to his work within his own companies, Darnaby spends a considerable amount of time on the road presenting guest lectures to many top graduate schools, including Harvard Business School, INSEAD, and Northwestern's Kellogg School of Business, as well as many business and government meetings. His lecture topics include innovation leadership, leading high performance people, building market-driving businesses, and global brand strategy. He finds it a privilege to be able to share his thoughts and knowledge with the future generation of leaders.

Rick Darnaby now resides in Montecito, California, with his wife, Marilyn, who is also an OSU alumnus. They enjoy a very active lifestyle with many hobbies, including traveling, fitness training, target shooting, skiing, and spending time with their children. Their children are currently evenly distributed between Chicago and New York.

CHAPTER THREE
FOREVER ORANGE

The color orange denotes energy and change. The following MBA Alumni have either stayed at OSU or returned to OSU to use their wisdom, talents and energy to create change. Thank you for effectively educating and empowering generations of Cowboys.

We make a living by what we get, we make a life by what we give.

—*Winston Churchill*

A JOURNEY OF A THOUSAND MILES MUST BEGIN WITH A SINGLE STEP

Bob Curtis Hamm—I was born and raised in Oklahoma City, attending Lee Grade School and Capitol Hill High School. My father was a sheet-metal worker and my mother was a buyer for the John A. Brown Company Department store in Oklahoma City.

My fourth grade teacher greatly influenced me as a child. In those days, students were given IQ tests and assigned to classes based on their IQ scores. I was assigned to an accelerated class of sixteen students. Ms. Jayne told us that education was a way out of poverty, and we believed her. She gave us tickets to movies and the Oklahoma Symphony orchestra. Movies in the 1940s depicted college as a great place to learn and have fun. She was a major influence on me, and I thought, if I ever get to be a teacher, I want to be the kind that looks after my students. My aunt, who was a world traveler, also had a strong influence on who I became. She went to China in the 1930s and my desire, even as a little boy, was to visit China. She encouraged me to enter higher education, to invest in real estate, and to see the world.

I was able to enter OSU in 1951 for an undergraduate major in marketing, the discipline I enjoyed most. My first year at OSU was historic in that it was the first year the Library, the Student Union, and Bennett Hall were open. I was impressed by three brand new buildings. I worked in the kitchen and as dorm counselor at Bennett Hall to help pay for college expenses. In addition, I received $50 month for ROTC military training and taught 10-key adding machine classes in the Business School. I was active in student leadership organizations as a member of the Business Student Council, Delta Sigma Pi, Phi Gamma Delta Fraternity, and Blue Key campus-wide leadership organization (my mom encouraged me to be a member of Blue Key because their members were sharp). In 1955 I graduated with a Bachelor's degree in marketing and was commissioned a second lieutenant in the Army. I served six months of active duty, followed by 11 years in the reserves.

Following active duty, I interviewed at IBM. I arrived early because everyone said, "Don't be late for your job interview." I was standing outside a building at IBM and all of a sudden a pigeon came over and dropped something on my shoulder. And I thought, "Oh my, I'm not supposed to get this job." So I had to go in the men's room to get that all cleaned up. When I went to my appointment, they looked at me and said, "What happened on your coat?" I told them the story and they died laughing. They said, "Well normally we don't accept people who come in that way, but you'll be an exception." So I interviewed for the job and took a test required by IBM. I really wanted this job, so I called IBM and said, "How did I do on this test?" And they said, "You were number two out of 27." I said, "Well I'd really like to have this job." And they said, "The manager's wife is in the hospital, so he can't respond." I said, "I'll call back tomorrow." I called back every day for eight days. And finally the assistant manager said, "Well, why don't you just come to work for us because you show more persistence than anyone else." So that's why I got that job. I worked there for five years.

While I was working for IBM, I saved my IBM stock hoping to return to the University some day to complete an MBA. This happened when IBM wanted me to move to New York City and become a Managerial Auditor, but I was engaged and did not want to leave. OSU had the first MBA program in Oklahoma, and it was highly recommended by the media. At OSU, I taught basic computer science classes, which paid my way through the MBA program. Classes in accounting were hard, so I opted to give oral presentations because I was better at that than at working the problems. Our MBA group was older (25-30) and had more business experience than our professors. To take a break from our studies, a group of us in the MBA program liked to drive to Pawnee and have dinner at Click's restaurant; Click's has the best steaks in Oklahoma.

While I was in the MBA program the Head of the Marketing Department called me into his office one day and told me he thought I should go to The University of Texas and get a PhD and come back and teach marketing for him. I graduated from the MBA program in 1962, and then I got my doctorate degree in marketing from the University of Texas. The professor went bankrupt, but I ended up taking his place several years later.

One of my biggest challenges was fighting my childhood poverty issues and having the self esteem to believe I could get a doctorate at a major university. This esteem issue caused me to seek higher goals to prove to myself and the world that I was worthy of being in the academic world. Since I ended up being a professor, I think I was greatly influenced also by some of my professors. In my undergraduate days, it was normal to spend time in professors' offices talking in small groups about academics as well as life in general. It was like small groups with no one being the leader but everyone participating. We were being mentored but did not use that word.

In 1966 I was hired at OSU as a marketing professor. Three years later, I was promoted to Director of Graduate Studies. As a member of Dean Richard W. Poole's leadership team, we transformed the college into one of the top business schools in the nation. In 1974 the Dean selected me to be the Director of Business Extension and External Relations. I was promoted from assistant to associate professor in two years and then to full professor in five years. In 1980, I taught one semester in China and later returned to China as a Fulbright Professor for a year. My time abroad also included a year in Jordan with USAID.

Opportunity in the form of a job offer as Associate Dean for Graduate Studies at Oklahoma City University came to me, which I accepted and enjoyed for five years. After five years at OCU, I faced the biggest setback of my life, finding out that I had developed cancer. I was fortunate to be able to take a couple of years off at that point. Two years later, I returned cancer free to OSU as a Professor Emeritus, teaching two classes on business consultancy.

During my career, I've provided consulting services for many companies, organizations, and government agencies, including one year at NASA. I taught and did international consulting work in many countries throughout the world. Mentors are greatly important, as they encourage you to take those steps up the mountain. My aunt was my first major mentor regarding my real estate ventures. Dr. Edward Cundiff at the University of Texas was my greatest inspiration as an academic mentor, and there always seemed to be someone at each junction to guide me over the minefields.

Mentoring, like Christianity, I think is to help others become better people and to be a servant leader. My life has been full of doing what I wanted to do without major setbacks. My academic career always came first. It rewarded me with opportunities to teach in China, Jordan, Russia, and many other countries on Fulbright's, with USAID, and on International Rotary Scholarships. It was not typical for Oklahomans to be accepted for those awards at that time. The selection to the Oklahoma Higher Education Hall of Fame and the $250,000 for scholarships contributed by my former students is my greatest satisfaction and validation that my life was of value.

I offer the following advice, which has been important to me in achieving success and living a happy life.

- Get an education. It is one thing that no one can take away from you.

- Surround yourself with associates who can benefit you and receive value from your relationship.

- Never take yourself too seriously.

- Remember to look for the good in what is happening around you.

- Intelligence is a gift from God and must be used for good.

- You must have strong faith in yourself as well as in your Creator.

- Setting goals is one of the most important steps to success.

- Make a plan to achieve your goals.

- There are always exceptions you have to make to be successful.

Look forward several years and ask the appropriate question, "What is going to make this career valuable five years from now and what must I do to be a success now?" Whatever you do, work should be enjoyable. Find contentment and happiness in your efforts.

Bob Curtis Hamm
Contributed by Mazen Makhamreh

KEY SUCCESS FACTORS: Intelligence, Setting Goals, Faith, Making a Plan, Finding Joy in Work, Education, Not Taking Life too Seriously

WEBSITE: www.osugiving.com

SOCIAL MEDIA: Facebook—Bob Curtis Hamm; LinkedIn—Bob Hamm

EDITOR'S NOTES: Dr. B. Curtis Hamm lives in Stillwater Oklahoma. He is currently a Special Projects Consultant at the Oklahoma State University Foundation, raising money for student scholarships and for a new Spears School of Business building for future faculty and students. Dr. Hamm is a member of the Oklahoma Higher Education Hall of Fame and has received many other honors and recognitions, including Distinguished Graduate of OSU by the Alumni Association in 2005; Outstanding Educators in America; and Senior Fellow of the Center for Religion, the Professions and the Public. His many teaching accolades include the Redskin Congratulates Outstanding Faculty Award, National International Students Association Award, and the Dow Chemical Faculty Fellowship. He is held in high esteem by his former students, many of whom helped fund a $250,000 endowed scholarship in his name when he retired. Dr. B. Curtis Hamm has been selected as a Fellow by various academic institutions: The American Graduate School of Business, The University of Pittsburgh, The University of Missouri, and Oklahoma State University.

Dr. Hamm has a passion for travelling and teaching all around the world. He began his international career by taking high school and college students to countries such as Norway, Great Britain, the Netherlands, France, and Italy. He has taught graduate seminars in Russia, Singapore, China, Malaysia, and England. As a USAID professor at the University of Jordan, he helped begin their MBA program and was the first Rotary Fellow to Jordan. He additionally served as consultant to various universities in Argentina and the Czech Republic.

Dr. Hamm has served as a consultant to numerous organizations with international markets such as PepsiCo and Reynolds Aluminum. He has published numerous academic and trade articles on international subjects. His book, *The Art of Partnering,* has been translated into Russian, and articles such as "The Five Dragons of Asia" have received acclaim. Because of his great heart for international students, he was selected for the National International Students Association Award. His other awards include Yearbook Faculty Member of the Year and his mentorship of Blue Key members led him to be selected as the National Faculty Advisor of the Year. Dr. Hamm loves to tell stories; it's his favorite way of teaching and mentoring, especially when it comes to his experiences while traveling all over the world.

Bob has a cat named Meko, uses an iPhone for everything, and uses Skype to talk to people from Jordan to China, the internet to maintain some knowledge of what is happening in the world and Kindle for reading books. His son, Kevin Curtis Hamm, is married and recently had a child. Kevin and his family live in Hong Kong, where he is the General Manager of a corporation.

Dr. Hamm has influenced and been a mentor to many students and colleagues throughout the years. He is loved and respected by all who know him.

Whereas you are not only good yourself, but the cause of goodness in others.

—Socrates

BLESSED WITH SUCCESS

Lee Manzer—I was born in California, the son of migrant farm workers. When I reached elementary school age, my family moved back to Osage County, Oklahoma, where I received my K-12 education. I enrolled at Oklahoma State University, becoming the only member of my family to attend college, and received a degree in chemistry in May 1965. I was admitted to the OSU MBA program that spring and completed the degree in August 1966. I have many wonderful memories of my time as an MBA student. The MBA program was primarily designed for individuals with technical backgrounds, and the disciplines of chemistry, physics, and engineering were all well represented in my classes. The program was eye-opening to many of us regarding the intricacies of the business world.

After receiving the MBA, I was employed by Dow Chemical Company and worked as a chemist in Michigan. I soon moved from being a chemist for Dow to becoming a research assistant in the marketing department, and finally working in Dow's industrial sales division. The knowledge I gained while in the Oklahoma State University MBA program proved invaluable throughout my career at Dow Chemical and beyond, opening up many opportunities for me that I would not have had otherwise.

After working in the private sector for several years, I was determined to return to the academic world as a professor. This was something of a risk as it entailed a sizable reduction in pay, and I had a family to support. However, I had a strong desire for the academic environment and felt it was the correct decision. This movement toward the business academic world was a direct result of the MBA. I was accepted at several PhD programs, but returned to OSU and received the Doctorate in Business Administration (major in Marketing) in July 1974. In 1973, I had accepted a faculty position at Memphis State University.

In 1975, Bob Hamm, a member of Oklahoma State University's MBA class of 1962 and a professor at Oklahoma State, asked if I would be interested in a position at Oklahoma State's College of Business. It was an opportunity that could not be refused. Both my wife and I love Oklahoma State and jumped at the chance to return. I have taught at OSU for 35 years, and I do not anticipate retiring anytime soon.

I have taught over 25,000 students and made hundreds of presentations to the business world. It's been a great "ride." Throughout my career I have seen many changes in the business environment. The use of technology alone has greatly reshaped the economy, leading to greater opportunities for product development, marketing, and distribution. Social media, information systems, and e-business are just a few examples of this remarkable revolution. However, with this never-ending transformation in the business world, one may ask if there are any unchanging secrets for success. The answer is most definitely "yes." No matter the industry in which you work, your position within that industry, or your background, there are a number of principal factors that will lead to success. Examples of these factors are ethics and reliability.

A strong work and moral ethic, coupled with a passion for what you do, will nearly always take you near where you wish to go. My life is a prime example of this fact. I was blessed with goodly parents who, from a very early age, emphasized the importance of hard work and dedication to whatever I endeavored to do. I must thank their love and teaching of this simple principle, more than anything else, for whatever success I have had in my life.

A second example for success is keeping your word any time you give it. When you tell someone that you will do something, do it. This seems like a very easy prescription to follow, but far too often it is neglected in today's business world. By keeping your word, you build trust with your subordinates, coworkers, and supervisors. This trust will inevitably lead to greater responsibilities and opportunities as you progress in your career.

I have been extremely fortunate in my life. I have been blessed with loving parents, a wonderful wife whom I love, and fine children. I have also had very few obstacles and setbacks along the way. Because of these facts, I am not sure how much of my success I can take credit for. However, I know beyond a doubt that whatever part of my success I am responsible for stems from my adherence to such guidelines as stated above. Without them, my life would not have been as fulfilling or successful.

Lee Manzer
Contributed by Brock Marsh

KEY SUCCESS FACTORS: Work Ethic, Creativity, Integrity

WEBSITE: http://spears.okstate.edu/directory/41-marketing/602-lmanzer#schteach

EDITOR'S NOTES: Dr. Lee Manzer has had a very distinguished career at Oklahoma State University. He has served as department head, director of graduate studies, and director of the Small Business Institute. He has received 18 University and College teaching awards, including the University Teacher-of-the-Year Award three times (1978, 1979, and 2000), the Richard W. Poole Outreach Excellence Award (2006), and the Acton Entrepreneurship Faculty Award (2008). Additionally, Lee was recently inducted into the Oklahoma Higher Education Hall of Fame (2010).

Dr. Lee Manzer has had a profound impact on the many students and professionals he has taught throughout the years as a professor at Oklahoma State University.

Whoever renders service to many puts herself in line for greatness—great wealth, great return, great satisfaction, great reputation and great joy.

—Jim Rohn

PIONEER SPIRIT

Julie Flasch Weathers—My story begins with Julia, a young Austrian girl, who spoke no English and had recently been orphaned, traveling to a new country to enter into an arranged marriage with my future grandfather. This union brought much love and a large family, seven children of which my dad was the youngest. I was her namesake, born in Guthrie, Oklahoma, the second child of Harold and Joy Flasch. We lived in the house where my dad was born, on a farm overlooking the Cimarron River northwest of Coyle, Oklahoma (about two miles north of Langston University). My dad was a farmer/rancher who raised wheat and cattle primarily. My dad's father as well as his mother emigrated from the small village of Eltendorf, Austria. My grandfather, John Flasch moved near Coyle with his family. His older brother had married my grandmother's older sister, who also came to America.

Not uncommon at the time, my mother's father, Robert H. Childers, only completed the fourth grade and then had to go to work. He farmed and worked in the oil fields in Texas. A bit of an innovator, he later built his own water well machine and was a water well driller in southern Oklahoma. My grandmother, Lois Childers, was a hard-working homemaker who inspired her only child to "be all she could be." My mother taught for 43 years before retiring as a professor of English and director of the Honors Program at Langston University, where she had worked for 33 years. One of the first non-Black faculty members there in 1964, she was the first chairman of the Department of Communication and was named the Outstanding Faculty Member in Arts and Sciences in 1989.

We lived in the house where my Dad was born until I was 16 years old. When I was a sophomore in high school, my parents built a new two-story home near their old home. Recent Senior Olympic state champions, my parents included a recreation room in the new home, complete with a ping-pong table, where fierce competitions were held—and still are. I have a brother, Chris, 2 1/2 years older and a sister, Jeanine, 7 years younger.   Round-the-World ping pong tournaments are held with Chris, his wife, and their two teenagers; my sister, Jeanine, her husband, and their two children; and my husband, Shane, and our three boys. My mother (78 years old) and father (86 years old) and all the family have a lot of fun when we play one another.

I played both basketball and softball in high school and was named "Guard of the Year" for our area in my senior year, 1980, one of the last years for 6-on-6 girls basketball.

My dad and mom both insisted that good grades and a college education were expected and that setting goals and working hard to reach them were important in life. My dad loved sports and played with us often. My parents watched all our basketball, softball, and baseball games. My dad helped coach my brother's baseball games for nine years. In summers we worked hard on the farm, but I had an almost idyllic childhood. My mother guided me in setting goals and working toward them, especially in pursuing a higher education.

My academic career as an adult began in 1980 at the University of Science and Arts of Oklahoma in Chickasha, a small school where my best friend had enrolled. I had an academic scholarship as valedictorian of Coyle High School and had also managed to earn 21 credit hours at Langston University in summers while at home. One of my best memories of undergraduate life is playing on the tennis team at USAO. In my junior year I decided to major in Business Administration, and the following year, in 1983, I was named the Outstanding Graduating Senior at USAO.

After deciding on a business major, I knew I wanted to pursue an MBA.   With my undergraduate degree at 21, I enrolled at OSU. There I met Dr. Lee Manzer, who was the Director of the MBA Program at the time. He became my teacher and a great motivator. In 1985, I graduated from OSU with my MBA.

Faculty I will always remember include Dr. Jim Gentry for Statistics (one "tough" class) and Dr. Wayne Meinhart, in whose class I wrote a report on factor analysis. Also while at OSU, I met Becky Richards through the MBA program, where she served as assistant while I was working as a graduate assistant for Dr. Tom Pearce. Becky and I became lifelong friends and at one time, roommates. Dr. Pearce became an influence in my life as well. As his grad assistant, one of my duties was painting his office orange. It was, at that time, the only orange office in the Business building. His research was in labor relations, and we wrote a paper together, which was a real learning experience. In my second year I was a graduate assistant for Business Extension, working with Walter Shaw, Karen Ward, Lana Ivy, and Jill Hawkins under the direction of Dr. Jim Hromas. Other friends, like Paul Grizzell, Nick Colson, and Bill Cormany, I remember meeting after class for a friendly game of racquetball, basketball, or volleyball.

OSU has had a major impact on my life, being my graduate school of choice and my employer for over twenty years. I have met many interesting people from various backgrounds, which expanded my cultural education considerably.

Immediately following graduation from the MBA program, I interviewed for several jobs but really enjoyed my work in the Business Extension Office. As fate would have it, a position as Coordinator opened, and I applied for it. After working as a Coordinator in Business Extension for several years, I was promoted to Manager. Jim Hromas, the Director of Business Extension, encouraged me to keep pursuing more education, so I took courses in evenings toward the doctorate in Occupational and Adult Education, receiving an EdD in1994. Jim Hromas became Director of University Extension, and I was named Assistant Director of Business Extension. Later, when the position of Director opened, I became the Director of Business Extension.

As my career has grown, so has the Center. We have expanded to offering credit courses, distance learning, conferences, study abroad and travel, and executive and professional development. As programs evolved and administration changed, Business Extension experienced a name-change, becoming the Center for Executive and Professional Development in the Spears School of Business at Oklahoma State University. I have served as Director since 1994. Although not a business owner, I assist business owners through the Center which, I believe, runs on business principles as much as possible in a state government entity.

The OSU Center for Executive and Professional Development offers over 400 programs to 25,000 individuals with 23 full time staff and a budget of over $9 million. We offer programs through our seven departments: Accounting, Economics and Legal Studies in Business, Entrepreneurship, Finance, Management, Marketing, and Management Science and Information Systems.

One of the first programs I worked on as coordinator, and one that I am particularly proud of, was the Tulsa Business Forums, a speaker series which has now just celebrated its 25th anniversary. Our first speakers in the series in 1986-87 were Alan Greenspan (before he was Chairman of the Federal Reserve Board), Malcolm S. Forbes, Jr., and Robert Crandall, President of American Airlines. Among our many other speakers have been a number of nationally and internationally known business and government leaders such as Margaret Thatcher, Colin Powell, Lee Iacocca, Condoleezza Rice, and Mikhail Gorbachev. This program is widely known and attended today, both in Stillwater and Tulsa, and is recognized as one of the more visible contributions OSU makes to our community.

Other recent conferences include a business healthcare conference and an energy conference; a sustainability conference (which will feature Boone Pickens and Robert F. Kennedy, Jr.) is scheduled for April 2011. In 2011, we are celebrating the 20th anniversary of our Women's Business Leadership Conference, offered in cooperation with the Oklahoma International Women's Forum. We also offer an Executive Education Partnership Program and a Governor's Executive Development Program in cooperation with OU, both of which have been very successful over the years.

Our distance learning courses now number almost 200 annually with enrollments of over 7,000, including more than 260 MBA students in 33 states and 3 countries. This year we are offering 14 study abroad and travel programs through the Spears School of Business. We are fortunate to have excellent faculty, resources, administration, and staff to help support all these outreach initiatives.

The OSU Center for Executive and Professional Development has won 17 national awards and 18 regional awards for programs and/or faculty excellence. Internally, I think our office has kept the goal of having a quality organization and working hard with integrity. Externally, the economy certainly affects our enrollment in noncredit and executive development, so offering credit courses is important to maintaining financial stability for our outreach unit.

None of this hard work paid off overnight. I am very fortunate that the excellent staff in our office have that same above-and-beyond, service quality orientation that will take us far in regard to clients, both internal and external.

My parents continue to support me and my family. We built a home on their farm near Coyle over 12 years ago, and their close proximity gives me the flexibility to have a career that I thoroughly enjoy while raising a family. The support of my husband, Shane, and my three boys, Ryan, 15, Jared, 12, and Brendon, 9, is very important.

Setting goals and following through on those goals, hard work, building professional relationships, and earning the respect of those with whom you work are qualities that have served me well and that I would recommend to anyone beginning a career. As a manager, I have found it is essential to surround myself with individuals who believe in the goals of the unit and in establishing and maintaining a pleasant, team-oriented work environment. Be happy when your co-workers and employees achieve. Let them know how proud of them you are when they accomplish "great things."

While there have been a few problems with employees in the past regarding the amount of time spent on the internet, these were resolved by verbal reprimands. Usually these persons move on once they realize that the culture of our office is one of working during working hours. However, I use LinkedIn and both our office and Spears School of Business use Twitter and Facebook to market our programs and keep people up-to-date on current happenings in the Spears School of Business. The use of Facebook for our study abroad and travel programs has been quite successful.

A good work ethic allows us to lead by example, and a passion for our work is important to enable us to come to work every day and summon the energy and desire to accomplish "great things." Honesty and integrity are key to success, as is dedication to customer service. Dr.

Lee Manzer, Professor of Marketing at OSU, is one of our star performers in Outreach. He has emphasized customer service again and again, and we try to live by that example daily in the OSU Center for Executive and Professional Development.

I believe my successes have been due to the blessings of God and the support of my family, as well as to working with people who believe in a common mission. I truly enjoy the work I am doing, because the challenges and opportunities are different every day, and I am committed to not only meeting those challenges, but increasing the opportunities. I also believe that no man or woman is an island, doing it all alone. While hard work and passion are important, I believe we all answer to a higher power. Certainly my firm belief in God has sustained me through difficult times. I know I have been blessed, first in the family life that served as my foundation and now in both my career and my personal life.

Julie Flasch Weathers
Contributed by Karen Steed

KEY SUCCESS FACTORS: Family Support, Learning the Values of Hard Work, Team Work

WEBSITE: cepd.okstate.edu

SOCIAL MEDIA: Facebook—Center for Executive and Professional Development; LinkedIn—Julie Weathers

EDITOR'S NOTES: Dr. Weather's accomplishments include national awards such as the Outstanding Program Development award from Tulsa Business Forums, the Merit Award from the National University Continuing Education Association, and more recently the Energy Conference National Award from the Association for Continuing Higher Education. She has served as officer and board member for the Stillwater Chamber of Commerce and as Alumni Association President of Coyle schools. Julie was selected and participated in Leadership Stillwater and was named Woman of the Year by Cimarron Business and Professional Women. Dr. Weathers has served on numerous committees and made presentations at national and international conferences. She is married to Shane and has three adorable boys.

The only thing that stands between a man and what he wants from life is often merely the will to try it and faith to believe it is possible.

—*Richard Devos*

BRINGING THE WORLD TO OSU

James G. Hromas—While growing up on a small farm in Waukomis, in northwest Oklahoma, I never thought that my career would be spent in higher education. In fact, I just assumed I would follow in my father's footsteps and be a farmer. By high school and in conversations with my father, it became clear that the farm operation was too small to support other family members and that I should consider going to college. He agreed to help as he could with the cost of this venture. Neither of my parents had attended college.

In choosing where to go to college, I wanted to go to OSU. Many of my friends attended OSU and were very happy in Stillwater. Besides sports, I was very involved with music and held 1st chair trumpet for two years in the Oklahoma Allstate Concert Band. Phillips University, in Enid, was well recognized for its music education program and offered me a scholarship to attend. So, I chose Phillips University and enrolled. I could live at home and continue to work on the farm, and this made financial sense.

But after weeks of contemplation, I just couldn't get attending OSU out of my mind. Getting away from home and music seemed important at the time. With less than three weeks before class was to begin, I got in my '57 Chevy and headed to Stillwater, went to Whitehurst, and told them I wanted to enroll. I was so naïve—but that's when it started: August 1962. I started out in general Arts and Sciences and after some investigation, switched to the acclaimed accounting degree program.

Following a January graduation in 1967, I enrolled in OSU's MBA program. I had heard many good things about the program and the faculty, and was excited to broaden my business education knowledge base. After one semester the Army called, and I joined the Oklahoma National Guard. After the active duty period, I joined the Accounting

Division of AMOCO Corporation in Tulsa. About a year later, a call came from an OSU official offering a staff position to assist with advising the OSU fraternity system—and it was accepted immediately. Corporate life as an accountant was not what I had expected, and I was so excited to be able to continue the MBA program. In 1970, following a half-year internship scholarship at the NASA Johnson Spacecraft Center in Houston, I graduated and took a position with the College of Business Administration as Assistant Director of Business Extension. The position was charged with working with faculty to develop and deliver professional development for business, government, and associations. In 1981, I was promoted to director of the unit and served in that position for ten years. During this time, we were able to achieve significant growth in the number of people served and dollars generated; important partnerships were developed and many programs are still offered. The Tulsa Business Forums and the Oklahoma City Management Briefings were two of the most significant program achievements. During this ten year period, I was able to complete my PhD in Business Administration and joined the faculty in the Department of Marketing. Dr. Julie Weathers, a fellow OSU MBA, took over the unit and she and an outstanding staff continue to expand the programming. Particularly with the distance MBA program, they have taken the outreach program to a new level of excellence.

In 1991 I was named Director of Extension for the OSU campus. This job included outreach, public service, and distance education programs through the Colleges of Arts and Sciences, Business Administration, Education, Human Environmental Sciences, and Engineering, Architecture, and Technology. University Extension had direct responsibility for Independent and Correspondence Study and Central Office services. My title was changed to Dean of University Extension in 1994 and in 1997, and I assumed additional responsibilities for International Studies and Economic Development. At that time our unit was assigned to the beautiful building known as the Center for International Trade Development.

In 1997 OSU President Halligan asked me to form a faculty group to develop a new school to be known as the School of International Studies (SIS). I had become fascinated with international studies and development from following the career of my father-in-law, who was an international scientist and administrator with the Rockefeller Foundation. The School was approved in July 1998 by the OSU Board of Regents and involved a framework to unite all OSU colleges to engage in international education strategies. The School now has 100 M.S. students, half international and half American, with over 30 countries represented. Over 450 students participate in Study Abroad programs and more than 100 students are involved in the English Language Institute. Outreach programs have featured internationally known speakers, and millions of dollars have been generated to grow outreach program efforts. To increase the intellectual capital of the program, the school founded the Henry Bennett Fellows program. Over 25 outstanding business and government officials have been inducted including Steve Forbes, Colin Powell, and Condoleezza Rice. The school was chosen in 2009 as one of the top 10 international outreach programs in the country.

I retired in August, 2010, after 40 years of service to a university that had given me so many opportunities. When I joined Business Extension, I thought this would be a perfect place to find the small business career I had in mind. Having worked for big government and big business, I thought I would be a better fit for a small business environment. What I found was that I had many of these elements at OSU. In addition I felt that what we were doing would have a lasting effect on the development of the state. The university also supported my involvement in community, state, national, and international organizations and activities. I was fortunate to serve as the chair of Leadership Stillwater, the Stillwater Chamber of Commerce and the Stillwater Industrial Foundation. I also served on the board of directors for Leadership Oklahoma and on several of the Governor's economic development advisory boards. At the national level, I chaired the Outreach Council of the land-grant association, APLU, and served on the board of directors for the University Continuing Education Association, UCEA. In 2010, the association presented me with both the Regional and National Service awards.

I was also privileged to serve on the International Advisory Board of the College of Business Sciences at Zayed University in the United Arab Emirates. This is my second term on the International Board of Directors for Sister Cities International (SCI), which includes more than

600 US cities and 2000 international cities. Its purpose is to develop twinning agreements to promote world peace. I currently have a two-year OSU appointment as the first to hold the L. L. Boger Professorship in International Studies, working primarily with SCI.

The 40 years went by way too fast and I'm so lucky to have had these opportunities. I credit all of my education degrees for preparing me for this career. One particular thing the MBA program did was force me into a class environment that required me to interact with others in exploring endless difficult problems. It was a very competitive setting and helped me to evaluate and find valuable solutions. I applaud the 50 years of the outstanding MBA program and remain very proud to be one of its graduates.

James G. Hromas
Contributed by Lindsey Liotta

KEY SUCCESS FACTORS: Passion, Work Ethic, Leadership, Networking

SOCIAL MEDIA: LinkedIn—Jim Hromas

EDITOR'S NOTES: Dr. James Hromas resides in Stillwater, OK with his wife, Kathryn. He has a daughter, Lindy, who lives and works in Tulsa and who is also an alumnus of Oklahoma State University.

Dr. Hromas has had an impressive career at Oklahoma State, using his drive and passion to make a significant impact in several areas. As a long-time supporter of Outreach activities, Jim is an outstanding mentor in encouraging other continuing education professionals to become involved in UCEA at the state, regional, and national levels.

Jim's accomplishments at all levels are exceptional. In 2008 he won the John L. Christopher Outstanding Leadership Award and is certainly an inspiration to those who work in Outreach and continuing education to aspire to his type of leadership. Other awards include OSU Arts and Sciences Center for African Studies and Development Appreciation Award, 2007; OSU School of International Studies Student Commitment Award, 2006; OSU African Student Association Appreciation Award, 2006; OSU School of International Studies Student Vision Award, 2005; recognition as Maestro Honorifico by the Universidad Popular Autónoma del Estado de Puebla, 2006; and the

Global Vision Award, OSU Global Agriculture Organization, 2004.

Dr. Hromas was involved in several international programs and activities, several of which helped gain recognition for OSU in the national and international community. Some of his international activities include developing and raising funds for The School of International Studies, serving on the Board of Directors for Sister Cities International, providing leadership and support for the Oklahoma International Strategic Plan, and being active in the Oklahoma Department of Commerce. Dr. Hromas has traveled the world, speaking and working in Brazil, Canada, Ethiopia, Iraq, Italy, Japan, Mexico, Poland, Russia, Taiwan, Thailand, Ukraine, and the United Arab Emirates—lists of his accomplishments and activities seem endless. He has spent his life and his career representing Oklahoma State with his outstanding leadership and service at the regional, national, and international level.

What you get by achieving your goals is not as important as what you become by achieving your goals.

—Zig Ziglar

SUPERMOM AND
THE RECIPE FOR SUCCESS

Betty Simkins—As the youngest of four children and the only girl, my family had great expectations for me. I learned from the get-go to stand up and fight for what I believe in, no matter the obstacle. Both of my parents were doctors and in my family, hard work and dedication were not just words, but a way of life. As expected, upon graduation from high school I attended the University of Arkansas, studying chemical engineering (not in the least a "fluffy" major). After graduating in 1980, my husband and I moved to the great state of Oklahoma to go to work for Conoco. While working at Conoco, I began a discussion with my supervisor about my options for the future. My supervisor had an MBA and thought that perhaps I would benefit from obtaining one myself. Frankly, I had only a vague idea of what an MBA was or how it could or would benefit my career, but Oklahoma State University was right down the road. Perhaps I should give it a shot!

I remember my time at OSU fondly. Dr. Lee Manzer was the Director of the MBA program. I met some really great friends and mentors who provided immeasurable knowledge and guidance in the course of my life decisions. Dr. James Jackson was my MBA thesis advisor as well as a close friend and confidant who would prove crucial in providing direction on my future career path. Upon graduation in May of 1983, I accepted a position at Williams Company in Tulsa, OK, as a member of the planning team. The combination of an engineering degree plus the MBA was very appealing to them. However, after only two years of work, my husband and I discovered that we would have a new addition to our family. I was thrilled with the prospect of a new life challenge, but was now uncertain as to what direction my career path would lead me. I knew that with a new baby at home, perhaps working full time would no longer be a viable option. I investigated my options, and with the guidance and direction of my husband and mentors, I decided to pursue a position as a teaching adjunct at the University Center at Tulsa (UCAT). Little did I know that eventually this would become OSU-Tulsa! I taught as an adjunct for several years, during which time my family continued to grow. My husband accepted a position in Texas, and I continued to teach as an adjunct for the University of Texas at San Antonio.

Eventually, I decided that I wasn't getting any younger. What did I want to do with the rest of my life? I had every intention that once my children were a little bit older, I would rejoin the corporate world. However, I had no idea how much I would love teaching! After more consideration, my husband and I decided to move our family to Ohio so that I could pursue my PhD at Case Western Reserve University. I never anticipated the challenges I would face during those years in Ohio. My beloved mother developed a degenerative disease that would eventually rob her of her life. My husband and I added a fourth child to our family at this time (a big surprise!). I liked to humorously refer to her as the third essay of my dissertation because I had her at that point in my studies. To say I was "stressed out" would be an understatement of epic proportion. However, with the loving support of my husband and family, I obtained my PhD in 1997. Then we began to discuss where we should go from there.

My first thought was "Let's go back to Texas!" All of those cold and dreary Ohio winters had done a number on me. I needed to get back to the warmth and sunshine of the "sunbelt." However, while investigating potential job opportunities, I discovered an opening at my MBA alma mater. I made a quick call to my former thesis advisor and mentor, Dr. James Jackson, to inquire about the open position and the "climate" of the department. He spoke highly of Dr. Janice Jadlow, the department head, and thought I would like working in the department. After a lengthy discussion, I had no hesitation in submitting my resume. Not to be overly optimistic, I sent off a couple of others as well, but was overjoyed to receive an offer to teach as an Assistant Professor at OSU. (I am now the Williams Companies Professor of Business/Professor of Finance at Oklahoma State University!) Interestingly enough, my current office is the same one that my mentor, Dr. Jackson, occupied while I was working with him on my thesis. Also, I have to point out that Dr. Janice Jadlow has been a great mentor and colleague to me too—

just as Dr. Jackson thought. Both Dr. Jackson and Dr. Jadlow have been very important to my career—both as mentors and friends.

Now, several years later, my three older children have grown up and flown the coop to experience their own life opportunities. My husband, my "3rd essay" daughter (born just three months after my mother passed away), and I are dedicated to finding a way to make it work in Stillwater. There have been other job offers, struggles with a dual income family, layoffs, and other day-to-day problems; but we love our life, we love our community, and we look forward to the opportunities ahead. With a network of close friends and colleagues, as well as the support of family, I am truly in the place where I was destined to be. This may not have been the future I pictured as that naïve young Arkansas schoolgirl, but I have discovered many things about myself along the way. Not only was that ingrained work ethic important to my success, but I would never have made it this far without discovering the love of teaching and research, maintaining a positive attitude and enthusiasm even while facing hardship and adversity, and developing those relationships both personal and professional that have helped me along the way. Most importantly the love and support I have received from my husband over the past 30 plus years has given me the ability to continue pursuit of the career that I love. In addition, I am blessed to know that I have also made a difference in the lives of my students and that they consider me to be a mentor as well.

Betty Simkins
Contributed by Jennifer Schneider

KEY SUCCESS FACTORS: Work Ethic, Integrity, Passion, Enthusiasm, Positive Attitude, Networking, Supportive Family

WEBSITE: http://spears.okstate.edu/~simkins

SOCIAL MEDIA: LinkedIn—http://www.linkedin.com/in/bettysimkins

EDITOR'S NOTES: Dr. Simkins has been married to her husband, Russell Simkins, for over 30 years. They have three grown children, Luke, Walt, and Susan, as well as a daughter, April, who still lives at home. Betty enjoys walking and jogging in the Oklahoma heat! Dr. Simkins has received numerous awards and honors for her teaching, research, and publications including most recently receiving the Regents' Research Award this past November (2010), the Regents Distinguished Teaching Award (2001), the Outstanding OSU MBA Faculty Award (2002) and the Merrick Foundation Teaching Award (2001). She has authored or co-authored more than 40 publications. Her current research interests include enterprise risk management, financial and energy risk management, international finance, and corporate governance. Her stated primary goal in teaching is to bridge the theory/practice gap so that students better understand how to apply what they learn in the classroom to their jobs when they graduate.

A career is a marathon, not a race with a clear finish line in sight.

Stephen J. Miller

REFLECTIONS ON A SUCCESSFUL ACADEMIC CAREER

Stephen J. Miller—I have been asked about what inspired me to pursue a career in academics. Rather than a single moment or event, it could best be described as a culmination of decisions, made at various stages of my life, when my opportunities and interests aligned.

Upon my graduation from high school in Oklahoma City, my parents fully expected me to advance to college, even though neither of them had collegiate study. The singular choice was "where" to study. My desire was to stay close to home and friends and to be mindful of the financial sacrifices my family made to pay my way. An older brother of mine had just graduated from OSU the previous year, so with the blessings of my family and friends, I headed off to Stillwater.

My initial plan was to study mathematics. However, when advanced differential equations came on the scene, my interest quickly changed to business. During my study at the undergraduate level, I was active in the Phi Delta Theta social fraternity and thoroughly enjoyed the social and service opportunities it provided. Many of my fraternity brothers were in business, and the fit seemed good. I married Lynne, my loving wife of 49 years, during my senior year and as a newlywed, my thoughts turned toward our future plans together. Upon graduation in 1962 with my Bachelor's of Science in General Business, I took a close look at the job opportunities available. I felt my opportunities for quality employment would improve if I focused on graduate education, and for the first time, truly sought to excel in the classroom. I was not sure at that moment what I really wanted to do with my career, but felt that the advanced education would surely meet my needs. I made the decision to stay at OSU for my Master's in Business Administration degree as a personal and financially feasible option. As a side note, my wife was able to secure a secretarial position in the Office of the Dean of Business.

In 1962, the MBA program focused on broad-based managerial study with little opportunity for specialization. However, since my favorite course work at the undergraduate level was in marketing, I sought graduate level courses in the field where feasible. The MBA program was very new at OSU when I enrolled in 1962 and there were only three marketing faculty at the time. Thus, few options were available. I applied for and received a graduate assistantship and was very thankful for the financial support and the opportunity for close faculty interaction. Additionally, the chance to teach a Principles of Marketing course arose. The change of perspective from student to instructor greatly expanded my thoughts on the coursework in new ways, and I found real enjoyment and satisfaction in teaching.

While on an assistantship, I had much greater interaction with the faculty, including a young marketing professor who sparked my interest in pursuing a career as a professor. Being closer to my own age than most of the other faculty, I was able to visualize, through many involved discussions with him, about what a career in academics would be like. He strongly encouraged me to continue my education with the goal of a career in the academic field. In 1963, I completed my MBA and began that next career step of getting my PhD.

Lynne's family was from California, so I limited my university considerations to West Coast doctoral programs. After focusing on UCLA and UC Berkeley, I decided on UCLA and was again fortunate to be selected for a research assistantship. Over the next four years, I completed my doctoral degree and continued to do occasional classroom instructing. After earning my PhD in Marketing, I was hired as an Assistant Professor at Penn State University. Of course my early years at Penn State were focused on instruction and research.

In 1971, Lynne and I chose to return to Oklahoma when I was offered the position of Associate Professor in the Administrative Sciences department of the College of Business Administration. My position required balanced attention to instruction, research, and outreach. After 10 years I moved into administration in various capacities including Department Head, Associate Dean, and Center Director.

During the last 25-30 years of my academic career, increased opportunities in the areas of instruction and service arose. These included distance education and international education. Neither matched my prior academic study and research, but the initiatives were deemed critical to the university and both were appealing. In many ways, both areas were at odds with the traditional perspectives of that time. A number of professors and administrators had doubts about the educational value of distance learning and felt it offered an inferior product to the traditional, face to face, classroom environment. Likewise, international issues were viewed cautiously as weak in academic quality and primarily "boondoggles."

One individual who supported the further development of both distance learning and international outreach was Dr. Robert L. Sandmeyer, Professor Emeritus and Dean Emeritus of the College of Business Administration, now the Spears School of Business. Dr. Sandmeyer had a strong desire to develop and position OSU's business programs for the future. Through his involvement with the Association to Advance Collegiate Schools of Business (AACSB), he came to recognize that these were areas where OSU could establish itself as a leader in higher education and better serve students' educational needs. I worked with him extensively on both areas of attention and have found it quite rewarding.

In particular, I was willing to step outside my academic comfort zone and accept the challenges that he presented in expanding and refining our programs. Dean Sandmeyer provided an unwavering base of support for me and others.

Early offsite distance learning involved the use of televised classroom lectures known as "Talkback TV." The video was beamed out to remote sites at Conoco, Halliburton, and Phillips. The technology was advanced for the day, but limited in that while the students could see the instructor, he or she couldn't see the students. If questions arose, the student needed to pick up a telephone handset to communicate with the instructor. Additionally, the broadcasts were of on-campus lectures to full-time students while the off-site viewers were mid-level managers. Obviously, the two groups bring different perspectives and experiences to the classroom. As the number of locations grew, the limitations on delivery and interaction became significant. I worked to develop changes to the delivery methods to improve the distance learning quality and began lectures uniquely to off-campus students. As newer technology became available, I continued to implement the advances to improve the student's educational experiences.

This does not mean that my initiatives were always accepted without resistance. I realized that in challenging the traditional classroom model, I was going to face significant skepticism from administrators and peers alike. To make the required progress, I took risks with implementing the new technology, experimented with delivery methods, and redesigned classroom interaction methods. I was always willing to stand before my peers and the administrators to discuss what I tried and whether it worked or didn't. I had to accept that not all of my ideas were going to find approval, and I sometimes had to take an unpopular position to fight for what I thought was best. Today, the Spears School of Business provides distance education programs at both the graduate and undergraduate levels with a high degree of faculty involvement and I'm proud to have been part of the pioneering faculty.

As an outgrowth of my experience in distance education, I have frequently been a presenter at OSU, and elsewhere, on challenges faced by the faculty in this arena. Additionally, I have demonstrated teaching adaptations as technologies. In recognition of my innovative initiatives, in 2004 I received the Great Plains Region V Teaching Award and in 2005 was selected for the UCEA National Excellence in Teaching Award.

Another success was my design and implementation of the Executive Interaction Program. It was intended to develop the presentation skills of students and to stimulate professional and social interaction among MBA students, faculty, and business executives through on-campus visits of top-level executives, case analysis scenarios, and MBA students' presentations of their analyses to the visiting executives. Today, campus visits by top-level executives are viewed as fairly commonplace, but in the 1970s, it was very cutting-edge. The opportunity to make and defend presentations as team members and to articulate their rationale and justifications to active business executives has significant benefits to the students. It has become a fundamental component of the program and has greatly expanded since its introduction.

The second area of focus that consumed my time over the latter years of my career was in international education. This instructional and outreach focus again was supported by Dean Sandmeyer, and the deans that followed. In 1991, the business school established the Office of International Business Programs and I am honored to have been allowed to direct that office over a 15-year period.

During this time, I did extensive foreign country lecturing, spearheaded OSU initiatives growing out of three federal grants received, and building university contacts and cooperative relationships in instruction/research   In 1991, I joined Dr. Jim Jackman, Associate Professor of Legal Studies, in establishing the first business study abroad program at OSU. Over time, hundreds of students and over 35 faculty members have participated in the program. A few years later, I initiated programs in Japan and France. The latter program still has strong enrollments. Today, the school provides 14 different foreign study programs for students and professional development opportunities for participating faculty. Additionally, on-campus and study-abroad international business course offerings have moved from two in 1990 to 15-20 today.   In 2004, I was awarded the Outreach Excellence award by the Office of International Education and Outreach.

A person who deserves much credit for the distance education initiatives and for international education is Dr. James Hromas, who received Bachelor's, MBA, and PhD degrees from OSU and, retired in 2010. As the Director of Business Extension and later as the Dean and Director of the School of International Studies, he has been an outstanding leader and supporter of my involvements in those areas. I worked closely with him in the creation and development of the School of International Studies at OSU and the graduate program in International Studies. His focus and commitment were invaluable to me and to OSU.

Upon my retirement from OSU in 2007, Dr. Hromas encouraged me to join the School of International Studies on a part-time basis and I served as Director of Graduate Studies for 2 1/2 years. This provided me more extensive involvement in university-wide international initiatives.

It was very satisfying to finish my on-campus career as the Director of a program that was only a distant vision when I first began teaching at OSU.

During much of my career, the administrators that I worked for have provided support of my initiatives and encouraged creative approaches to advancing education at OSU. They identified their goals and turned me loose to find a way to achieve them. As I progressed in my career and took on more administrative roles, I tried to keep my guidance similarly limited to providing opportunities for others to succeed without constraining the methods of achieving that success.

Challenging the traditional role of a professor in the classroom does not lend itself to always being the most beloved by others. Recognition for my work was usually reserved for after-the-fact when, over time, things had been proven to work. This did not bother me significantly, as I was passionate about the value of the goals I was aiming to achieve and had the support of my immediate peers and family.

I believe it is very important to keep balance in your life between work, family, church, community, and country. I have a wonderful and supportive family life. My wife, Lynne, has my love and unending gratitude for all of her years of support and companionship. My daughters, Stephanie, Heather, and Jennifer, all graduated from OSU and have been successful in the business world, their communities, and in their family lives. I often had to work long hours, but I kept my family time as special. Work is only part of your life; your family transcends your career and retirement years.

One should be engaged in your community and give back when you can. In that regard, I serve as the Executive Director of the Governor's International Team for the State of Oklahoma. Its dual mission is international economic development and the attraction of direct foreign investment by bringing together private sector, governmental, educational, and non-governmental organizations in Oklahoma. Additionally, I am a 20-year member of the Oklahoma District Export Council and have served on other state and community organizations, providing leadership when appropriate. Serving the citizens of Oklahoma in this role is one way I can help to give back to the state.

It is important to identify goals in life, but be flexible. Your passions, interests, and life situations will change over time. Allow yourself to revisit your goals and adjust them accordingly. Have confidence in yourself and be willing to stand up for what you believe. You may not always win the day, but you will have stood for your convictions and will likely succeed in the long run. A career is a marathon, not a race with a clear finish line in sight.

Stephen J. Miller
Contributed by Randy Tiedt

KEY SUCCESS FACTORS: Willing to Challenge Academic or Work Traditions, Willing to Take Risks, Balancing Career Objectives with Family Life, Passion, Focus.

EDITOR'S NOTES: Dr. Stephen Miller is a Professor Emeritus of Marketing at Oklahoma State University. He was born in Enid, Oklahoma and moved as a child to a small farm near Oklahoma City. His father had his own moving and storage business for over 25 years. Growing up on the farm, he had many daily chores and had to learn to work independently at an early age.

Dr. Miller's instruction and research activity has integrated marketing strategy and international business. He has lectured in many countries and traveled extensively to Pacific Rim, European, and Latin American countries. He has been a frequent coordinator and instructor in the Spears School of Business study abroad programs to France, Japan, Mexico, and the UK. Dr. Miller has authored over 40 academic publications and technical reports dealing with marketing and related issues. He has been frequently recognized for his higher education contributions including being named a Regents Service Professor and receiving the President's Service-Outreach Faculty Excellence Award and the UCEA National Teacher of the Year Award.

Dr. Miller works closely with the business and governmental communities to enhance their export activities and global competitiveness. He is a member and past chairman of the Oklahoma Governor's International Team and also serves on the Oklahoma District Export Council. Dr. Miller has conducted many management development seminars for industry and has organized seminars and conferences on international activities. Finally, he has hosted individuals and delegations from different countries during their visits to OSU and the state.

Dr. Miller served the university in a number of administrative capacities including as Head, Department of Marketing; Director, International Business Programs; and Director, M.S. in International Studies Program. Additionally, he has been an educational leader in the application of telecommunications technologies to distance education. The latter involvement has included extensive distance learning instruction at the graduate level throughout the United States.

Dr. Miller has been actively involved with Rotary International, serving in local leadership roles. He is also active in his church and has served as president of his congregation and also as a church elder.

Motivation will be highest when you align your innate God-given gifts, abilities, and passions with the opportunities that are available (or that you create).

—Tom Brown

THEY PAY ME TO DO THIS?

Tom Brown—"Well, you know you're just a frustrated marketing profes-sor, don't you?" I was working as marketing coordinator at Stillwater National Bank and Trust Company. Bob Hamm, my mentor in the MBA program at OSU, happened to be in the bank that day back in 1987. Becoming a university professor was something that I had in the back of my mind as a potential career, even though I thought I'd pursue it a little later in life. Bob must have recognized that; I'll always appreciate his not-so-subtle nudge to get on with it.

I trace my passion for scholarship and my appreciation for hard work back to my youth. I was raised in Chandler, about 40 miles southeast of Stillwater. In 1972, my father purchased a furniture store in Chandler; he's been there ever since. He and my mother worked dili-gently to make the store a success in order to provide for our family. I began doing small jobs around the store dusting the furniture and sweeping the floors when I was about 12 or 13 years old. Growing up, our lives revolved around our church and the store. Thanks in large part to the influence of my parents, my life today centers around my love for God, my family, and an appreciation of the value of hard work.

My parents certainly promoted studying hard and going to school. They weren't able to go to college, so it was important to them that I continue my education after graduating from Chandler High School. School usually came easily to me so I was happy to continue. I began my undergraduate studies at OSU in the fall of 1979 and continued to work in the furniture store. I would leave Chandler for Stillwater on Sunday nights, headed toward Parker Hall, my "home away from home" for four years. I would study and go to class during the week, returning home on Friday to be with my family and work all day Saturday at the furniture store.

I received my Bachelor's Degree in marketing in 1983. At the time, the job market wasn't all that great and I was being particular about what I wanted to do, knowing that grad school was always a nice fall-back plan. Plus, my then-girlfriend (and future bride) DiAnn was about to begin her undergraduate studies at OSU . . . no surprise, I ended up sticking around. After a year in the MBA program, I took a full time job at Stillwater National Bank, thanks in large part to an assist from Bob Hamm. After that, I completed the MBA program one course at a time, finishing up in 1988. For some, starting and completing an MBA immediately after the undergraduate degree may work out fine. For most people, though, I strongly recommend waiting a few years and gaining valuable experience. During the first year of my MBA program, it felt as though school had never stopped; I was simply a "fifth year senior." When I began to work and take classes simultaneously, however, the coursework took on new meaning—I had a context within which I could make connections between what I was learning in school and experiencing in the work place.

Immediately after completing my MBA—and not too long after Bob's words of wisdom—I left the bank to pursue the PhD. As I mentioned before, academics sort of came naturally to me. After consulting with John Mowen, another of my mentors (and one of my current faculty colleagues), and others, DiAnn and I loaded up the U-Haul and headed north to the University of Wisconsin at Madison. It was a tremendous opportunity to be mentored by Gil Churchill, one of the world's leading scholars in the marketing area. School went well and DiAnn and I were forced to grow up and depend on each other so many miles away from home. After a lot of work, time invested in close friends, and loads of fun, we left Wisconsin in 1994 with PhD and our first son (Drew) in tow.

I spent the next three years in Dallas at Southern Methodist University. SMU has a terrific business school and I really enjoyed my colleagues there. Work was going well and our family was thriving, adding another son (Taylor) and a daughter (Avery). In the spring of 1997, though, we were given the opportunity to return to Stillwater and OSU (yes, you can "go home again") and we've remained here ever since (adding another son, Brady, in the process). I now have the opportunity to mentor others as Bob Hamm mentored me, continuing the cycle (Bob was also an MBA student here years ago).

I recently was asked if I could share a challenge that I had to overcome. Nobody likes to remember the difficult times, but I'd like to offer some advice about something I learned the hard way. One of the key tasks in obtaining a PhD is the completion of a dissertation. The dissertation research must be approved in advance in what's known as a "proposal defense." When I developed the initial ideas about what I wanted to do, I worked very closely with my advisor to develop a plan. The problem, however, was that I wasn't listening very closely to the other members of my dissertation committee—they were telling me (in their own nice ways) that what I was doing wasn't enough to satisfy them. Failing that first proposal defense (the committee didn't use the word "fail," but that's what it was) was probably the worst day of my professional life, but in hindsight there's a valuable lesson to be learned about keeping arrogance in check and listening to input from others, especially when they hold more power than you do! Seek out mentors—you need someone that motivates you, someone that you can trust to tell you the truth. Find people in your church, your profession, a business organization, whatever is appropriate . . . but everyone needs someone who has lived it and can give you insight and direction.

In my profession (which mostly involves conducting research and publishing it in scholarly journals, as well as teaching college students at all levels), the primary keys to success include motivation and a "threshold level of intelligence" as Churchill used to tell me. Frankly, of these two success factors, motivation is more important. Getting out of bed in the morning and being excited about what you do is incredibly central to success in any field. Motivation will be highest when you align your innate gifts, abilities, and passions with the opportunities that are available (or that you create).

Completing the MBA was very important for me, as it confirmed the career path I would later take. I plan to keep on doing what I'm doing until God leads me in another direction, which is always possible. I'm one of those people who wake up in the morning and say, "I can't believe they pay me to do this!"

Tom Brown
Contributed by Grant Sparks

KEY SUCCESS FACTORS: Motivation, Getting out of Bed in the Morning, Being Excited about What You Do, a "Threshold Level of Intelligence", Finding Mentors

WEBSITE: http://spears.okstate.edu/directory/41-marketing/749-tomb#present

EDITOR'S NOTES: Tom is Ardmore Professor of Business Administration and Professor of Marketing in the Spears School of Business at Oklahoma State University, as well as International Research Fellow in the Oxford University Centre for Corporate Reputation.   In addition to his BS and MBA from Oklahoma State University, Tom holds an MS and PhD from the University of Wisconsin—Madison. Tom's current research interests include corporate identity, corporate reputation, and the customer orientation of service workers. His research has been published in a wide range of scholarly journals.

Currently, Tom teaches marketing theory (PhD program), services marketing (MBA program), and marketing research (undergraduate) at Oklahoma State University. He is co-founder (with Peter Dacin) of the Corporate Identity / Associations Research Group. Tom currently serves as president-elect of the Academic Council of the American Marketing Association. He is coauthor (with Gilbert A. Churchill, Jr., and Tracy A. Suter) of *Basic Marketing Research* (7th ed.).

Tom lives in Stillwater, Oklahoma, with his wife DiAnn and their four children: Drew, Taylor, Avery, and Brady. They are active in leadership positions with Young Life of Stillwater and Sunnybrook Christian Church.

Combined with hard work and a higher education, your relationships with others can give you the background and experiences needed for achieving your dreams.

—*Ronald Bussert*

BUILDING RELATIONSHIPS FOR SUCCESS

Ronald Bussert—My name is Ron Bussert, and I am the Vice-President for Administration and Finance for the Oklahoma State University—Tulsa campus. In this capacity, I oversee a variety of administrative functions such as the business office, human resources, and marketing as well as the police, the physical plant, and IT services. I completed my MBA from Oklahoma State University in 1979 and have worked in many different professional roles during my career. If there is one key factor that has contributed to my career, I think that it would have to be "relationships." Combined with my education, the real and honest relationships (much deeper than networking) I have been blessed with over the years have shaped my experiences, provided growth opportunities, and helped mold me into the person I am today.

I was born and raised in southeast Kansas. Growing up, we lived in the small towns of Cherryvale and Independence, where my father worked for an oilfield pipeline company. When I was in the 5th grade, my father (who worked very hard and was a great relationship builder) was transferred to Houston and then to Shawnee, Oklahoma. While attending Shawnee High School, I was elected Governor of Boys State. After high school, I attended OSU and with my parents' support, became the first in my family to obtain a Master's degree.

In 1978, I graduated from OSU with my Bachelor of Science in Accounting. I really did not know what I wanted to do after graduation. The work environment was very competitive, and I felt that I needed more education to be successful in the marketplace. I knew that Oklahoma State's MBA program was highly regarded in this region of the country and I decided to apply.

It was while studying accounting at OSU that I met Dr. Usry, with whom a very meaningful and important relationship developed. Milton Usry was an accounting professor, author of our accounting text, and advisor who helped me "find my way". He encouraged me during my course work and supported me during the application process for the MBA program. Dr. Usry cared about his students and their lives. Without his direction and support, I doubt I would have entered the MBA program.

My first position after graduation was with the Public Service Company of Oklahoma as a budget analyst. By age 24, I was the Director of Finance for the City of Chickasha, Oklahoma. I attribute this management opportunity to my MBA education. It broadened my horizons beyond accounting. In a significant way, my MBA provided me the skill set for management opportunities early in my career, leading to more significant roles in later years.

After the Director of Finance position, I worked at the State Auditor's office, in public accounting during which I completed my CPA, and I then moved on to Bank of America (previously First Interstate Bank and Boatmen's Bank of Oklahoma) as an Internal Audit Manager and then Director. During my years at the bank, I earned my law degree at night from Oklahoma City University and got to know Ken Townsend, the president of the bank. Ken was supportive while I went to law school and later promoted me to Assistant General Counsel for Oklahoma City and the western half of the state. He had worked his way up in the bank, starting literally in the mail room, and demonstrated that hard work, a little risk taking, and good relationships were his keys to success.

An extremely influential mentor in my life is Russell Perry. I worked with Russell both in the public and private sectors. Russell is a self-made success, owning radio stations, a bank, and a newspaper in Oklahoma City. Russell chaired the Audit Committee of the Board for the bank while I was Audit Director. Russell later was asked to be Oklahoma's Cabinet Secretary of Commerce for Governor Frank Keating's administration. Through my relationships with Russell and with Oklahoma's Secretary of State Mike Hunter, OSU graduate and long-time friend, I received the gubernatorial appointment as Executive Director of the Oklahoma Department of Commerce. As Executive Director of Commerce, I had the opportunity to work in economic and community development and to represent Oklahoma with Governor Keating and

Secretary Perry nationally and internationally. Many new relationships were formed during my time at Commerce.

Both Russell and Ken impressed me with their business savvy, willingness to work hard and take risks, and their ability to forge quality relationships. They both achieved tremendous success. Their examples were strong indicators to me of the importance of hard work and meaningful relationships.

After serving in the Oklahoma Department of Commerce, I had the opportunity to work in higher education as the Vice President of Fiscal Affairs for East Central University in Ada, Oklahoma. After a couple of years, I moved to my current position at OSU—Tulsa. While I was qualified for these roles, the strong relationships I built over the years allowed me to gain the references that assured me the opportunities in higher education.

I love working in higher education (previously an adjunct professor at the University of Central Oklahoma and the Oklahoma City University School of Law), particularly at OSU, and plan to finish my career in this field. Not only do I work in the capacity for which I am trained, but I also continue to develop relationships in higher education, with business and community leaders, and by interacting with students. It is quite gratifying to be part of an organization that makes a difference in people's lives, like it made in mine. Through my relationships and experience, I have been blessed to have a rewarding career.

Getting a good education is about having options, choices about where to go and what to do. In large part due to my higher education, my career has progressed with significant roles in the private and public sectors that I have enjoyed. Getting a higher education opens doors that may not be open to everyone, but it is not often education alone that leads to success. In addition to an education, my MBA provided me the opportunity to develop organizational skills and to excel in my career with opportunities to build life-long business relationships and friendships. The friendships that I made led me down a rewarding career path. And it is not a one-way street. It takes real relationships and friends.

Combined with hard work and a higher education, your relationships with others can give you the background and experiences needed for achieving your dreams.

Ronald Bussert
Contributed by Austin Parks

KEY SUCCESS FACTORS: Higher Education (BS, MBA, JD), Hard Work, Relationship Building

WEBSITE: www.osu-tulsa.okstate.edu

SOCIAL MEDIA: Facebook—osutulsa

EDITOR'S NOTES: Dr. Bussert wants to thank his wife of 23 years, Ellen, and two sons, Jack and Paul, for their love and support. Dr. Bussert is an avid college sports fan and loves to spend time supporting his two sons in their high school marching band. Bussert is active at Bixby First United Methodist Church and is a life member of the Oklahoma State University Alumni Association, where he serves on the Board of Directors and has served on several of the association's committees. He has been a member of several business and community organizations and serves as the Board Chair for the Tulsa Global Alliance, which manages Tulsa's Sister Cities, visits from student and business exchange programs, and contracts with the U.S. State Department to assist foreign visitors who come to Tulsa.

CHAPTER FOUR
ATHLETICS, ACADEMICS AND LIFE

Athletics have impacted the lives of many, whether they be spectators, participants, coaches, or administrators. The following MBA alumni have excelled in athletics, academics, and life.

Every great dream begins with a dreamer. Always remember, you have within you the strength, the patience, and the passion to reach for the stars to change the world.

—Harriet Tubman

BELIEVE IN YOURSELF
AND LOVE WHAT YOU DO

James Michael Holder—Born in Odessa, Texas and growing up the son of an oil field worker, I never imagined that I would be fortunate enough to work at Oklahoma State University and enjoy a four-decade career associated with athletics. Little did I know the hard work, trials, and tribulations of my family, trying to make a living in the oil patch, were developing the drive and competitive nature I have today.

Following graduation from high school in Ardmore, OK, I pursued a marketing degree from OSU and was a representative on the OSU golf team. On the course I was fortunate to learn many life skills from my coach, Labron Harris. I have always been motivated by a fear of failure. Coach Harris helped me believe in myself and made it possible for me to win the 1970 Big Eight Conference individual championship, as well as a third-team All-American selection my junior and senior years and honorable mention All-American my sophomore year.

Obtaining an MBA from Oklahoma State was never a goal; it was more an alternative during a difficult time for the average young American during the Vietnam era. Following completion of my undergraduate degree in 1970, I decided to continue with my MBA in order to keep a step ahead in the event my draft number was called. The MBA program presented a new challenge for me. As an undergrad, I never spent time in the library. The MBA program quickly changed my perspective, as I soon found myself spending late nights studying in the library trying to survive the rigorous academic standards of the program.

Most of those who complete an MBA go on to work for a company or venture out and try to establish their own businesses. However, after graduating, I was offered an opportunity to succeed Labron Harris as the OSU golf coach. Through the next 32 years, coaching golf never felt like a job to me, it was more like being paid to pursue your hobby. As a golf coach, I surrounded myself with competitive, focused student athletes who made it possible to compete for championships and create a lot of great memories. The success of the golf program opened the door for me to become the athletic director at OSU.

In September 2005 I was selected to succeed Harry Birdwell as Director of Intercollegiate Athletics at Oklahoma State University. I really enjoy my new job and it is gratifying to watch our athletes succeed not only on the field but also in the classroom. I have been fortunate enough to see athletes compete at OSU not just from Oklahoma or even the United States, but from around the world. These student athletes work hard day in and day out, from early morning practices to long, multi-day road trips for games, and still continue to make time to study for exams. This kind of dedication makes it easy for me to come to work each morning ready to help make a difference in their lives.

Being the golf coach and now the athletic director has taught me the importance of giving back. Without the generosity of our donors it would be impossible for our teams to compete for championships. Building relationships and fundraising was a cornerstone for my success as a golf coach and it is even more important in my new role.

Golf is a game that teaches honesty, hard work, personal reliance, self-motivation, discipline, and other values that are necessary for success. It is one of few sports where you are your biggest competitor. If your mind is not completely focused, it is virtually impossible to play at a high level. Golf teaches sportsmanship. You learn to be humble in victory and gracious in defeat because humility is usually only one shot away. Good sportsmanship is paramount if you want to realize your full potential as an athlete. If you lose respect for your opponent then you will eventually lose respect for yourself. OSU has a tradition of excellence, as evidenced by the 48 National Championships, and it is important for us to carry ourselves in a manner that reflects positively on the university. As AD, it is important for me to establish a culture within the athletic department that shows respect for the opponent and encourages our coaches and athletes to play by the rules.

I have always been competitive, with a passion for athletics. I have been fortunate to be surrounded by a lot of great people that made it possible for our teams to succeed at a very high level. I believe that moving from town to town as a child and learning great life lessons from my parents made me who I am today. They made me believe that it was ok to dream big and expect those dreams to come true. I want OSU to be a place where dreams come true for all of our students, especially those willing to dream the impossible and willing to work hard enough to make it happen.

James Michael Holder

Contributed by Seth L. Davis

KEY SUCCESS FACTORS: Work Ethic, Competitiveness, Desire for Success, Fear of Failure, Surrounding Myself with Successful Competitive People, Loving What I Do

WEBSITE: www.okstate.com

EDITOR'S NOTES: Coach Holder is 1 of 5 coaches in any NCAA sport to win a National Championship in 4 different decades. Mike and his wife, Robbie, donated $500,000 for the first fully endowed scholarship for Cowboy football in honor of the late Vernon Grant. The Holders have also donated $1 million for an entrepreneurship endowed chair at OSU Spears School of Business.

The achievements of an organization are the results of the combined effort of each individual.

—Vincent Lombardi

GAME CHANGER

Andrew Solheim—"The man who changed the game of golf." This is how many people know of my grandfather. Karsten Solheim, the man some have credited with changing the game of golf, is my grandfather. Karsten Solheim was a great man. He was dedicated to his family, was a man of faith, intelligent—and he was a worker. His simple desire to create a better product was the foundation for the family business, Karsten Manufacturing Corporation, more commonly known as PING. My grandfather was a mechanical engineer in the aerospace and computer industries. He and PING are credited with numerous innovations that have become industry standards. His insistence on adhering to strict engineering principles and tight manufacturing tolerances raised the level of product performance and quality throughout the golf industry.

As you can imagine, I had—and still have—some big shoes to fill. The game of golf is integral to my family. At an early age, I knew that golf would in some way be a large part of my life. So, I have tried to always enjoy the game. Golf can be frustrating if you let it. I have learned to enjoy it; I try to enjoy it. I began working summers at the family business when I was fourteen. I do not really remember how it happened or whose idea it was for me to begin working. All I knew was that I was getting paid, and I liked it. I spent summers working at the company and going to golf camp in Stillwater, Oklahoma. Stillwater was a long way from Phoenix, Arizona, where I was born and raised. It is 1,025 miles to be exact and has a different climate and completely different way of life. However, it was because of those summers at golf camp in Stillwater that I was led to Oklahoma State University.

I wanted to attend college somewhere out of state and Stillwater seemed like a good place. I had friends there that I had met during golf camp and was somewhat familiar with the area. It was nice not to go to a new place totally blind. I got my bachelor's degree in general business and while there met my future bride, a diehard Cowboy's fan from McAlester, Oklahoma.

It was apparent to me from a young age that I would be working in the family business. I was very blessed that I did not have to worry about where I might or even if I might find employment. I was not sure what role within the company I would have. That was still the question. I started college planning on following in my grandfather's and father's footsteps as an engineer, but quickly realized I had other interests. During this time, the infamous OJ Simpson trial was underway and I had thoughts of becoming a lawyer. In the end, I decided that a degree in Business Administration would better prepare me to take my place in the company. I knew I could be a contributor in product development and in the business side of the business.

Following completion of my undergraduate degree, and after I'd worked for a couple of years, my dad began pushing me to get an MBA. I was never a big fan of school, but I looked at it as an opportunity to go back and live in Stillwater for a couple of years. It turns out, my dad was right about an MBA helping to prepare me for my future responsibilities, and it was great to be back in Stillwater for a while too.

My time in Stillwater was one of the changing events in my life. When I went back to school, my wife and I moved back to Stillwater, started my MBA program, and had a baby in about a month. We loved our time there. We lived there for 18 months and made many friends we still keep in contact with today. One of the best experiences I had during the time I spent getting my MBA was the "Summer in China" program. The country was completely different than what I expected. I had visions of an underdeveloped nation. But even during that time, probably 9 years ago, it was developing at a quick pace. The experience was insightful, something I will never forget, and I was with an incredible group of people. The MBA provided a wonderful foundation on which to begin building my career: I learned the fundamentals of business, of new ways of doing things, and more about marketing and technology. Most importantly, I learned how to work with others.

Entering the family business may sound simple; and in some ways, I suppose it was. I knew I had a job. However, as a Solheim, you are expected to work. It was hard work and perseverance that built the company that started in my grandfather's garage. A family business has its challenges; it is, after all, first and foremost, a business. All families have their challenges, even when they are not in business together. We discuss, we challenge, and we argue with each other. The family aspect is one thing that I believe has contributed to the success of the company. We have a strong bond and loyalty to the success of PING. We also truly love what we do.

Family goes beyond direct relatives; all who work at Karsten Manufacturing are considered family as well. I am proud to say that my grandfather, from very early on, decided to treat his employees well so that they could take care of and provide for their families. Most of our employees have been with us for fifteen years or more. It is from this family legacy that I hold true to what I consider a core value and a necessity for success: treat others with respect and treat them how you would like to be treated.

Family is important to me. I consider my family my greatest success and achievement. In August of 2010, we celebrated our 12th wedding anniversary, and I am the proud father of three beautiful girls. If there is one thing I hope I can successfully teach my girls, it is to treat other people how you want to be treated. It is imperative in business but also in life.

In today's fast-paced world, many may find it difficult to find time for life outside of work. However, if an up-and-coming professional asked me what advice I would give, it would be to make time for your family and to create family memories. My wife's and my free time revolves around our daughters. Whether it is a dance recital, movie night, learning to ride bikes, or getting their first deer, all the memories are priceless.

PING is constantly working to stay at the top of the game. We have had many successes over the years, and the PING name is synony-mous with quality and innovation. As the business unit leader of soft goods, I am tasked with managing and growing our market share in a somewhat less obvious product line than the clubs. Soft goods include golf bags and other apparel. One of the biggest challenges is that internally, soft goods have lost the focus of our other product lines. It is an area that hasn't received the attention that it deserved and because of that, we have lost market share over the last 8 to 10 years. It is my job to turn this pattern around and regain our status in the market.

The people I consider my mentors are very important to me. I could not name just one person as my mentor; many have taken time to share their time with me. It is imperative to take time to learn from those who have more experience than you. It has been critical for me to have those people I can bounce ideas off of or can ask for advice. I still have much to learn, but I am willing to share what I do know with those who ask as well.

Technology is constantly improving the game of golf and our business. We have only scratched the surface of potential opportunities available because of improved technology. The tools that we have today to test and develop equipment are so much better than they ever have been. Technology allows us to build a better product and build it faster. We know before we build a product what it is going to do and how it is going to perform.

The ever-increasing number of opportunities allowing us to connect with the PING user is also paramount to our continued success. We have what we call "the locker room," an interactive platform on our Website that allows golfers to share with other people what equipment they are using, offer critiques, or in many instances advice or information about their experiences. Our Twitter account and Facebook are found under PINGman. These are great tools for reaching the younger generation who are the next generation of golfers and our customers. We have been very fortunate that we have not had any major social media disasters or shortfalls.

Along with treating others as you would like to be treated, I believe that we should treat the environment around us well. At PING, we try to be an active part of the community. The Solheim Family Foundation does work throughout the world. We have completed two or three Habitat for Humanity houses, and we strive to be as environmentally friendly as we can. We work to reduce the amount of waste that we create, and we examine the different uses of chemicals and what types of chemicals can be used. We have obtained ISO 14,000 designation, which verifies PING's commitment to Environmental Management Systems to protect our environment for future generations.

I have been blessed with a wonderful family and a great family heritage. My father probably states it best in the afterword of the biography, *Karsten's Way*. "Trust in the Lord with all your heart, and lean not on your own understanding. In all your ways acknowledge him and he will direct your path. This is what guided my father and continues to guide our family."—John Solheim

Andrew Solheim
Contributed by Robyn Scribner

KEY SUCCESS FACTORS: Hard Work, Treat Others with Respect

WEBSITE: www.ping.com

SOCIAL MEDIA: LinkedIn—Andrew-Solheim; Facebook— Andrew.Solheim

EDITOR'S NOTES: Andrew Solheim lives in Phoenix, Arizona, with his wife and three young daughters. His grandfather, Karsten Solheim, founded PING in his garage during his quest to make a better putter. Karsten Solheim passed away in 2000, and now Andrew's father, John, is President of Karsten Manufacturing and Andrew's older brother, also named John, is Vice-President.

The Solheim family is synonymous with the words "golf" and "putter." Today, PING develops some of the most advanced and innovative equipment available, designed to improve the game of golf. Karsten Solheim was dedicated to making the game of golf fun. The family continues this legacy today. The Solheim Foundation contributes financially and supports organizations around the globe.

Fortune favors the prepared mind.

—Louis Pasteur

PUTTING A PREMIUM ON PREPARATION

Trip Kuehne—I have been lucky enough to play golf at the highest level, competing against the world's greatest, and unlucky enough to fall victim to one of Tiger Woods' historic comebacks. But as much as I love golf, I love Wall Street even more. I am known for giving up my dream of playing professional golf, but my dream wasn't to play on the PGA Tour. While visiting New York City as a 10-year-old, I fell in love with two things: the Statue of Liberty and Wall Street. The vast flight and transfer of wealth at the historic financial district fascinated me and made me realize that my dream was to play on Wall Street.

Although I chose a different career path than professional golf, golf has been one of the most significant influences on who I am today. I am still an avid golfer, but for fun. I take pride in having been a student-athlete and believe there is something special about people being able to perform at a high level both in athletics and in the classroom. As a competitive person, I picked up great habits through golf such as always preparing myself to perform at my best. I experienced success and failure frequently as an athlete and learned how to learn from the experiences. Dedication, preparation, balance and dealing with adversity are qualities from athletics that I have been able to successfully translate to business.

Golf was also the road map that guided me to and through Oklahoma State. From high school, I went to Arizona State for two years to play golf, but an injury and my brother led me to OSU, where I flourished and stayed through graduate school. It would be lying to say an MBA was always in my plan. I needed to enroll in a graduate program to be eligible to play on the golf team. But I am more than glad that I did. My experience in the MBA program put me in a position to be more successful from a performance and salary standpoint. More importantly, the MBA program gave me two more years to grow up and focus.

Graduate school was more challenging than I originally thought it would be. It didn't take me long to figure out that the program was more than just more classes to take. It was my introduction into the real world. My commitment to the golf team only magnified its difficulty. Being a student-athlete traveling so much, I started my MBA career behind. I was weeks behind and even a full session behind in some courses, but thanks to hard work and some relationships I developed with faculty and students, I was able to persevere. One example was my experience taking calculus. I had never taken a calculus class before and had to basically teach myself with the support of some great people because I was behind and couldn't make it to the lectures. It was definitely difficult, but my success is a testament to my friends, the faculty, and the university in supporting me and wanting me to succeed.

I would not be where I am or who I am today without the wonderful relationships I have developed along the way. It is immeasurably important to have people you respect, especially those hard-nosed mentors, to reinforce character qualities and encourage you. The opportunities presented by these people and their reinforcement of what it takes to be successful were affirmations of the respect I'd earned. For me, a few of these mentors were, of course, my father, Coach Holder, hedge fund manager Stan Drunkenmiller, and Vinny Giles. It was confirmation and reassurance that I had made the right decision to focus on my pursuit of Wall Street when Coach Holder told me, "I don't believe in quitting and would never tell someone to, but if you want to move on and focus on your career, you have my blessing."

Thanks to my experiences and relationships from OSU, golf, and my mentors, I am fortunate to be in the position that I am. I knew what my dream job was at 10 years old, and I'm living my dream at my own company, Double Eagle Capital Management, LP in Dallas. The habits I learned as an athlete are a big part of what got me here. The mind-set of an athlete is identical to that of a successful money manager, and I go about my job the same way I went about golf. I have to have a plan, I have to prepare, I have to perform, and I have to learn from my successes and, more importantly, my failures. The world I am part of is extremely competitive, so I have to compete. Although I am living my dream, competition is what keeps me motivated. Moving forward, I want to do more than live the dream and continue my goal of making Double Eagle Capital Management, LP a top performing fund of hedge funds. I am just going to keep on and, simply, I want to be the best.

In addition to getting to where I wanted to go in life, I am in a position now where I get to provide opportunities for others to reach their goals. I believe it is important to give back and actively support several charities and foundations. The Terence Newman Rising Stars Foundation, which profiles 10 high school freshmen with various support programs and a college scholarship upon graduation, the Juvenile Diabetes Research Foundation, and Friends for Kids are just a couple of charities and foundations in which I am actively involved. Being able to offer opportunities to others, especially the opportunity for an education, is rewarding.

The success factors I previously brought up aren't exclusive to money managers. They apply to all aspirations in life and especially in business. Successful people use their greatest assets, whatever they may be, to put themselves in positions to succeed. Along with doing that, my advice is to find your passion. Find something you love and pursue it.

Trip Kuehne
Contributed by Blake Koppitz

KEY SUCCESS FACTORS: Ambition, Passion, Dedication, Balance, Preparation, Focus, Teamwork, Respect

WEBSITE: www.doubleeaglecapital.com

SOCIAL MEDIA: LinkedIn—Trip Kuehne

EDITORS NOTES: Mr. Kuehne is a decorated golfer with accomplishments including NCAA All-American, USGA Champion, NCAA Champion, member of Walker Cup and World Amateur teams, Ben Hogan Award Winner, and Big 8 Student Athlete of the Year. In business, his Ace Fund has been in the top few in returns since its inception. Thomson Reuters named it the top fund of its kind in 2009. His brother, Hank, and sister, Kelli, are also decorated golfers; together the Kuehnes are known as the First Family of Golf. Trip has a son, Will, and his wife, Dusti, played basketball at Oklahoma State, graduating with a Bachelor of Science in Agricultural Economics.

Keep your dreams alive. Understand that to achieve anything requires faith and belief in yourself, vision, hard work, determination, and dedication. Remember all things are possible for those who believe.

—*Gail Devers*

LEGEND LIVING THE AMERICAN DREAM

Johnny Halberstadt—I was born and raised in Johannesburg, South Africa. I grew up in a very interesting time, when the country was transitioning to an open society—a time of significant turmoil. When I was young, my attention was mainly sports orientated, particularly on running, as that was where my talents lay. I started off in competitive running when I was in my early teens. I was also involved in the Boy Scout movement. Both of these pursuits had a very positive influence on me. Running motivated me to challenge myself and take my development step by step.

It was a huge thing for me to get a full ride scholarship to run at Oklahoma State University in 1971, thanks to the help of fellow South African runner and Oklahoma State alum, Peter Kaal. At the time Peter was rated 3rd in the world among high school runners, with a 4:01 time in the mile. I had credibility with Peter, and he convinced Coach Ralph Tate to recruit me to Oklahoma State. But I still had to prove myself because I was a little guy, and I think the coaches might have thought that I wasn't going to make it. However, those doubts were probably dispelled after I was able to run a time faster than the school record in my very first outing on the track.

My first memories at Oklahoma State were that everyone talked with a strong accent. It felt like I had been thrust into a western movie and it was difficult to make myself understood! I remember thinking that surely I would wake up one morning and everyone would be talking the same way I did. It didn't happen. The other thing that really struck me was the amazing friendliness and kindness of everyone I met, especially my teammates. OSU became a special place for me very quickly. I also remember the first Thanksgiving and not having any plans. I didn't really know what Thanksgiving was, being from South Africa. I thought the free time would be great and I would just train more. But when my teammates in the dorm asked me what I was doing for Thanksgiving and I told them, everyone was fighting over me to go home with them for the holiday. For me, that just epitomized the way people are in this country—the American spirit.

After my undergraduate degree in General Business, I still wanted to run competitively on the international level. I decided to stay in America, get my MBA at Oklahoma State University, and also compete in track on an international level in the USA at the same time. The MBA program at Oklahoma State University attracted top students from around the globe from all walks of life. At that time, many of the students came from either agricultural or petroleum engineering under-graduate backgrounds. I remember many case studies in the MBA program at Oklahoma State that developed critical thinking. These case studies and projects for local businesses gave me confidence. I don't believe I could have done any better at any other university.

When I went back to South Africa, the MBA degree opened doors with a multinational American pharmaceutical company. I first got a posi-tion in marketing, and then later was appointed national sales manager. After being in big business for a few years, I decided that it was time to be more on the entrepreneurial side. I founded and managed a small chain of successful specialty running retail stores in South Africa called "Heart and Sole."

In South Africa my running career flourished. The country was banned from international competition through sports boycotts because of apartheid. Apartheid and South Africa had the attention of the world at that time. After winning the South African cross-country championships in 1979, I was supposed to receive Springbok Colors, the highest award in South African sport. A few months earlier, three top black runners had been awarded Springbok colors, the first blacks, I think in any sport, to receive that honor. One of those men, Matthews Motswarateu was offered a scholarship in the U.S. However, he was denied a passport by the South African government on the grounds that he was a citizen of the apartheid homeland of Bophuthatswana and thus did not qualify for a South African passport. Because of the treatment of Matthews, I refused Springbok colors. If it was okay to showcase to the world that South Africa at last had black recipients of the highest sports award in the country, it was hypocrisy to then claim that they were not really fully fledged South African citizens. After my decision became known, a firestorm of controversy erupted that to me was quite unexpected, as was the support that flowed in seemingly from around the world. At home, the situation became quite tense with people either fiercely opposed or fiercely supportive of my position. Despite the pressure that bore down on the South African government from so many quarters, they would not relent on the issue. However, Mr. Motswarateu eventually was able to accept a scholarship at an American university, but only because he was given special papers by the US Government to travel to the USA without a passport.

Looking back after so many years, it seems like refusing the colors was an easy decision to make, but at the time it was not so clear-cut, with potentially serious repercussions. It was probably one of the first times that South African government officials saw that the apartheid system, in sports anyway, was not going to work. But it wasn't just because of me. I just happened to be the guy at that time to stand up. The good Lord put me in that situation. If it hadn't been me, it would have been someone else. The recent movie *Invictus* depicts President Nelson Mandela uniting all the racial groups in the new South Africa, through support of the Springbok rugby team (a sport played predominantly by whites) at the 1995 World Cup tournament. My controversy in South Africa took place about fifteen years earlier.

At the peak of my running career I was running 130 miles per week and found that the running footwear available at that time was not very good. I started tinkering around in search of a better shoe and came up with a channel sole concept that was patented in America. The licensing of the channel sole concept eventually allowed me and my family to move to America. But due to unforeseen delays in cash flows, I had to find another way to make a living. I worked with my South African friend Mark Plaatjes to found the Boulder Running Company in 1995. (Mark, who also emigrated to the USA, had won the marathon at the World Championships in 1993.) This turned out to be a fortuitous move as our company has been quite successful.

At the Boulder Running Company we specialize in treating runners and walkers of all skill levels like premium athletes. We were the first running specialty store in the country to offer free state-of-the-art video gait analysis, to ensure everyone gets the right shoes for their feet, rather than shoes suited to someone else. We match and tweak shoes and gear to match a person's unique gait and profile. Mark helped a lot with developing this system since he is a physical therapist. Our model for retail is to deliver outstanding customer service with a staff committed to excellence. With a great team of enthusiastic people on the sales floor, we strive to give everyone a memorable customer experience. We endeavor to really "WOW" our customers, to give them "what's in it for me" attention. We work hard on being true match-makers for people's feet, since that delivers in a very tangible way, a better quality of life for our customers.

In 2006 we were fortunate enough to garner the national Running Store of the Year Award (out of about 750 stores nationwide) and in 2008 Mark and I were jointly named as Esprit Entrepreneur of the Year by the Boulder, Colorado Chamber of Commerce.

My future plan is to concentrate on the big picture and hand over the day-to-day running of the business to a management team we have nurtured. As we have expanded and have been able to employ really good people, it has been easier to delegate and allow people to run with their responsibilities and develop and grow in their area of expertise.

America is a wonderful country. If you want to do it, you can do it here in the United States of America. I was exposed to so many things and many opportunities and the MBA program helped me recognize those opportunities. I believe that we are here to be the best that we can be and to strive to make the best of our God-given talents.

I enjoy excellence in whatever form, whether it is in business, sports or the arts. I am fascinated by people who are excellent in what they do. America has more of that than anywhere else in the world.

I will always be a South African at heart, but I gained American citizen-ship in 2000 along with my family. That is something of which I am very proud.

Johnny Halberstadt
Contributed by Terry Britton

KEY SUCCESS FACTORS: Faith, Confidence, Integrity

WEBSITE: www.boulderrunningcompany.com/boulder/

SOCIAL MEDIA: Facebook—Boulder-Running-Company

EDITOR'S NOTES: Mr. Halberstadt immigrated to the USA with his family in 1994. He lives in Boulder, Colorado, where he started the Boulder Running Company with his longtime friend, Mark Plaatjes, in 1995. The Boulder Running Company now has four locations and 56 employees, 35 of whom work full time. Mr. Halberstadt gives back to the community both in the Boulder area and in South Africa.

While working on his undergraduate degree in General Business at Oklahoma State University, Mr. Halberstadt was a six-time Big 8 Conference Champion in track and cross-country and the 1972 NCAA 10,000 meter champion. Because of his performances, he is still regarded as one of South Africa's greatest all-round distance runners. He placed 3rd in the Boston marathon on only his 3rd attempt at the marathon distance and has run a sub-4 minute mile. Some of his best times are 1 mile: 3 minutes and 59 seconds; 5000 meters: 13 minutes and 44 seconds; 10,000 meters: 28 minutes and 50 seconds; half-marathon: 63 minutes and 35 seconds; marathon (26.2 miles): 2 hours 11 minutes and 46 seconds; and 100 kilometers (62 miles): 6 hours and 47 minutes.

Success is focusing the full power of all you are on what you have a burning desire to achieve.

—Wilfred A. Peterson

THE COACH'S KID

Chad M. Weiberg—Growing up the son of a basketball coach meant that I knew the definition of hard work; experiencing my early childhood in southern and eastern Oklahoma cultivated this trait that we as Oklahomans identify with. I was born in Paul's Valley. Even if you are from Oklahoma, chances are you might have never heard of this town. My father was the men's basketball coach at Paul's Valley high school, just starting his career. Having a father as a coach came with its fair share of benefits and challenges. Growing up in a small town meant that as the "coach's kid," everyone knew you. But being that "coach's kid" is what has shaped me and made me who I am today.

As I mentioned, there were some challenges to being a coach's kid. One of those challenges was the periodic move. In the coaching profession, moving is part of the game. For me and my family, this meant that we had to get used to the reality that we were never really going to settle in. Of course, a part of me resented this; growing up, I had to leave friends . . . just as I was making them, and I hated all the good-byes each time we moved. By the time I was an 8th grader, my father had become an assistant coach at Oklahoma State University. This was the mid-1980's, before the smaller Gallagher Hall became the expanded Gallagher-Iba Arena. I loved the time in Stillwater and the love affair with the Cowboys was on. But by the time my freshman year was coming to an end, it was once again time to move. We moved to Tonkawa, Oklahoma, where my dad became the head coach and Vice President of Student Services at Northern Oklahoma College. So after looking forward to graduating from Stillwater High School, I spent my high school years in Tonkawa, where once again, I made lifelong friends.

Looking back, I now realize how much moving actually gave me an advantage. Over the years, I became acclimated to moving and it prepared me to be a flexible person. And contrary to what you might expect, moving actually aided me in building relationships. Not until I got to college did I realize that always having to move made meeting new people second nature to me. In my world, if you did not learn how to build relationships, you weren't going to have much fun.

Once I graduated from high school, all of these relationships that I had built over the past years of moving came together at one place: Oklahoma State University. It was during this transition that I found my calling in life. When I came to Oklahoma State, my big brother in the Kappa Sigma house was the Interfraternity Council President and he appointed me to the student athletic advisory council as the IFC representative. Because he knew I had an interest in sports, he figured I would be the right fit. Through this came an opportunity to have an unpaid internship with the athletic department at Oklahoma State.

During the internship, I was fully convinced that sports was my professional calling. I felt it was important to do what you loved and having a passion for it was extremely important. I realized what I needed was more experience in the field. Fortunately, my uncle, whom I consider a mentor, was involved with athletics administration and was working at that time for the Big Ten Conference. Because my experiences told me that I would rather be in administration that coaching, when the opportunity presented itself to go to Park Ridge, Illinois, for the summer and do an unpaid internship with the Big Ten Conference, I took it. These experiences confirmed that athletics administration was what I wanted to do. By the time I started my junior year, I had begun gaining valuable experience. I was blessed and fortunate to have a father and an uncle who would help guide me and get me started in my profession.

Like many, luck is part of my story: I was fortunate to be in "the right place at the right time." Shortly after graduating from OSU, a position in the development office at OSU Athletics opened. I applied and Dave Martin, who is still the Sr. Associate Athletics Director at OSU, gave me my first job. It was a dream-come-true. I felt I would have opportunities in athletics, but to be able to start out at your alma mater was truly special.

I worked for OSU Athletics for four years. Then, I was presented with the opportunity to work for the OSU Alumni Association as the Director of Field Operations. It was a difficult decision for me to consider leaving the athletics profession; however, I believed that this position could open further opportunities in the broader profession of institutional advancement. It was during this time, that I also felt it was important for me to continue my education. Working for OSU, the timing was right. It was more convenient for me than most part-time students as I was already on campus, but more importantly, it was the opportunity to learn real-world applications of business practices, plus be exposed to a variety of different cultures and work with people from different backgrounds. Also, the MBA program provided dynamic instruction that I was able to put to use immediately. One of my favorite memories of the MBA program was the study abroad trip to Toronto, Canada, where we got to speak to executives about their experiences and success. In addition, I felt pursuing an OSU MBA would keep doors open should I decide to pursue a profession outside of institutional advancement.

It was while working for the OSU Alumni Association that my life was changed forever. On January 27, 2001, while traveling in Texas visiting OSU alumni, I got word that my younger brother and nine other men had been killed in a plane crash. You see, my younger brother, Jared Weiberg, had the same passion that I had for sports, and he was a student assistant for the men's basketball team. The team had played the University of Colorado earlier that afternoon and was on its way back to Stillwater when the aircraft went down 30 miles east of Denver. Oklahoma State took three small planes to this road game. Two made it back to Stillwater safely that night, but the plane my brother boarded that evening was not one of them. Jared and I shared the same passion for athletics and were products of our father's zeal for basketball. Nothing can ever prepare you for such a tragedy. I was enjoying having my youngest brother about to join me as an alumnus of OSU. In addition, he was living with me while he was in school. I knew when I went home that he was never going to pass through our front door again.

It's hard to remember what life was like before the accident. The accident is a part of me, of my life, and has radically changed me and my outlook on life. Now, life isn't all about wins and losses; I realized that at the end of the day, sports was really just a game. The accident gave me a new viewpoint about what is really important in life. I now realize how fortunate I am to have a job I enjoy and to have a wonderful family and great friends. All too often in the past, I would have taken these things for granted. Forever changed, I now work and play with the realization that life is not guaranteed. When I feel down or think that something is just impossible, or when I have had a bad day, I think about my youngest brother, Jared. I am living and working for more than just myself, but also for my little brother's legacy.

Following the 2001 tragedy, the Oklahoma State University Alumni Association was kind enough to allow me time to deal with the tragedy. I am grateful to so many who helped me and my family in those darkest days. Then, in 2002, with my MBA and a new attitude toward life, I went to work for the Oklahoma State University Foundation as the Director of Development for the College of Business. I did this for one year, and then moved on to become Director of Development (Athletics) for the Oklahoma State Foundation. I was back in athletics.

Less than a year into that position, with personal events unfolding in my life (meeting my future wife), I made the biggest decision in my professional life. I decided to move to Manhattan, Kansas, home of Kansas State University (KSU). At KSU, I accepted the position of Director of Corporate Relations for the KSU Foundation. After 13 months in that position, I was offered an opportunity to work for the K-State Athletics Department and, once again, found myself back in athletics—first as the Director of Major Gifts, then as Assistant Athletics Director of Development and currently as Associate Athletics Director of Development.

As Associate Athletics Director of Development, I have had the privilege of experiencing professional successes, including record highs in annual giving and garnering contributions for a new athletic training facility for men's and women's basketball. But what I do realize is that I did not get to this point in my career on my own. Many outstanding people invested in my life, starting with my parents and my uncle, who now works for the Pac 10 (soon to be the Pac 12). Joe Haney, Jerry Gill, and Larry Shell at Oklahoma State, among others, all contributed to my professional successes. Along with these and other great mentors, I learned success factors that still permeate every decision I make: honesty and transparency. In my industry, these two aspects are the foundation of building trust, which is pivotal for success.

As for the future, I plan to continue to work hard at what I am doing, and see what happens next. I feel like that hard work has always been the key to opening doors. When the doors open, it's the opportunity to walk through and try to be successful, so I will continue to do just that. Hopefully, I will continue to be blessed.

Chad M. Weiberg
Contributed by David Manison II

KEY SUCCESS FACTORS: Honesty, Transparency, Hard Work, Trust

WEBSITE: www.kstatesports.com

SOCIAL MEDIA: LinkedIn—Chad Weiberg

EDITOR'S NOTES: Chad lives in Manhattan, Kansas, with his wife, Jodi, and their two young children. Jodi and Chad love to travel and have a particular love for Italy. Mr. Weiberg is a past recipient of the outstanding young alumni award from the Spears School of Business at Oklahoma State University and is also the Big 12 representative for the National Association of Athletic Development Directors (NAADD).

CHAPTER FIVE
SUCCESS IN CORPORATE AMERICA

Thank you to those in the corporate world who employ numerous MBA graduates and make a difference by giving back. The following MBA alumni have made a difference not only at Oklahoma State University, but also in corporate America.

Show up every day for whatever you are supposed to be doing, and do the best you can for the organization.

—Jim Alcock

COMMITMENT AND ACCOUNTABILITY

Jim Alcock— I was born in Tulsa, Oklahoma, where my family and I lived for a short time before moving to Jackson, Mississippi. I spent most of my grade school years in Jackson before we went back to Tulsa, where I finished junior high and high school. I grew up in a strong family consisting of my two parents, an older brother, and a younger sister. My parents were great examples for me to look up to because they were both the first in their families to graduate with a degree beyond high school. My father received his Master's in geology, and my mother became a registered nurse. In addition to setting an example by receiving their education, my parents influenced me by the way I was raised. My mother and father always set high standards of hard work, accountability, and doing the right thing. My mother worked some as a nurse, but mainly was an excellent home-maker who cared for and guided us. Sometimes my father would take me with him on his work visits to oil well drilling sites. I learned a lot watching him work with the drilling crews and making decisions about what to do next. After graduating from high school, my older brother went on to college at Oklahoma State University and then continued his education by receiving his Master's in forestry from Oregon State.

Because of the examples set by my both my parents and my older brother, there was no doubt in my mind that regardless of what I majored in, I would go on to get a Master's degree. I graduated from Edison High School in Tulsa and went to OSU, where I received my Bachelor's in economics. After graduating and with the encourage-ment of several OSU professors, I looked into options for my Master's degree. The program I was drawn to the most was the Master's in Business Administration because of the new director who had been hired in 1964. He was very impressive with his pitch about the MBA program, including the companies that would be coming to interview at OSU.

I met my wife, Linda, while attending school at OSU, where she was working on her degree in Family Relations and Childhood Development. One of my favorite memories of school is spending time with her while we studied in the library. Some other memories I have from the MBA program include working with fellow grad students and how the professors really cared about us, testing us in and out of class. They would give us real-life examples as to how academic material translated over to the business world.

I graduated with my MBA in 1965. Immediately after graduation, I married Linda and started a job with Humble Oil (later Exxon USA) as an economic analyst and moved to Baytown, Texas. My MBA made a big difference when I applied for this job. Employers use the MBA as another screening device, thinking that the person who gets this degree has done so in a more strenuous academic environment. Although a BA in economics was beneficial, it did not open many starting positions. I do not think that I would have received my job offer from Exxon without my MBA. After I started work, I realized that my time at OSU in undergraduate and graduate school put me in a position to compete favorably with MBAs from higher-profile schools as well as engineers from all over the country. My Master's did make a difference in my starting salary at Humble Oil/Exxon, but after the first few years, my salary was based purely on my performance.

Besides helping get me a good starting position, the MBA greatly helped me put the pieces of the business puzzle together—it showed me the importance of each business function and the importance of working with people in a positive manner. Also, the analytical thinking required in school was critical to my career.

I received my first supervisory job as head of business analysis within the first couple of years with the company. After this, I received a series of geographical relocations into supervisory and management positions: financial coordinator positions, the Accounting Department Head in New Orleans, and then Controller of Exxon USA Upstream Operations. In 1982, I left Exxon USA and moved to Exxon Corporation and worked in several corporate controller management positions before becoming Controller of the Exxon Chemical Company. In 1988, I moved to London, England as the Executive VP and Finance

Director of Esso UK, which ran Exxon's petroleum operations in the UK. In this position I was responsible for systems, treasurers, controllers, tax, purchasing, and general administration.

The last three jobs I had with Exxon were Assistant Controller of Exxon Corporation, Controller for Exxon International, and finally in 2000, after Exxon and Mobil merged, I was named the Controller for ExxonMobil's worldwide downstream operations. This job involved a controller's responsibility for refining, marketing, lubes and specialties, supply, and downstream research. After working for Exxon for 36 years, I retired in 2001.

One thing I feel has helped me to succeed in my career is that early on I did not have any goal in mind other than doing my best in whatever came my way and showing I could contribute to the company. I wanted responsibility, and I wanted to make a difference, so when I was given an assignment I made sure that it was completed to the best of my ability and in a timely manner. Later on in my career, I started looking at higher level jobs; as long as I thought I could do them well, I wanted the additional responsibility. My guiding principle was to be ambitious in terms of contributing to the part of the company where I was currently serving. I felt that if I was successful in making a positive difference, then my success would likely follow.

Everyone faces challenges to being successful. One of the biggest personal challenges I faced was the balance of family life and business life. My wife, Linda, and I approached this challenge the same way. We wanted success in both, and although it was difficult at times, we realized that both our family and business lives were going to need commitment, cooperation, attention, accountability, and the happiness of the people involved. A major challenge in my business and personal life was the adaptability required in my career—learning the technology and economics of the oil industry, experiencing different kinds of jobs, and working with people from all over the world. There were many other business challenges, but the top career challenge was participating in the Exxon Mobil merger and creating an even more dynamic company from two rather different corporate cultures. And after this merger, I was responsible for making sure the staff knew the ExxonMobil standards and expectations.

Looking back, there are also many things to be pleased about. Due to the influence from my parents, I went to OSU where I received my BA and MBA. I have been happily married to my wife for 45 years, and we have raised two fine boys, Todd and Blake. I have also had the benefit of a long career with Exxon, where I worked with exceptional people in a thriving, well-managed company that contributes an important product to the economy. And I was able to retire early. Linda and I have traveled around the world on business and pleasure. I have also spent time volunteering in a variety of ways: children's schools, coaching sports, civic and community clubs, and Habitat for Humanity.

I feel that the biggest key success factor in achieving these accomplishments is 100% commitment to your current responsibility. I believe in the old saying about how 80-90% of success is just "showing up." Show up every day for whatever you are supposed to be doing, and do the best you can for the organization. Of course thinking long term and having a vision and plan are important, but it starts with taking care of today's business. A piece of advice that was always helpful to me in both my personal and career lives is to consider your actions in terms of how they would play out as a newspaper headline. Would you be proud of your actions being publicized, or would you rather they were not known?

Jim Alcock
Contributed by Sabrina Cundiff

KEY SUCCESS FACTORS: 100% Commitment, Showing up Every Day and Doing my Best, Thinking Long Term, Having a Vision/Plan

EDITOR'S NOTES: Jim Alcock's wife, Linda Hoefer Alcock, is an OSU graduate in Family Relations and Childhood Development. She was a teacher for 2 years and then became a successful homemaker, raising 2 sons, Todd and Blake. Todd, 42, is married to Jennifer, and they have 2 boys, Brett and Garrett. Todd is Project Manager for Bank of America and Jennifer, after a banking career of 10+ years, is a busy and successful homemaker. Blake, 40, is working to become a teacher and coach after having spent time with several companies—mostly at AT&T—in marketing operations and auditing, plus his own small start-up.

Jim enjoys golf, watching sports, traveling throughout the world, reading, and volunteering. He is just finishing a 6-year term, including 3 years as Chairman, on the Board of Chatham County Habitat for Humanity. Also, Jim was the instigator/organizer behind the creation of the ExxonMobil Controllers Alumni Scholarship Fund involving other Exxon OSU alumni. The fund, with matching gifts from ExxonMobil and Boone Pickens, is forecast to grow to over $2.5 million by 2014.

Live and work but do not forget to play, to have fun in life and really enjoy it.

—*Eileen Caddy*

INTEGRITY, RESPECT AND
THE COWBOY CODE

Rand Berney—Growing up on our small spread on the wind-swept plains of Kansas near the Nebraska border, I knew just about every one of the 3,000 people who lived in the nearby town of Phillipsburg, Kansas. And they knew my family, especially my dad. You see, Phillipsburg is widely known for putting on Kansas' Biggest Rodeo each summer. On the cowboy circuit, Nat, my dad, had rodeo'd with the best, even earning the title, "Kansas' All-Around Cowboy." In addition to being a top money winner in the toughest events—saddle bronc, bareback, and bull riding—he lived by the cowboy code of honor. Surrounded by some of the truest cowboys of the West, I was influenced and inspired by cowboy values and work ethic.

Carrying out the daily chores that go along with having horses and acreage, I had plenty of opportunities to learn what it means to be a good worker and respectful of others, as well as helpful and courteous. In our small community, wealth was not measured by money or possessions; it was measured as freedom from want. We treasured family and relationships. We understood value and reputation were earned by telling the truth, being humble and trustworthy, and never taking unfair advantage of anyone or any situation.

In my dad's eyes, respect was a particularly important quality, respect for laws and respecting every person without regard to his or her background. Whenever my mom and dad welcomed visitors to our home, they were treated with equal respect, whether they were the clean-up crew from the rodeo or entertainers like Fess Parker, who I thought of as Daniel Boone, or Ken Curtis, known to most of us at the time as Festus Hagen from the popular television show "Gunsmoke." Dad always went out of his way to put visitors at ease to be themselves. People responded to his open acceptance and genuine respect for them individually. The words I use to sum up these values today are integrity and respect, and they are the foundation for how I do my job, live my life, and relate to the world.

During my junior year in high school, I had two life-changing experiences. First, I became a Christian and dedicated my life to Christ. Second, I met a girl—*the girl*, the wonderful woman named Patti who would eventually marry me. Nearly 40 years later, I see these events clearly as turning points that reinforced the foundation of integrity and respect laid by my family and community.

After graduating from high school in 1973, I chose to further my education at Kansas State University in Manhattan. After two capstone accomplishments in 1977, marrying Patti and graduating with a Bachelor of Science in accounting, I began my first job at Kansas-Nebraska Natural Gas Company (now KN Energy) as a supervisor and soon was promoted to a financial manager position. I did not hesitate when the opportunity arose in 1981 to move to Bartlesville, Oklahoma to join Phillips Petroleum Company (now ConocoPhillips) as a senior staff accountant for Exploration & Production. After being born in Phillipsburg, Kansas, in Phillips County, I seemed destined to go to work for Phillips Petroleum, although I found it ironic that if any place should have been named Phillipsburg, it was Bartlesville.

After serving in several financial management positions in Exploration & Production and Gas & Gas Liquids, I decided to pursue my Master of Business Administration (MBA) at Oklahoma State University (OSU). I believed an MBA would deepen my understanding of business, expand my skills beyond what I gained on the job, especially in the international arena, and provide networking opportunities. I highly recommend participating in the MBA program at OSU for any professional who wants to demonstrate management potential. One of the major benefits of earning my MBA is the confidence I gained. Our professors prepared us to be future leaders of business and industry.

During my time as an MBA student, my favorite professor was Dr. Lee Manzer. He had practical advice to give, and it was a great honor to be his student. I took classes on the Stillwater campus, commuting with classmates and co-workers from Bartlesville several nights a week, getting to know them better. I also took some classes by Talk Back TV, a distance learning system enabling faculty at OSU's campus and Phillips students in Bartlesville to connect remotely.

Following completion of my MBA in 1985, I continued to work in Gas & Gas Liquids and Finance. In 1986, I was promoted to a director position in Corporate Tax. My MBA skills and exposure complemented those acquired through experience and gave me the confidence to transition to the next phase of my career. From 1992-2009, I was honored to be elected and hold positions in the company as Associate Tax Officer, Assistant Treasurer, Assistant Controller, General Auditor, and Vice President and Controller. In 2009, after 29 years of service, I was named to my current position as Senior Vice President of Corporate Shared Services.

Every person must recognize and overcome career challenges. Many of my peers have lived outside the U.S. I have not. In the oil and gas industry, it is valuable to have international experience. As a global enterprise, we have a large number of operations, businesses, partners and employees outside the U.S. Growing up in a small town that lacked diversity, it seemed as though everyone I knew looked at the world the same way. To overcome this challenge, I traveled extensively abroad and invested time to understand and become familiar with other cultures and different ways of looking at problems. It is vital to understand how people look uniquely at the world. Respect for the value and contribution of diversity and the ability to adjust to cultural differences is essential for working in a global company.

The most important thing I have learned throughout my life is the importance of family. Without my wife and two kids, I would not be who I am today. I have seen many people lose sight of this and sacrifice family to get ahead in the business world. For every position I have accepted, there is a silent partner involved—my wife, Patti. We have always been a team. On days when I have been too busy to come home for lunch, she would bring a sack lunch and we could talk about the kids' schedules. I made it a priority to participate in events in my children's lives.

I think about my life like a bicycle wheel with many spokes, each representing parts of my life: spiritual, social, fitness, health, employee, being a good father, friend, husband and so forth. If the only spoke I worry about is the employee spoke and I ignore the others, the wheel will collapse over time. Balancing work and family truly is key to managing all aspects of my life.

When asked to provide career guidance, I have seven key success factors to share:

1. *Integrity*—Always be honest and do what is right, especially in a financial management role. Even though results may not always be pleasant, they will be right. Without integrity, all the other success factors are worthless.

2. *Respect*—Treat each individual with respect. Do not jump in and decide matters before listening to all sides. Have a genuine interest in others, their well-being and continued development.

3. *Capability*—Build your foundation by getting a great education and continually look for ways to expand your qualifications in your chosen profession.

4. *Confidence*—Make sure you have a comprehensive under-standing of your area of responsibility. If not, pursue training to be more competent. In my case, obtaining certifications (CPA, CIA, CMA and MBA) gave me confidence that I understood all relevant rules and regulations.

5. *Diversity*—Surround yourself with leaders and talented people with different backgrounds and perspectives.

6. *Opportunity*—They are endless, you just have to watch for them and prepare accordingly.

7. *Flexibility*—Be flexible enough to tackle something you did not know was coming. In my case, becoming the general auditor was unplanned. However, when the opportunity to advance to the controller position arose, my background as a general auditor proved invaluable.

As I mentor OSU undergraduate and graduate students, I hope that by helping students build on their own foundation, they will develop into future leaders who operate their businesses and live their lives with integrity and respect. Just as my life seems to have come full circle from humble beginnings as the son of a real cowboy to becoming an OSU Cowboy, may the simple and honest cowboy code resonate in this next generation of OSU Cowboys.

Rand Berney
Contributed by Katy Kenslow

KEY SUCCESS FACTORS: Integrity, Respect, Capability, Confidence, Diversity, Opportunity, Flexibility

WEBSITE: www.conocophillips.com/EN/Pages/index.aspx   and www.kstate.edu/media/newsreleases/oct10/berney103010.html

SOCIAL MEDIA: Facebook—ConocoPhillips

EDITOR'S NOTES: Mr. Berney and his wife recently donated $5 million to KSU. This money will provide support for the two highest-priority capital projects on K-State's Manhattan campus: the renovation and maintenance of the welcome center at Memorial Stadium and the initial construction of the basketball training facility.

Perseverance is not a long race; it is many short races one after another.

—Walter Elliott

STEPPING STONES:
FROM MUD TO MANAGEMENT

Howard J. Thill—It all started in the mud business. For those of you not familiar with the oil and gas business, "mud" is the nickname for the sophisticated fluids utilized in drilling for oil and natural gas to cool the bit, lift the cuttings and stabilize the hole. This is where I began my almost 30 year career in the oil and gas industry, as a drilling fluids sales/service engineer with Phillips Petroleum Company in 1982. As I've advanced from one position to the next, one of the things that underpinned all aspects of my professional career has always been my education. In addition to receiving Bachelor's degrees in marketing and accounting from OSU, it was my MBA that helped unlock the door to the business development and investor relations side of the business that I love to work in today.

Growing up in the oil town of Bartlesville, Oklahoma, I was always intrigued by the oil business. I saw what kind of career a business background could lead to, and it looked fulfilling. Like many starting college, I didn't have a crystal clear view of which career path I would take, but eventually I earned a marketing degree from OSU. It was after getting this degree that I started in the "mud business" with Phillips Petroleum Company. After a few years in the oil patch, I realized that having just a marketing degree wasn't going to take me where I wanted to go, and I went back to OSU part time for my accounting degree. Both my father and older brother are Certified Public Accountants, and I thought this would be a good career path to pursue. After a few years in various accounting roles at Phillips, I again felt the need to pursue additional education to help advance my career as I realized—no offense to my accounting friends—I wanted to do more than debits and credits for the rest of my life. I decided an MBA was a way to further demonstrate my abilities and unlock additional value.

After finishing my MBA from OSU in 1996, I was offered a job in business development. This opportunity presented itself not only because of my previous experience, but in large part as a result of earning my MBA, and it ultimately led me down the path to investor relations. This job was a very large change from the accounting world I was used to and gave me much more exposure to senior management as well as a broader look at the Company. I really enjoyed this strategic side of the business; it gave me a true appreciation for the global reach and scale of the Company. My operational and accounting experience had placed me at the door, but it was my MBA that provided the key to unlock the door to this exciting new world.

Throughout my career, I've found it important to keep my options open and be on the lookout for new opportunities. One of these opportunities came in 1998 when Phillips posted the job of Manager of Investor Relations. My soon to be mentor had run the office of Investor Relations for Phillips in New York for many years and the office was now being relocated to the headquarters in Bartlesville. I remember vividly, down to what I was wearing, the meeting to discuss investor relations and what was expected of the position. This was a major turning point in my career path and a great opportunity that I would have missed had I not continuously sought further career advancement.

The next few years presented some of my greatest learning experiences. Dealing with investors and the highest levels of management at Phillips gave me the sense of just what it takes to run a business and to judge its accomplishments or failures. I wanted and strove for the next level and realized it wasn't going to be at Phillips. I wasn't willing to allow someone else to make what I felt was a bad career decision for me and so I went to work seeking opportunities outside Phillips. This was a difficult decision, after almost 20 years with the company and being a third generation Phillips employee, but we were not seeing eye-to-eye about my career path.

Having developed an extensive network over my three plus years in investor relations I started contacting people to spread the word that I was looking for an investor relations or analyst position and to let me know if they heard of any opportunities. At dinner one evening in New York, I mentioned to a friend and investment analyst that I'd made the decision to seek other opportunities. Within a matter of days he phoned me that Marathon Oil Corporation was looking for someone with exactly my skill set for a position in investor relations, and as they say, the rest is history. Had it not been for the proverbial networking and informing my friends and colleagues that I was looking for a new position, they would have assumed I wouldn't leave Phillips.

I truly believe that if you have a job you love, you're going to do that job well. I've moved from that first position as manager of investor relations at Phillips to my current position as Vice President of Investor Relations and Public Affairs at Marathon and couldn't be happier with that progression and what I do for a living. I love visiting with investors and analysts about the business and it provides the opportunity to travel all over the U.S. and world to discuss the Company and industry. My career path has been somewhat unorthodox, but I believe my diverse background has given me the skills necessary to fully understand the industry and Company.

My career has definitely been a growing experience, and has come as stepping stones rather than one big "a-ha" moment. By keeping myself open to new opportunities along the way, I have been able to pursue the career that I really enjoy and not just what a company thinks is best for me. I believe it's very important to take charge of your career and to put yourself out there for new opportunities when you don't like where your current career path is taking you. Even if you have 20 or more years with a company as I did, you ultimately have to do what is right for you.

Having great mentors along the way was also crucial to my success. One of the best pieces of advice I received was from the corporate controller who advised me I should look into moving to the Exploration and Production department for the international opportunities I had been seeking. The permanent international assignment never materialized, but the opportunity to help establish international offices and to broaden my experience was invaluable. Likewise, my investor relations mentor at Phillips was very influential in helping me hone my skills for dealing with investors and to take me to the next level, and frankly, as a reference for my current position. It's very important to have someone you trust to share not only your career goals but also life changing events. Without my network of mentors and friends in the industry, I wouldn't have found out about the position with Marathon. Finally, my success wouldn't have been possible without hard work, perseverance, integrity and honesty. Integrity is very important in any job, but particularly so in this field of work. If I tell an analyst or an investor something, they can take it to the bank. Honesty is also crucial. If you don't know the answer to a question, don't be afraid to tell someone you don't know the answer, but tell them you can find it or find someone who has the answer.

As I worked my way up from the mud business to senior level management, I've always kept and eye open for better opportunities and have taken charge of my career when needed, even when that meant leaving a company after 20 years. I believe it's important for everyone to take charge of their career and not just blindly follow what the company may think is best for you. Getting my MBA from OSU was a big step along that path as well and really opened the door to the strategic side of the business that I really enjoy. As you pursue your own career, remember that education should be an ongoing process, and you can never stop learning.

Howard J. Thill
Contributed by Eric Sipos

KEY SUCCESS FACTORS: Hard Work, Perseverance, Integrity, Honesty

WEBSITE: http://www.marathon.com/About_Marathon/Corporate_ Profile/Corporate_Officers/Howard_J_Thill/

SOCIAL MEDIA: LinkedIn—Howard Thill

EDITOR'S NOTES: Outside of his career, Mr. Thill enjoys spending time with his five children; two are also OSU graduates and one is a current student and continues to maintain his OSU football and basketball season tickets to spend more time with them. He has also been very active in his parish and his children's school, having served as Treasurer for eight years. He is involved in the Junior Achievement program and serves on the Houston Chapter's board of directors. Through this program Mr. Thill is able to reach out to underprivileged youth in the community and teach them the fundamentals of business, showing them how it comes together with their community to create a better environment and promote good citizenship. He's also been active in the OSU alumni association, having served as past president of the Washington county chapter in Oklahoma.

One of Mr. Thill's greatest accomplishments was passing the CPA exam on the first attempt. He also received an Institutional Investor ranking after his first full year at his current position of VP of Investor Relations and Public Affairs. This prestigious ranking is voted on by peers in the investor world, and they voted Mr. Thill the #1 investor relations professional in the integrated oil and gas industry.

We are each gifted in a unique and important way. It is our privilege and our adventure to discover our own special light.

—*Mary Dunbar*

FROM BUST TO BOOM

Bruce Yee—Mine is the story of an American Dream, a rags-to-riches story reminiscent of Horatio Alger. It is the tale of determination, of passion, and of drive to succeed.

While I have no complaints about my upbringing, it was not the childhood everyone dreams of. The neighborhood I grew up in was not exactly conducive to success. There was a lot of crime, violence, and shortsighted decision-making. The possibilities were limited, to say the least, and being able to imagine a different, better worldview was difficult. My mother, Linda, was forced into raising my two siblings and me by herself, all while holding down several jobs. I watched as she ground out every day, trying to provide a better life for us. It was never easy watching her struggle through long days and into the night. I was moved by her sense of determination, affected by the way she sacrificed herself. I know this is where I get my sense of service. She instilled in me the desire for education. She knew that the best way to pull yourself out of obscurity was to empower yourself with knowledge. Not only was she vocal, she also practiced what she preached—receiving her MBA from the Spears School of Business at OSU-Tulsa in 1997, all while working full time during the day to support her family. My mother is my mentor, my friend, and my role model.

It was that example that led me to OSU. But it was not an easy decision. I knew that college was going to be on my dime, as my mother did not have the financial means to support me through school. That said, I sought out every scholarship and loan available and followed my love of business to OSU. It seemed natural to pursue a degree that would set me up for success and I landed on accounting. I received my BBA from the Spears School in 1996. While ecstatic about earning an undergraduate degree, I had always known that an undergraduate degree would not get me where I ultimately wanted to be. To earn that competitive edge, I knew that I would need an advanced degree. With my mother already enrolled in the MBA program at OSU-Tulsa, there was never any question as to what would follow: I enrolled as an MBA student. I was fortunate that two of my closest friends from undergrad chose to follow me. Angela Courtin, an engineer, and Jennifer Coonce, a marketer, decided to pursue an MBA as well. I remember how all of us struggled through Dr. Rick Wilson's Production Operations Management course. Thankfully we all had each other's backgrounds to pull from, as linear operations was not anything I had ever studied before. But it was not all coursework and strife for the three of us. In 1997, after Angela had heard about Gator Growl at the University of Florida, she convinced Jen and me to help her start a similar program at OSU. We decided to call our event Orange Peel, an entirely student led and run entertainment production. While there were definitely struggles getting that first event off the ground, it was well worth it. That first year we brought in comedians Bill Cosby and Norm MacDonald and followed up in the second year with Jeff Foxworthy and the band Blackhawk headlining the event. The event actually outlived our tenure at OSU and was held on campus annually from 1997 to 2009. I'm not saying that my part in Orange Peel was the cause, but it sure did not hurt me in my being selected as OSU Homecoming King in 1997—a true honor. I was humbled by being chosen. Unfortunately, Homecoming King did not mean the riches and laissez-faire lifestyle afforded to actual royalty, and after six years of college it was high time to find a job.

Mr. Jim Alcock (an OSU alumnus) was conducting interviews for positions at the Exxon Corporation my second year in the MBA program. Thankfully, Mr. Alcock saw something in me and offered me a position at Exxon. I did not know much about Exxon, but it was a job and a paycheck, which, as a poor college student, meant that I jumped at the opportunity. Armed with my fresh MBA and an undergraduate background in accounting, I was placed in Exxon's controllership area. I must admit to being a bit nervous that first day. Exxon recruited from all over the country, including the most prestigious business schools. But my nerves were calmed that first day as the initial briefings made it clear that our degree only aided us in getting hired; it was performance on the job that would be rewarded, not pedigree. It took me a while to understand how good I really had it. I realized that I actually enjoyed the work that I was doing. But more than that, I finally realized that what I'd learned at OSU was not just a bunch of academia, but that it had actually prepared me for my endeavors at Exxon. I looked back and understood the value of my MBA. The team projects, the complex case studies, the late night paper writing sessions were not just exercises in scholastics, but rather tools to prepare me for the situations in the real world.

I have been blessed with success at Exxon. I love working with the people there. I love that I am challenged everyday and love that I am allowed to move around business units within Exxon so that I can broaden my own horizons. Most of all, I love that I am afforded multiple opportunities to give back. Following in the steps of Mr. Alcock, I have taken up the mantle of recruiting. I serve as the Financial Recruiting Team Captain at OSU for ExxonMobil, working diligently to procure jobs at the company for fellow OSU graduates. But I always look back at my childhood and take great satisfaction from giving back to those individuals who desire to better themselves the way that I did. I decided to endow a scholarship at OSU for students who want to pursue their education but do not have the means to do so. I know that had it not been for my education, I would still be in the same situation that my mother faced. But thanks to her example and my OSU degrees, I am able to give back and bring others out of their less fortunate situations.

I have learned a lot in life, but a life is not lived until one passes those lessons on. In that light, I wish to pass along some of those things that I find most important. First, my mother taught me never to settle. She taught me how to be independent and do those things required to get me where I wanted to be. She taught me the value of education and its ability to improve my quality of life.

The biggest takeaway from my college years is that it's the friends you make and the experiences you share that follow you the rest of your life. I still find ways to meet with Jenny and Angela. In fact, we joke that we are tri-coastal. Jenny lives in New York City, Angela rests her head in Los Angeles, and I now reside in Houston. We keep in touch regularly, and try to make it out to see each other at least once a year.

In my work at Exxon, I have learned the importance of leadership and communication skills. Exxon hires its future leadership and in that light expects its employees to take up the torch when it is passed to them. This requires every employee to prepare themselves for the challenges of leadership, as the opportunity to execute is always waiting. The ability to work in teams, to turn weaknesses into strengths, to deliver a product when the resources are not there is the challenge presented to all Exxon employees, and one that I have taken to heart.

I relish the opportunities to lead at ExxonMobil and hope that others do as well. Included in that role as leader, I cannot stress enough the importance of the continual refinement of communications skills. I always tell my recruits that they might be the smartest, most gifted analyst to ever grace this company's doors, but if they cannot take those ideas and succinctly present them to management so that the ideas are adopted, then they are really of no use to the company. It is only through practice and patience that one learns how to clearly communicate, but it is time well spent.

Finally, I have learned to be flexible. I force myself to look beyond just getting the job done and look towards ways to make the job better. I have learned to accept challenges that stretch my preconceived limits; otherwise I will never grow. I seek out mentors for advice and have learned to accept failures as opportunities to learn. I realize that my career is only one part of the happiness puzzle. I also find joy in my family, friends, and community.

Bruce Yee
Contributed by Graham Glaser

KEY SUCCESS FACTORS: Leadership, Communication Skills, Desire for Knowledge, Sense of Humor

EDITOR'S NOTES: Along with being a true success story at ExxonMobil, Mr. Yee takes pride in his many accomplishments while at OSU. Bruce was a founder and member of the OSU MBA Ambassadors and was selected to present a case at a competition in Washington, D.C. For his contributions to OSU since graduation, Bruce has been honored as a Spears School of Business Outstanding Young Alumni. He and his best friend, Lara, enjoy traveling, entertaining with friends, and exploring the Houston food scene. He looks forward to a continued relationship with Exxon and hopes to retire from the company he so enjoys working for.

CHAPTER SIX
ALUMNI EXTRAORDINAIRE

Living the lives many dream of—New York City and Dolce Vita, Hollywood and MTV, Washington D.C. and the U.S. Congress—the following alumni prove that the career possibilities with an MBA are unlimited.

You are unique, and if that is not fulfilled then something has been lost.

—Martha Graham

BUILDING A PATH TO SUCCESS

Jennifer Coonce—Business is exciting, the politics of business is fascinating, and the challenge of leading a team towards a common goal is exhilarating. Climbing the ladder is a great game, until you get to the top and realize that you don't like the view. When it happened to me, I wasn't willing to wait around until retirement in a position that I was not passionate about. I decided to jump off the ladder and forge a new path that fit my skills and my passion.

As a child, I would set up "shop" in my room and "sell" dresses to my sister and my mother. I always wanted to run my own shop. My journey towards my goal continues and after a few distractions, I am moving forward with focus and determination. I was raised with a strong work ethic and strong time management skills. My parents worked full time and my siblings and I were very active. From junior high through the MBA program, I almost always had a retail job, a marketing position, or even a paper route. To this day, I derive a lot of my self-worth from my work performance and am proud of my successes. Along with my part time jobs, extracurricular activities reinforced my parents' lessons regarding the importance of teamwork. My competitive nature was amplified by these activities. However, I learned how to gain consensus without dictating to other members of the team.

Learning how to solve problems was the most valuable lesson from my childhood. My father is a very curious man and could figure out how to fix anything—a trait shared by my grandfather. Watching them work through problems demonstrated to me that although I may not know anything about a particular issue, with patience and time, I can figure out a solution—even if sometimes the solution is duct tape or band aids.

I was offered a scholarship to the MBA program during my senior year of undergraduate school. Continuous learning is a core value of my family. But in all honesty, I love school and was looking forward to the opportunity to study and practice business theory. The OSU MBA program gave me the confidence to trust my intuition and to pursue challenges outside of my comfort zone. The program also taught me to defer to individuals who were more knowledgeable in specific areas. The interactive nature of the program allowed me to leverage my team working skills and put into use the theory we were being taught. The team projects, case studies, and class discussions emphasized for me the importance of listening while still leading. During many class sessions, the passion and intensity with which my colleagues held tight to their views was frustrating; however, I learned during those somewhat contentious sessions how to manage diversity in backgrounds and ideas in order to arrive at the strongest solution. The skill of learning from the diverse experiences and knowledge of my team members while being patient for the team to arrive at a good decision has served me well throughout my career. The program taught me how to lead without dictating—a key skill for business and life.

After graduating from the MBA program, I was recruited to work as an Information Risk Management Consultant at KPMG in Dallas, Texas. Although I had a marketing background, I was confident I could quickly learn about computer security and leverage my communication skills in order to succeed in this new industry. After a few years and a couple of promotions, KPMG asked me to move to New York City, where I quickly found other opportunities to grow. One of my clients, UBS Wealth Management, hired me as an Information Security Policy Officer, and I was later promoted to Chief Information Security Officer for the business group. While climbing the ladder at KPMG and at UBS, I realized that just "winning" in the corporate game wasn't really winning at life if I wasn't passionate about the work. While I loved the people and the problem solving, I realized that my ultimate goals of continuous learning and leadership were not being fulfilled and I needed to start anew.

I have always strived for positions that require a high learning curve. After leaving UBS, determined to find a role I could be passionate about and one that could benefit from my previous experiences, I took a year to explore my interests and study those areas—very similar to my MBA experience! Once I focused on retail and realized my passion for business and fashion would allow me to leverage my current skills and continue growing, I set out to find a way into the industry. As I researched the retail industry and began building my business plan for my own store, I met the owner of Dolce Vita, a large footwear and apparel manufacturer. After six months of conversations and coffee, he offered me a position to run his five retail stores. At the time, my last job in a retail store had been more than 10 years earlier, but my previous experiences gave me the confidence to know I could do the job.

The environment at Dolce Vita is very autonomous, and the owners allow me to run the stores as my own. This position requires continuous learning and teamwork and allows me to use my leadership skills in ways that I haven't experienced before. The work is extremely challenging and rewarding. As with the first partner who hired me at KPMG, the owner of Dolce Vita believed that given the opportunity, I could help him build a better business, and I hope I am doing just that. I believe that mentorship shouldn't be limited to one person in your organization—I believe that you should be looking to different individuals to leverage their skills and knowledge to help you find the best answers for your challenges. My grandmother gives me some of the best advice about my current job, while my boss provides great advice on how to navigate personal challenges. You should never assume that a person's role in your life is defined by their title. Strive to learn from everyone around you.

My business card at Dolce Vita does not have a title and I have a desk in the middle of a loft space with no privacy. From the outside, my new position is a far cry from UBS with the trips to Zurich for meetings, the executive furniture, and the office view overlooking lower Manhattan. And I couldn't be happier. Well, maybe if I owned my own store. But that is coming; I know it.

The best advice I can give to young MBA students is to expose yourself and your ideals to as many people as possible. Be curious about others and their life experiences. Strive to learn something new every day and strive to be a teacher to someone every day. Continue to question what you want and the path you are taking to get there. You never know when or where inspiration will come for solving a problem, learning something new, or even starting a new career, so embrace all of life's experiences.

Jennifer Coonce
Contributed by Scott Robin

KEY SUCCESS FACTORS: Teamwork, Continuous Learning, Integrity, Respecting Different Perspectives and Backgrounds, Sense of Self-Worth, Competitiveness, Problem Solving Skills, Listening while Leading, Leading without Dictating

WEBSITE: www.dolcevita.com

SOCIAL MEDIA: Facebook—Dolce Vita; Twitter—shopdolcevita

EDITOR'S NOTES: Jennifer was awarded the Outstanding Young Alumnus award from the Spears School of Business, Oklahoma State University, in 2006. She plans to continue working for Dolce Vita until the opportunity presents itself to fulfill her ultimate goal, which is to own her own store.

Follow your passion and success will follow you.

—Arthur Buddhold

NOT JUST ANY PEP RALLY

Angela Courtin—I remember it like it was yesterday. The sound of over seventeen thousand people screaming, cheering, laughing, and enjoying one of the first pep rally events of its kind— *Orange Peel*. Bill Cosby had just left the stage as Norm McDonald walked on, and *Dog's Eye View* was warming up backstage. I could not help but smile ear-to-ear, take a deep breath, and sigh. A year's worth of organizing, one hundred thousand dollars worth of fund raising, hundreds if not thousands of hours of effort by dozens of students, and it all came together on that night. I looked over at my friends and exclaimed, "We pulled it off!" We could've walked on air. We were proud of our enormous accomplishment. Looking back, *Orange Peel* became the pivotal point in my life that would later catapult me into my career.

I was born in Dallas, Texas, and traveled all over the world growing up. My father was an Air Force officer and managed air fields, so we moved every few years. Most of my family are architects and engineers, so it was fairly easy to decide what I wanted to do with my life. My parents really wanted me to pursue engineering, but I was more interested in architecture at that time. In 1991, I compromised and enrolled in a heavy course-load in Architectural Engineering at the University of Texas.

Two years into my degree, I flew up to Stillwater to help my sister, Sarah, move into the dorms at Oklahoma State University (OSU). I enjoyed the campus and people so much that I decided I wanted to go to school there as well. I found that I enjoyed creating experiences more than structures, so I transferred into Civil Engineering. My brother, Raymond, also transferred to OSU—from Texas A&M. As I was finishing my undergrad degree, I got the idea to overhaul our annual pep rally. I wanted it to be something that OSU had never seen before, something big, bold, and memorable. I started my MBA and the first *Orange Peel* team in 1996, and it became my life for the next two years. *Orange Peel* not only became a great tradition and source of entertainment for the local community, but it also became a giant learning lab for students to work and gain experience. Everyone involved with *Orange Peel* could apply the skills they learned every day in class.

I found that the topics I learned as an MBA student were far more applicable than my engineering degree. I was able to apply all of the concepts I learned throughout my MBA to *Orange Peel* immediately. Advertising strategies, choosing the right people for a job, winning negotiations, leading by influence—all were concepts I learned from my MBA classes. I knew I wanted to pursue something in that field, so the more I learned, the more I could apply. My MBA really provided a foundation on which to build my career, and it gave me the tools to advance quickly through the ranks. I continue to use those skills every day.

Every time I think of *Orange Peel*, I quickly remember all of my wonderful friends and great mentors: Dr. Keys, Dr. Basu, and Dr. Manzer, just to name a few. I remember a story Dr. Manzer told us during class about when he was working as a salesman for Dole. He spoke about his wife's obsession with Coca Cola and how he forgot to pick up a bottle on his way home after a long day of work. Just as he turned the key and walked through the front door, he found his wife asking for her bottle of Coca Cola. Regretfully, he turned around, walked back out to his car, and drove to the store to get his wife her bottle of cola. All he'd wanted to do was sit down, put his feet up, and relax, but this is what he learned: In the moments where the outcome is certain, the only choice you really have is your attitude toward achieving the objective. Dr. Manzer's lesson has stuck with me over the course of my career, and I've learned that the more you have the right attitude as you grow, the easier it is to achieve your goals.

After I completed my MBA, I wanted to do something that I loved. I decided to answer an ad in the *Washington Post* to become the Field Organizer of the 8th District of Maryland. The pay was far from great, just one hundred dollars per week, but I was not very interested in money, and I was very passionate about politics and advocacy. It was a great experience and led me to become the Finance Director of the

8th District's Democratic Party. I was also involved with the Human Rights Campaign as the Associate Development Director for the Federal Club Council. I certainly was not making a lot of money, but I loved what I was doing. In 2000, I left Washington DC and moved to Los Angeles to work for another advocacy organization. I helped raise money for the 2002 Democratic National Committee mid-term elections. It was a challenge to encourage people to donate when you were not winning, and it was difficult to connect them to a larger goal rather than an immediate one.

I continued with my love for politics and advocacy, but I still had that itch for producing from my experience with *Orange Peel*. In 2004, I served as MTV's Vice President for *Rock the Vote*. The people I worked with at *Rock the Vote* became the catalyst for my producing career. A year later, I became Associate Producer of the HBO series, *Big Love*.

The connections I have made from early on to today have been the catalysts for my career growth. I have found that the relationships you make along the way are just as important as the product you create. Getting to know your peer group in your environment is essential because those people, especially when you are young, go on to be big titles. Even now, I use networking to help place people in jobs. For instance, if I hear that someone is looking for a certain skill set, I can usually point them to someone who can get the job done, just as others helped me make the leap into producing.

A year after my producing career with HBO, I landed a job with MTV as the Vice President of Integrated Marketing. Two years later I accepted a job offer from MySpace as their Senior Vice President of Marketing, Entertainment, and Content. It was very interesting and challenging. The technology was constantly changing and progressing, and moved so quickly that it was hard to keep up with. I always had to make sure that my staff was staying in line with customers. We worked hard to keep up with new trends so that we could continue to relate to MySpace users. At that time social media was exploding, so we acted quickly to harness that power. It was a wonderful experience and every day was a new opportunity.

In July 2010, I received an offer to come back to MTV as the Senior Vice President of their Integrated Marketing Group. I am incredibly happy and content with my current position and feel strongly about MTV's success. I find myself challenged every day, both profession- ally and creatively, and look forward to continuing to develop innova- tive execution for our partners. I plan to continue building a career and family that I can be proud of, while balancing the two and also making meaningful contributions to our local community and society at large.

As I look back on the path my career has taken, I feel incredibly blessed as a professional. I was able to lead my career choices based on my life's passions. I will admit I have been very lucky in terms of timing and opportunity. People in every company I worked for became mentors and friends. A lot of them took chances on me because I was young. I knew I could do great things and I wanted to prove that to them. Every step I took was a step forward.

If I were to give anyone advice about their career, I would say to do what you love. You give so much time and energy to your career, that you must do something that will inspire you the majority of the time. I found that when you take a job because you love the work, everything else seems to fall into place because you are so much happier. If you have life goals, the path that you are on will get you there—just remember that it may not make sense at the time. When you are young and ambi- tious, you will want to do everything, but keep in mind that being patient and listening is just as important as pushing forward. Follow up after a meeting with LinkedIn or a phone call. Do not do it just for networking's sake, but take interest in others' ideas. If you stay within your field or industry, remember that it's a small world. Most importantly, be sure to nurture the relationships you make along the way. There are still a few people I have kept in contact with since *Orange Peel*.

Angela Courtin
Contributed by Matt Syme

KEY SUCCESS FACTORS: Attitude, Passion, Integrity, Networking, Work/Life Balance

WEBSITE: www.mtv.com

SOCIAL MEDIA: Facebook—Angela.Courtin; LinkedIn—Angela Courtin; Twitter—acourtin

EDITOR'S NOTES: Angela's work was recognized in 2004 *Out Magazine*'s OUT 100, the annual list of the year's most interesting, influential, and newsworthy LGBT people. Since 2007, she has served as President of the Board of Outfest, Los Angeles' Gay & Lesbian Film Festival.

Angela has delivered the keynote at OMMA, has been featured at the *Economist* Forum, and has been cited in a wide array of articles, books, and publications focused on social media. She has been a guest lecturer at Harvard Business School and the USC School of Media Studies. Angela was named one of *Power Up*'s 10 Amazing Gay Women in Showbiz and selected as the recipient of the Spears School of Business Outstanding Young Alumnus Award.

We gain strength, and courage, and confidence by each experience in which we really stop to look fear in the face . . . we must do that which we think we cannot.

—Eleanor Roosevelt

MAKING A DIFFERENCE
IN THE NATION'S CAPITOL

Leslie A. Woolley—Congressman Wes Watkins, an Oklahoma State alumni, approached me one day and said, "If I am chosen to serve on the House Banking Committee, I need someone who has knowledge in this area. Would you work for me and focus on this?" Thus, I was transplanted from my roots in Ada, OK, to Washington, D.C. That was over 30 years ago.

I was born and raised in Ada, OK. It was a great place to grow up. My parents, grandparents, and extended family were my greatest influence. Our family spent many Saturdays in Stillwater for OSU alumni meetings and lunches and Cowboy football games. I have found that my groups of friends from my school days in Ada, through my school days in Stillwater, to my inner social circle friends today, are very important to me and have had a great impact on and brought tremendous support for my career and my success in my work within the Washington, D.C. area.

I attended Oklahoma State University for both my undergraduate degree in Business Administration and for my Master's in Business Administration. I did so because my roots are in this area. Drummond Hall is named after my grandfather and most of my family has attended this university. It felt only natural to become part of such a distinguished group of alumni and attend Oklahoma State. I graduated in 1976 with my MBA, the only family member to obtain the degree to date, although several members have been in the undergraduate program. It seems like only moments ago.

As a result of attending graduate school, I had a large group of business contacts, both within the university and in the community. One of these was Congressman Wes Watkins, who was from Ada and attended the same church as my family. He mentioned to me that if he were to serve on the House Banking Committee, he would need someone with a business background. He did indeed serve on the House Banking Committee, and I was asked to join his staff. I began my employment for him on January 17, 1977, working for him on all matters within the economic and financial services industries. That was my start, and I continue to work on many issues regarding the financial services industry to this day.

As a result of my work for Congressman Watkins, I was exposed to a vast number of issues surrounding the banking and finance industries. During my tenure in Washington, D.C., I have seen the inner workings of the Treasury Department, the Federal Deposit Insurance Corporation (FDIC) and the Resolution Trust Corporation (RTC), as well as overseeing the federal financial regulatory agencies like the Securities and Exchange Commission and the Federal Housing Finance Board. I have been heavily involved in the legislation enacted with respect to the banking and financial industries. I was instrumental in evaluating and working on the Bank Insurance Fund (BIF) and Savings and Loan Insurance Fund (SAIF) Recapitalization Act of 1997, The Commodity Trading Modernization Act of 1999, as well as the Sarbanes-Oxley Act of 2002. I actually have a copy of the Sarbanes-Oxley Act signed by both Senator Sarbanes and Congressman Oxley. This signed document is a cherished memento of many hours of hard work and lots of discussion.

One interesting fact about having an MBA is that I am somewhat unique amongst my Capitol Hill peers. Most of the people I work with are lawyers. I have had to explain that I was asked here to add finan-cial services knowledge to an otherwise legal legislative process heavily weighted toward laws and lawyers. It has been interesting to say the least.

One of the hardest things for me has been that if a politician gets defeated in an election, you essentially lose your job. This comes as a mixed blessing: I have been very fortunate to get picked up by other congressmen and senators on the House and Senate Banking Committees and have done financial services work for 5 democrats and 2 republicans. I have also worked in the Administration for the

Treasury Department as well as an independent agency for the FDIC. This has given me the ability to see the banking and financial industry from both sides of Capitol Hill, across party lines, inside and outside the Administration and the private sector. I have really been fortunate to be able to work around such talented and dedicated people and to learn so much about the financial services world.

Some of the keys to my success have been that I try to be substantive and know the issues. I try to come to every meeting fully prepared and able to discuss the topics at hand. This characteristic gives me credibility. Credibility is everything in Washington. If you don't have credibility, it becomes known very quickly, and this city will not tolerate that. I am also good at identifying, analyzing and discussing the substantive and political pros and cons of the issues with the people for whom I work. Your word is your trade around here as with any other business.

I would advise others to find the type of work that you are very interested in and passionate about and follow that dream. If you really enjoy your work, you are steps ahead of your peers. I have been here for 34 years and have really enjoyed it. While my roots are in Oklahoma and Oklahoma State University, I have been very fortunate to work in this area where our country is governed.

Having seen lots of economic and financial ups and downs in our country during this period—I was here during the Savings and Loan crisis of the 1980s and the recent economic and financial services crisis of 2008—has given me a real perspective on the inter-workings and regulation of the financial services industries. My recent work includes the Dodd-Frank Financial Reform and Consumer Protection Act that was signed into law in July of 2010. This act encompasses several aspects of the financial world that I have been involved with. Chief among these have been the workings and transparency of the financial derivatives world as well as the treatment of consumer financial services and stabilizing our economy and financial industry.

As for technology and communication, Washington is on the cutting edge of both. We are one of the first areas of the country to get updated technology. We adapt the communications technology to fit our needs which then become the next roll-out for updated technology. Washington operates on electronic systems like Blackberries and iPads. While I manage our staff that maintains our social media sites for the Congressmen, I am not directly involved in maintaining these areas. While technology improvements are wonderful and have expanded our knowledge of others views and the news around us, my talented technology staff takes care of those sites. I certainly respect them for their talent in the technology world.

I believe firmly in giving back to the OSU and D.C.communities. I have been involved in the Women's Giving Circle of Alexandria, a group that provides educational grants for needy Pre-K and Kindergarten programs, and in the Women in Housing and Finance group, which provides grant money for financial education for low-income women. I have hosted several classes of OSU political science students in DC to discuss the political process. I have been the President of the Oklahoma State Society in Washington as well as the President of the Washington, D.C chapter of the Oklahoma State University alumni association. I have also proudly served on the Executive committee and the national Board of the OSU Alumni Association. So you can see my roots are firmly and proudly planted in the Oklahoma State University community.

Leslie A. Woolley
Contributed by Mark E. Wood

KEY SUCCESS FACTORS: Credibility, Knowledge of Industry, Ability to Analyze and Deliver Pros and Cons of Issues, Balanced Perspective, Trustworthy

WEBSITE: www.house.gov/cleaver/Cleaver%20Green/index.shtml

EDITOR'S NOTES: Leslie Woolley has worked for Senators Bob Graham, Zell Miller, and Joe Lieberman; Congressmen Wes Watkins, Bill McCollum, and Emmanuel Cleaver and the House Financial Services Committee. She has also served as Director of Policy and on the Executive Committee for the FDIC (for the first woman Chairman of the FDIC) and on issues surrounding derivatives for the Treasury Department. Leslie has lobbied for the Investment Company Institute, a trade association representing the mutual fund industry, Chemical Bank (now JP Morgan Chase), and the Conference of State Bank Supervisors representing the State Banking Supervisors. She has also worked with *former Treasury Secretary, Larry* Summers; Commodity Futures Trading Commission Chairman, Gary Gensler; former FDIC Chairman Ricki Tigert Helfer, and Acting Comptroller of the Currency, John Walsh, among many others.

Leslie has been at the center of some of our nation's greatest financial and economic crises and has been instrumental in bringing forth legislation that is intended to address many of the financial ills that plague our nation. Leslie has championed causes within the financial services and banking community and brings a wealth of knowledge and experience to her position and to the legislative process in our nation's capital.

CHAPTER SEVEN
BIG BUSINESS

The following alumni spend many hours giving back to Oklahoma State University, making a difference in the lives of our students and the companies they represent.

The way of the world is meeting people through other people.

—Robert Kerrigan

THE IMPORTANCE OF RELATIONSHIPS

Danielle Hollingsworth—I was born and raised in Arkansas City, Kansas with one brother and one sister in a very loving and supportive environment. We were all actively involved in sports and very competitive. During my senior year of high school, I decided to attend the University of Kansas. I began college as a computer engineering major, then switched to computer science. I finally decided to major in business administration, with an emphasis in marketing, graduating in 1995. During my senior year at the University of Kansas, I decided to continue my education and applied to several MBA programs. After speaking with one of my marketing professors, at his urging I chose to go out of state to get my Master's degree.

After several site visits to different campuses, including the University of Oklahoma and Oklahoma State University, I chose to attend OSU to receive my MBA. I felt very comfortable with my choice because of the faculty and professors I met with and the financial aid the university offered. During my site visit to OSU, I met Dr. Manzer, a marketing professor, and really connected with him. I truly felt OSU was the school for me. I enjoyed my two years at OSU and absolutely loved the structure of the program. The MBA degree program gave me a well-rounded education in every area of business. The breadth of the education made it possible for me to choose among several different career paths. I still have many friends I met through the MBA program. The two years spent in the MBA program were more fulfilling both academically and socially than my previous four years of college.

Upon graduating from OSU, I participated in many campus interviews with companies, including Payless, Conoco, and Koch Industries. At Koch Industries, I initially interviewed for a Marketing Analyst position. After two visits to Koch's Wichita headquarters, we were still searching for a position that suited my aspirations, so I made a third visit to

Wichita to talk to the Internal Audit department. Like OSU, I knew that Koch Industries was where I wanted to be; it was just a matter of finding the right role. I decided to accept the audit position with Koch in June 1997. In my role, I was responsible for both internal financial and IT audits. I didn't necessarily see myself in an auditing role upon graduation, but the experience provided vast learning opportunities. As we built our IT auditing function, I became more involved in individual technology audits. I developed many personal connections within the IT department and enjoyed working alongside the people there. I always thought IT might be a department where I would like to work at some point in my career, and my role on the Internal Audit IT team allowed me to begin focusing my attention there. A year later, Koch decided to outsource the audit function, which left me looking for a new position. This was the first challenge I faced in my career. It was a daunting obstacle after only a year and a half in the workforce. The well-rounded experience I'd received at OSU helped prepare me for this challenge and allowed me to identify other opportunities within Koch. Like the first time I interviewed with Koch, we worked together to find something we both believed was a good fit for my skills, talents, and career aspirations. I was thankful my MBA degree gave me the flexibility to transfer my skill set and knowledge to another department and discipline.

With the relationships I developed in the IT department, I decided to refocus my career and began working as a software developer implementing our corporate financial system. During this time, I worked within several Koch companies, including Koch Industries, Koch Petroleum Group and, ultimately, Flint Hills Resources. After approximately five years of developing, I was moved into a management position at FHR where I was responsible for a number of financial systems and six software developers. I faced daily challenges in making sure that both my team and I contributed to the success of the business. I constantly challenged both myself and my employees to make sure that everyone was doing their best to help the company succeed. I really enjoyed this position and developed a passion for my job, which made my work even more enjoyable.

In October 2010, I was promoted to a new position within Flint Hills Resources. The role is still within our IT organization, but I am now a

Program Manager. In this role, I continue to be responsible for a number of our commercial applications, as well as eight Business Systems Analysts. This new role has given me additional opportunities to utilize my interpersonal and relationship-building skills through the added responsibilities of maintaining IT's relationships with our Accounting and Commercial groups. Several key success factors have, I believe, helped me in accomplishing this goal. I believe you must have integrity and honesty in your job. I learned these qualities growing up and have always felt they are the two most important qualities a person can possess. You must also have humility and know when to ask for help. No one knows all the answers, but answers can be obtained if you are willing to admit you don't know everything and you are humble enough to ask for help. I also believe I have been able to maintain a great balance between work and home. Time outside of work, usually spent with my husband and kids, makes my job much more enjoyable.

Koch has also given me opportunities to give back to the Wichita community through the company's philanthropic efforts. I have participated in the humbling experience of helping build houses for Habitat for Humanity. The IT department is also actively involved in the Salvation Army's Angel Tree. Every December, we volunteer our time to assemble the toys purchased for the Angel Tree children. During the fall, we are also given opportunities to contribute to the Kansas Food Bank food drive through friendly competitions between Koch companies.

If I could offer one word of advice, it would be to understand the importance of building strong interpersonal skills and developing sincere relationships. Open communication, good listening skills, and treating others with mutual respect are key interpersonal skills that allow for productive relationship building. Developing these relationships with the people I have met throughout my career has helped me advance more than I thought possible.

Danielle Hollingsworth
Contributed by Alex Williams

KEY SUCCESS FACTORS: Integrity, Honesty, Humility, Mutual Respect, Balance between Work and Home, Strong Interpersonal Skills

WEBSITE: www.fhr.com

SOCIAL MEDIA: Facebook—Danielle Banister Hollingsworth; LinkedIn—Danielle (Banister) Hollingsworth

EDITOR'S NOTES: Danielle's husband, Todd, is the Vice President of Lending at Southwest National Bank in Wichita. They have two children, Amanda age 8, and Lukas age 6. Danielle helps coach both of her kids' soccer teams and between the two, stays very busy. She also enjoys running and biking in her free time. For 11 of the 13 years since she graduated from OSU, she has played a key role in the OSU recruiting team. She helps lead the team in identifying students for both full-time and internship opportunities for various business groups and disciplines within Koch. She, along with 15 to 20 additional OSU alumni, travel back to OSU throughout the year to give classroom lectures and student organization presentations and to participate in career fairs and campus interviews. She strives to help connect students to those key factors that will help bring them future success in the professional workforce.

Every job is a self-portrait of the person who does it. Autograph your work with excellence.

—Author Unknown

MAKING A DIFFERENCE

Julie Polk—I was born and raised in Stillwater, Oklahoma. My parents were both OSU alums; my mom graduated with a degree in Business Education and my dad was a pre-dentistry student. They met after graduation, in Dallas. When they were making the decision about where they wanted to live, work, and raise a family, they decided to move back to Stillwater. I'm not sure that I ever had any choice in being an OSU fan; it came naturally to me. I went to preschool on OSU's campus and have bled orange and black ever since the day that I enrolled at OSU as a freshman.

Teachers had a big impact on me from the beginning. I can vividly remember my elementary math teacher who made math fun. She ignited an interest in math in me that remains to this day. In high school, I did well in my math classes, as well as in computer science. One day, my computer science teacher brought an OSU degree sheet to class and talked about a new major the university was offering in something called Management Information Systems. He told me I would be good at MIS and encouraged me to look into it. I did, and soon after, enrolled at OSU as a freshman MIS major.

Once I got to college at Oklahoma State, I instinctively knew that I would go on to graduate school, specifically to get my MBA. It just seemed to make sense. I graduated with a Bachelor's of Science in Business Administration: Management Information Systems in May, 1999. I graduated with honors and felt confident that I had built a strong skill set. I was offered two good positions, both in MIS, and both with oil and gas companies I had interned with. But I wasn't convinced that I was ready to apply my knowledge and skills within a company. I declined the offers and enrolled in the full-time MBA program, graduating with my Master's in Business Administration in December, 2000.

What I remember most about the MBA program at OSU is my class-mates. They made the program for me. The people in my classes were from all backgrounds and nationalities, and some had years of real-world work experience that I didn't. Some students had traveled internationally with their jobs, and they came from a variety of indus-tries that I knew little about. The MBA students felt like a family to me. I didn't have as many social or extracurricular obligations in graduate school, so I was able to completely focus on my classes and projects. I very much enjoyed the program.

Another benefit of the MBA program was that it exposed me to a number of industries and positions that I wasn't familiar with. I realized that there were a lot of industries out there besides oil and gas. My jobs after graduation have allowed me to work in more of a consulting role, interacting with industries like health care and technology. I prob-ably wouldn't have had the opportunity to explore different industries if I had entered the workforce directly after undergrad (I would probably still be in oil and gas). After taking a year and a half to complete my MBA, I accepted my first full-time position, making 50% more than the offers I had declined out of undergrad.

Upon receiving my MBA from Oklahoma State, I accepted a job at KPMG, a global network of firms providing audit, tax, and advisory services. I was based out of Dallas. KPMG was not one of the compa-nies that visited OSU's campus to actively recruit students, but I was referred to the company by another OSU MBA graduate. I started as an IT auditor, working alongside financial auditors to audit the computer and security systems of our clients.

After two years at KPMG, I accepted a job at ISNetworld, which was in its start-up phase at the time. ISNetworld connects corporations with reliable contractors and suppliers from capital-intensive industries. Many people, including my parents, thought I was crazy at the time. I was leaving a very large, well-established firm (and taking a significant pay cut) for a start-up firm with eight employees. It was a huge risk—certainly the biggest risk in my career to date. Why did I do it? I did it because I wanted to make a difference. I wanted to provide a service to a client (as opposed to reviewing a service clients already have). As an auditor, I was very restricted in what services I could provide. I could point out problems, but I was never involved in implementing the solutions. I was ready to make a big impact and feel fulfilled at the end of my work day. That need to make a difference started during my graduate work at OSU. The broad education that I received inspired confidence that I hadn't had before, so I felt comfortable with more responsibility and was able to branch into new areas of business in order to perform to the best of my ability. The most important part in my decision to change careers was the fact that I believed in the product, the service, and the company that was ISN.

I knew about ISN through contacts I had met at OSU. Dr. Raj Basu had been my advisor during my undergraduate career, and we stayed in touch through the MBA program and after graduation. He introduced me to Joseph Eastin, another OSU graduate, when I moved to Dallas to work for KPMG. Joe and I stayed in touch and he recruited me to ISN in 2003.

When I started at ISN, we had eight employees. I began as a National Account Manager, doing sales and business development. I was given more and more responsibility as we moved into new vertical markets and, in 2005, was made Director of Business Development. Currently, I serve as the Director of Quality Assurance and Quality Control for ISN. We now have 180 employees in 5 office locations and 4 countries, and we work with over 30,000 contractors. My decision to change careers has certainly paid off, and then some.

I don't necessarily have someone in my life that I would call a mentor. I do believe that it is important to be surrounded by good people who challenge you—whether they are mentors, bosses, or coworkers; teachers in school; or your college advisors. People like my high school computer science teacher and Raj Basu at OSU pushed me in certain directions and forced me to move out of my comfort zone.

The people I work with at ISN constantly inspire me. Everyone I work with is dedicated to the company's growth, instead of their own, personal advancement. There is a real team environment; everyone is involved in the idea process. It is something that we look for when hiring employees. We don't need just skills—we need team players, people who have an overall goal of making a positive difference. We need employees who can adapt to a variety of roles and communication styles. It can be a humbling experience to learn teamwork in the work force; you have to find a balance between "me" and "us."

What sets OSU students apart from other business students? Their work ethic. Many OSU students come from small towns, or have an agricultural background, or have a family that has instilled in them the value of hard work. They have a hunger for education that other students lack. OSU students don't expect respect: they earn it.

My advice for current and future business students is to pick a company whose core values align with your own personal goals. I can't stress how important it is to feel good about what you do and who you work for. It makes all the difference in the world and success will follow if you are passionate about your organization and appreciate your position within that organization.

I also like the saying that "time invested is time well spent." It is up to you to create your ideal work environment. You have a responsibility to your organization to help create the best work environment for yourself and your peers. Customer service should always be a priority. In any position, it is critical to listen to your customer's needs and respond quickly. It is also important to have initiative in the workplace. You should always be willing to take on more responsibility than is specifically asked of you. When it comes time for advancement, you will be in a better position than a peer who does only what is asked of him or her.

Finally, you should *always be networking*! Be an active member in your community through a variety of organizations: join an alumni group, participate in philanthropic engagements, attend community events, and join several organizations. Keep contact with university faculty and advisors. They love to hear from you, and these are the people who are best connected in the business world. In the beginning, they can help you meet potential employers. Once you are established in your field, you can help others meet potential employees.

Julie Polk
Contributed by Casey Reed

KEY SUCCESS FACTORS: Personal Goals Aligned with Core Values of Employer, Invest Time, Customer Service, Take Initiative, Networking

WEBSITE: www.isnetworld.com

SOCIAL MEDIA: LinkedIn—Julie Polk

EDITOR'S NOTES: Julie was awarded the 2008 OSU Spears School of Business Outstanding Young Alumnus Award. She serves as an Advisory Board Member for Alley's House and is involved in the Dallas Chapter of the OSU Alumni Association. She lives in Dallas, Texas and is getting married in June 2011.

Never underestimate the power of passion.

—Eve Sawyer

BUILDING A LEGACY WITH CREATIVITY AND STEEL

Tiffany Sewell-Howard—Creativity is the heart and soul of an artist and the creativity remains, even if art stops being the central focus of your life. My undergraduate degree is in fine arts, and much of my early work following college was as an artist. Immediately after graduating from Oklahoma State University, I was a freelance graphic designer. Much of the art I created while in school was made with welded steel or cast aluminum, so perhaps working with these materials foretold that I was destined to return to Perry and my family's company, The Charles Machine Works, Inc., manufacturer of Ditch Witch underground construction equipment, machines made of steel and other materials.

While working as a graphic designer, I had the opportunity to start a business recycling scrap metal from the Ditch Witch factory. It was a small company with eight employees, but I learned that I really liked the business side of the operation. I also realized that my fine arts degree didn't give me the tools I needed to advance in business to the levels I wanted to reach. That was when I decided to return to OSU for my MBA. Being from Perry, Oklahoma, I had been insulated from the world, but in the MBA program, I found myself working on teams with students from around the world. My classmates from Korea, India, and South Africa had very different perspectives from mine, perspectives that would be important later when I joined Ditch Witch. I thought my education was to provide a new toolset for working in the business world—I wasn't expecting my world to become bigger.

After I graduated with my MBA, I joined Primedia, a Kansas City company that published 200 trade magazines. At that time, the OSU MBA program was receiving a lot of publicity for being a great value in education, and the program's reputation opened the door for me to get a position in Primedia's executive development program. Skills I learned in the MBA program helped me advance rapidly. If I had joined Ditch Witch after graduation, I never would have known whether the opportunities I was receiving were because of my family connection, or because of my skills. Being able to perform at a high level at Primedia gave me confidence not only to do the work, but excel at it. However, I felt the Primedia business model of growth through acquisition was not a good fit for me. Even if I wasn't a sculptor, I wanted the opportunity to be creative and build new things. I left Primedia during the big surge in web development during the late 1990's and became a freelance web page designer.

That experience led me back to Perry and Ditch Witch. I started as the e-marketing manager, creating web sites and doing all of our electronic marketing. It was a natural segue from that into the position of information technology director. I spent time as chief operating officer before assuming the chief executive officer position in 2003.

For me, nothing could be better than working with family. It is more than just a job and a paycheck; it is contributing to a legacy. And at Ditch Witch, we are so integrated into the Perry community, we are inseparable. I feel a great responsibility not just to the family business, but to our business family. Many of our employees are second and third generation employees of Ditch Witch. I feel a great responsibility to ensure that our company will continue to go forward and contribute to our community.

My challenge now is transitioning Ditch Witch from an industry-leading manufacturer to an expanding international corporation taking advantage of global growth opportunities. To live, a company must grow, and if it is not, it actually is dying. If we stayed the same size we are now, no one would feel motivated. In addition, I have to make sure that the company and its leadership maintains the family values that are the foundation of our success. That is why the children of our dealers attend a training program, so they can know Perry and experience being part of the Ditch Witch family. That is why we bring in dealers from around the world to host customers at the offices and factory. That is why we meet every year with the families of our employees to talk about the business and have my grandfather share the history and legendary stories of the company.

The family environment made it very difficult several years ago when we were faced with a downturn in the industry and had to lay off some employees. But it also meant that we faced those challenges with integrity and in a way that respected the employees, rather than treating them as part of the bottom line. The most gratifying thing I've done in this business was being able to hire those people back when business picked up.

Ultimately our success as a business depends on the work ethic I learned growing up on my parents' farm, having integrity in my day-to-day dealings with people, and having fun. If you conduct yourself with integrity, people will run through walls for you. If I'm happy and I'm enjoying what I'm doing, others will enjoy what they do. We've even put in the employee manual that, "It is okay to have fun here." You have to love what you do and have a passion for your work.

Otherwise, it is best to do something else.

Tiffany Sewell-Howard
Contributed by Aaron V. Sapp

KEY SUCCESS FACTORS: Integrity, Work Ethic, Having Fun

WEBSITE: www.ditchwitch.com

SOCIAL MEDIA: Facebook—DitchWitch; Twitter—ditchwitch; YouTube—CMWorks; Flickr— (official ditchwitch)

EDITOR'S NOTES: Tiffany is the proud new mother of twins and excited to get back to mountain biking with her husband. She is on the advisory board of the OSU Riata Center for Entrepreneurship and in 2011, will serve as the first woman chair of the Association of Equipment Manufacturers.

One's destination is never a place, but a new way of seeing things.

—Henry Miller

GOING GLOBAL WITH AN MBA

Dag Yemenu—My story begins in Ethiopia, an East African nation considered by some to be the birthplace of mankind. This is where I was born and raised, and where most of my extended family still live. My parents instilled in me the values of an education and a good work ethic, so when I was older, I entered college at Addis Ababa University, in the capital of the country, where I graduated with a degree in mechanical engineering. After college, I began my career as a mechanical engineer in the aviation industry before deciding to further my education and career by coming to the United States, and to Oklahoma State University, in 1999. Being a student at not only a new school, but in a new country, I had to learn from the ground up a number of things others take for granted—how to interact, how to handle myself, and how to bridge cultural barriers. This was one of my biggest challenges yet. But I succeeded. At Oklahoma State University, I received a graduate degree in industrial engineering and management.

After graduate school, I went to work at an energy company in Houston called Dynegy, a company which has had strong ties to OSU. It was a really exciting time, and what I considered to be my first "real" job out of college. Things were great, and I thought that this was the beginning of a long engineering career in a reputable Fortune 500 company. But just as soon as it started, it was all taken away. The unprecedented collapse of Enron and the resulting fallout destroyed a number of energy companies, and Dynegy was one. A year and a half into my new career I was laid off. I'd had a plan and high hopes. I was in their leadership program, and now all of that had come to a sudden stop. Everything was suddenly derailed.

But life's challenges can be the keys to great opportunities, and I decided to overcome this setback and keep moving forward. When I worked at Dynegy, most of what I did was power plant engineering design and project work. But I quickly noticed that on the projects that I was involved with, a lot of the decisions were being made by professionals who had a well-rounded understanding of what was going on, not just of the technical side of things. I wanted to have a good grasp of those things too—the marketing side, the finance side, how to approach people in general. That's what I wanted to get from an MBA—a well-rounded background that would allow me to take it to the next level in terms of my competency and understanding of business decisions. I had initially planned to work on my MBA part time while I was at Dynegy. So, instead of letting the lay-off get the best of me, I chose to take advantage of this situation. That's when I decided to return to OSU to get my MBA degree. Looking back now, it was one of the best decisions of my life. The MBA program at OSU was a great experience, and in a way, an eye-opener. Among other things, I was fortunate enough to be part of the team that competed, and won, the Big 12 MBA Case Competition held at the OU campus. We eventually ended up going to the George Washington Case Competition in Washington, DC. It was tough, competing against some of the big-name Ivy League schools. But it was a great experience to be part of a great team and to represent OSU. That was a big moment for me.

After graduating with my MBA in 2004, I went straight to work for a company called ISN Software (ISNetworld), where I still work. ISNetworld is a global, web-based business that functions as an online resource connecting corporations with contractors and suppliers. The president of our company, Joe Eastin, who is also an Oklahoma State graduate, was recruiting at OSU when I was a student. I interviewed with him and was offered a summer internship position. The internship experience gave me a great opportunity to learn how you really operate a business and how to work with and learn from a diverse group of professionals, like the president who had recruited me to ISNetworld. I certainly learned a lot from him. In business, you have to look around and see the respected people around you, the people that are a little bit more seasoned, and really observe and watch them. Try to build the kind of relationship with them where they trust you and you trust them. A lot of things that you would not learn in college, you can learn from these types of individuals. That is the best type of mentor: not someone who has been assigned to you, but someone that you have naturally built a relationship with.

At ISNetworld, I began as an intern, but had the opportunity to grow with the company after graduating with my MBA. I worked as a coordinator, a manager, and then a senior manager. I currently serve as a director of ISN's global Review and Verification Services (RAVS) group. ISN was a very small company when I first came on board, around thirteen people total. We now have close to two hundred employees and are still growing. It has been a great ride. We recruit almost every semester at OSU and interestingly enough, more than half of our executive leadership team went to school at OSU. This past January, we opened a subsidiary in the UK as part of our global strategy for growth in the region. With that, I currently have relocated to the UK and work out of our office in London.

These are some of my beliefs that I have learned along the way that I trust have contributed to my success, and that might be of value to others:

1. Have a vision; don't just walk along an unplanned path. Have a goal and a passion for whatever you want to do. Aim for that, and pursue it with excellence and an open mind.

2. Integrity is important. A lot of things will come your way that can derail you, but if you have integrity, you have a much better chance of successfully executing your vision and passion.

3. There will always be setbacks in life, but the important thing is to pick yourself up and dust yourself off. Persevere through your struggles and keep moving forward.

Dag Yemenu
Contributed by Curt Ralph

KEY SUCCESS FACTORS: Vision, Integrity, Perseverance

WEBSITE: www.isnetworld.com

SOCIAL MEDIA: Facebook—isnetworld

EDITOR'S NOTES: Dag Yemenu will be helping ISNetworld expand into the United Kingdom and other European countries. The family recently relocated from Dallas, Texas and currently resides in London, England. Dag is married and has a one-year-old daughter.

CHAPTER EIGHT
TAKE IT TO THE BANK

This group of outstanding alumni includes a Senior Analyst at FDIC; Bank CEO, President and Owner; Wealth Management Advisor; Owner of a Trust Company; and other financial experts including a Private Equity Firm entrepreneur. The experience, integrity, and passion inherent in each of these stories reaffirm confidence in our financial system.

I truly believe in capitalism and that if you are willing to work hard, are innovative, and have the never-give-up attitude, you can be successful at anything you desire.

—Bill Cormany

NEVER GIVE UP!

Bill Cormany—I have lived my life based on the principles of determination, dedication, and desire. By incorporating these principles into my life, I developed a "never give up" mind set. This mind set has helped me succeed and sustained me when I fell short of my goals.

I was raised in Massillon, Ohio, a small steel town south of Cleveland. Massillon is nationally known as "Tiger Town USA" because of its high school football legacy (Massillon Tiger Football). One of the "four horsemen" of Notre Dame and the NFL legend Paul Brown, among others, were all from Massillon.

While my parents did not work in the steel mill, a lot of our neighbors did. I heard stories of working in the steel mill and quickly made up my mind to go to college and get a degree.

My parents were very aware and supportive of my dream of completing college and securing a job in corporate America. I thought that my only avenue to college was through a sports scholarship so I dedicated my time and effort to football, wrestling, and golf. While I was dedicated, I never reached performance levels that warranted a college scholarship, but playing sports taught me a lot about determination, dedication, and desire.

In my junior year of high school, my father's company transferred him to Stillwater, Oklahoma. I was very happy to leave Ohio and move to a college town. The weather was better (more rounds of golf) and the people were extremely friendly. Most importantly, my dream of going to college became obtainable. After graduating from high school, I enrolled at Oklahoma State University. With the support of my parents and a "never give up" attitude, I achieved my goal of going to college.

I attended Oklahoma State University from 1978 to 1982 and received my Bachelor of Science degree in business with a major in accounting. Oklahoma State's accounting program was recognized as one of the best in the nation, and as a result I was heavily recruited by the then "Big 8" accounting firms. I ultimately accepted a position with Ernst & Whinney's (E&W) Tax Practice in Dallas, Texas. Within the first week of starting with E&W, I recognized that 90% of the new hires into the firm's tax practice had Master's or law degrees. I felt inferior to my peers and decided that I needed to have an advanced degree, but I was hesitant to return to school because I lacked the financial resources and I didn't want to forego the nice salary I was receiving.

In weighing the decision to go back to Oklahoma State for an advanced degree, I sought advice from anyone who would listen to me. Ultimately, my dad told me that "sometimes you just can't get all the ducks in a row" and you have to make a momentum move. So, in September 1983, I enrolled in Oklahoma State's Masters of Accounting program.

The week before I was to start the accounting program, however, I was still uncertain about obtaining a Master's degree in accounting and thought maybe I should consider a broader degree like an MBA. With time running out, I made an appointment with the head of the MBA program, Dr. Lee Manzer. Dr. Manzer pointed out that the MBA coupled with a CPA would open up numerous job opportunities for me. Following our discussion, I focused on where I wanted to be professionally in 10, 20, and 30 years. I didn't see myself being an accountant, so I committed to the MBA program. I didn't know it at the time, but that decision was one of the "best" decisions of my life.

I graduated from the OSU MBA program in May 1985 and moved back to Dallas, Texas, where I accepted a job in the management consulting group Kenneth Leventhal and Company. During this timeframe, the southwest commercial real estate market bubble popped. The value of real estate evaporated and developers were burdened with debts that far exceeded the value of the assets. My role at Leventhal was to work with CEOs and CFOs of some of the country's largest real estate development companies to create debt restructuring plans or "prepackaged bankruptcy" plans.

At Leventhal, I gained a lot of experience very quickly and soon developed a reputation as an expert in debt restructuring. I also soon found myself working seven days a week—and 12 plus hours a day became routine. I enjoyed the spotlight, but I had no life outside of work. I needed to find an opportunity that afforded me a more balanced life.

In 1988, I accepted a position with the Federal Government's Bank Regulator Agency ("Bank Agency"). My responsibility was to manage a pool of non-performing loans obtained from failed banks and savings and loans. 1988 was a banner year for me because I found a job that challenged me, but did not require 24/7 attention, and I was introduced to a lady who would eventually become my wife (and mother of our four children).

In addition to the two jobs mentioned above, my career continued to change and evolve as the economy changed and as I matured. I have held senior positions with various financial services companies, consulting firms, and banks. Some of my career highlights to date include the following:

- Negotiated and restructured debt with Union Pacific Railroad. This debt was secured by raw land in Denver, Colorado that eventually became the site of Denver's new airport.

- Negotiated and restructured a joint venture position with a private processing company called Affiliated Computer Systems (ACI). ACI eventually went public and most recently was acquired by Xerox.

- Consulted with the Gordon Jewelry family regarding litigation ignited by the Zale Jewelry bankruptcy.

- Provided consultation advice to the Maloof family on the attempted acquisition of the Tampa Bay Lightning (NHL) and the successful acquisition of the Sacramento Kings (NBA).

- Managed a $1.0 billion pool of debt securities consisting of senior and subordinated notes and industrial revenue bonds.

On a more entrepreneurial side, I am the managing member of the Colonnade Investment Group, LLC. Colonnade has completed two structured finance transactions (sale-leasebacks) totaling approximately $15 million. One transaction involved a Harley Davidson dealership in Palmdale, CA and the second was an emergency hospital in Gilbert, AZ.

Unfortunately, along with the success came some defeats or setbacks. I have accepted positions in my career with employers that have not honored their side of the business bargain. My "never give up" principle was challenged when I realized I was working for parties with misdirected moral compasses. I learned a valuable lesson through all of this—it was better to take the moral high road and find a position that better matched my moral and ethical standards.

Currently, I am back employed with the Banking Agency in Washington, D.C., where I am a senior analyst in the funding and investment division. My division manages a $45 billion fund for the agency. Additionally, we oversee and manage the agency's 401k plan. I hope to finish my professional career with the agency. I am very proud of the agency I work for because of its good corporate citizenship. The agency gives back to the community by supporting projects like Habitat for Humanity and providing educational programs to help communities better understand the banking system. Most importantly, in times of financial crises (for example, Lehman Brothers bankruptcy and the ensuing financial turmoil), people can feel confident that their savings in banks are 100% insured from losses up to $250,000.

I truly believe that if you are willing to work hard, you are innovative, and you have the "never give up attitude," you can be successful at anything you desire. Being an OSU MBA graduate opened up many career opportunities for which I would not have otherwise been qualified.

Bill Cormany
Contributed by Lorinda Wear

KEY SUCCESS FACTORS: Determination, Dedication, Desire, Never-give-up Attitude, Moral Standards

SOCIAL MEDIA: Facebook–Bill Cormany

EDITOR'S NOTES: Bill Cormany is an art collector and has built up a substantial collection that includes Russian Impressionism, Early California, and Western American art. Portions of his collection have been exhibited at The Museum of the Southwest in Surprise, Arizona, the Woolaroc Museum in Bartlesville, Oklahoma, and the Phippen Museum in Prescott, Arizona. Bill's art collection can be viewed at www.thecormanycollection.com.

Integrity is one of the most important character traits. Always tell the truth because truth will always prevail.

Roy C. Ferguson III

SMOOTH BUT DETERMINED SAILING

Roy C. Ferguson III—I was born and raised in Shawnee, Oklahoma, about 30 miles east of Oklahoma City and 60 miles south of Stillwater. I grew up in an agricultural business environment. My father, also named Roy, specializes in providing business and financial counsel to agricultural enterprises in order to guide them to financial success. So I guess you could say that I had business in my blood. But as I would learn later, business sense was not the most valuable asset I inherited from my parents.

Growing up in Oklahoma was rewarding for me on many levels. My parents provided my brother and me a very stable foundation upon which we could develop and learn. Education was important in my family, and early on in high school I found success in the class room. I earned good grades while balancing the competing demands of work and high school athletics. Participating in athletics taught me perseverance and an extremely valuable skill—how to get along with others. I worked very hard, guided by the example provided by my parents, and quickly infused that trait into my daily life. Overall, the strong and stable family life provided by my parents contributed significantly to my early successes and has continued to benefit me throughout my career.

Attending college was never a question for me. The only decision I had to make was which institution I would attend. I hoped that through hard work and discipline, I would find success in my future endeavors. So, armed with strong academic transcripts and a will to succeed, I followed my passion for business and applied to Oklahoma State University. I was attracted to OSU because of its reputation as a great university—and the fact that it was only 60 miles from my home. I majored in Business Administration with minors in economics and foreign language. OSU turned out to be an excellent fit for me. Despite the social upheaval in the United States in the late 1960's, OSU provided a great atmosphere in which to study.

Once again I worked hard and found success in the class room. I graduated top in my business class and decided to pursue an MBA from OSU because of its remarkable reputation for quality education. Furthermore, I was offered a graduate assistantship that helped pay for my graduate studies, which sealed the deal. I found the professors at OSU to be very committed to their students, and they provided ample opportunities for one-on-one instruction during which students could ask questions and master the curriculum. Guided by the traits first instilled by my parents and reinforced by my previous educational experiences, I worked hard and graduated from OSU with an MBA in December 1970.

Following graduation, and with two shiny, new diplomas from OSU hanging on my wall, I went to work for my father's agricultural business. This job provided valuable business experience, which I later used when working as a national bank examiner for the U.S. Treasury Department until I finally entered the commercial banking sector, which remains my professional niche to this day.

I entered the banking industry as an Assistant Vice President at First National Bank of Tulsa and was later promoted to Executive Vice President for Lending. My MBA from OSU certainly provided me with the business skills necessary to succeed in the banking industry. However, one of the biggest benefits from my OSU education was the interpersonal skills I acquired. Although technology is great and has provided many improvements to our everyday lives, human interaction is still an invaluable aspect of business operations.

Following my time at First National Bank, I moved to BancFirst, Tulsa, in 1992 where I am currently a Regional Executive Vice President. BancFirst has been an exceptional place to work. It is known as a super community bank that emphasizes de-centralized management and centralized support. BancFirst is the largest state-chartered bank in Oklahoma and operates over 90 locations in 50 communities.

I have been fortunate to avoid many of the stumbling blocks that have tripped up many great professionals in the business world. Instead of highlighting my professional successes, I prefer to highlight the factors that contributed to my success so that others may benefit from my experiences.

As I mentioned previously, my parents were my first and most significant inspirations. By watching how they worked together to find success in their personal and professional lives, I was able to emulate their example in my own life. I live by a famous saying which is often referred to as the Golden Rule, "Treat others as you would want to be treated." This principle has served me well, especially within the family atmosphere at BancFirst. BancFirst has a tremendous leadership atmosphere which can mostly be attributed to the founder of BancFirst and current Chairman of the Board of BancFirst Corporation, H.E. "Gene" Rainbolt, and his son, David Rainbolt, who is the CEO of BancFirst Corporation. I firmly believe that having a mentor in one's life is a critical component to success. A mentor will look after your best interests, provide the guidance you need to succeed, and help you accomplish your goals. For me, Gene Rainbolt has been that mentor. He originally started his company with nothing and has transformed BancFirst into a remarkably strong institution.

BancFirst was incorporated in 1984 and in 1985 merged with seven other banks. Over the next several years, BancFirst continued to acquire additional banks and holding companies until it reached its present state.   In 2010, BancFirst had assets of $5 billion and net income of over $42 million. Clearly, Gene and David Rainbolt know how to run a business! They have promoted an atmosphere at BancFirst where executives check their egos at the door and make business decisions influenced both by the positive impact on the community as well as on improvements to the bottom line. Their leadership has enabled BancFirst to sail on a steady course despite the recent economic downturns in the banking sector. Guided by a strong adherence to our core values, BancFirst has weathered the economic storm and has emerged as one of the strongest banks in the nation.

Looking back over the years, I have identified five key factors that have enabled me to succeed in the business world:

1. Integrity: Integrity is one of the most important character traits. Always tell the truth because truth will always prevail.

2. Work Ethic: By working hard and tirelessly, a person can achieve amazing results.

3. Perseverance: Never, never give up.

4. Golden Rule: Treat others as you would like to be treated.

5. Family: A strong family will support you through challenging times and help you to be successful in the business world.

Consequently, if I were to give advice to others regarding their career, it would be very consistent with the key factors listed above—keep your moral compass pointed north, have a strong sense of discipline, and treat others well.

Although I am very proud of my professional achievements, I am most proud of my community service activities. Some of my fondest memories involve community outreach that I have done personally and through BancFirst. I coached my children's youth sports teams eleven months a year for many years. Athletics helped instill a sense of discipline in the youth and provided them with some of the tools and skills necessary to be successful in life. I have also been fortunate enough to participate in many civic activities in Tulsa, including participation in the Tulsa United Way and various United Way agencies. These activities have given me great satisfaction, which has complemented the success in my professional life.

As I look ahead, there is no doubt that I want to continue to work for BancFirst. I have enjoyed working for this company and value the people I work with and the people we work for. I hope that this brief insight into my career and experiences can help influence and inspire the careers of the next generation of OSU MBA alumni.

Roy C. Ferguson III
Contributed by Brian Whisler

KEY SUCCESS FACTORS: Integrity, Work Ethic, Perseverance

WEBSITE: www.bancfirst.com

EDITOR'S NOTES: Mr. Ferguson has worked for BancFirst for almost 20 years and is currently a Regional Executive Vice President. He lives with his wife, Mary, in Tulsa, Oklahoma. They have two grown sons who are both graduates of the University of Oklahoma (where they were starters on the football team) and are now employed in the banking industry. Roy's wife, Mary, also graduated from Oklahoma State University and is a retired school teacher.

You're never really finished until you give up.

—*Sean Kouplen*

POISED FOR OPPORTUNITY

Sean Kouplen—I grew up in the very small town of Beggs, Oklahoma, where my dad still owns the family ranch. He was always very driven with high expectations for his children. At the time, you don't quite understand it; you feel no matter what you do, it's never good enough. But he instilled such a drive and work ethic in me. My grandfather would always say, "Sean, the ducks and the geese have a leader. You need to be a leader. You don't need to work for the other man; you need to be your own person." It was the kind of thing that, when you're young, you let go in one ear and out the other, but it clearly scripted me because I knew from very early on that I wanted to be my own boss.

I went to Oklahoma State after high school and studied Agricultural Economics, but had no real plans. I didn't know what I wanted to be. I was a student leader and Dr. Halligan, OSU's President at the time, asked me to attend a Board of Regents' dinner as his guest. As we sat with two regents, he asked what my plans were post-graduation. I had no idea and was too embarrassed to say so. I looked to my left and my neighbor's nameplate said "Bruce Benbrook, Chairman, Stock Exchange Bank, Woodward, OK." Suddenly, I remembered my grand-father saying, "Whenever you move into a new town, you've got to get to know the banker because they're more likely to loan you money if they know you." I thought it would be really neat to be the person everyone wanted to meet. I also noticed that Bruce had on a very nice suit. So I said that I'd thought about going into banking.

Dr. Halligan helped me get an internship with MidFirst Bank and I loved it. It wasn't a material event in his life; that's just what he did, he put people together. Helping me get an internship had no benefit to Dr. Halligan at all, but it totally changed my life. My family was not wealthy or well-connected. I often marvel at this because I compare Dr. Halligan's life to my role as president and CEO of Regent Bank. You always have more to do than you can get done. You constantly struggle with time management. For him to take the time to help me, I still don't know why he did it. It was so inspiring and it really impacted me to try to do the same thing in my life.

After college, I worked for several years and realized I had certain weaknesses. I felt an MBA would help me improve upon these areas and would give me a leg up in the corporate world. I already had a good relationship with the head of the Tulsa program, plus there was such a convenience factor of being able to attend here. OSU was and still is highly rated among MBA programs and it amazed me that you could attend this nationally ranked program with people you knew and close to home. I learned so much more in the MBA program than I did in undergraduate studies because I'd been out in the real world. All of the classes seemed so relevant. I have a ton of memories, many of team group dynamics, which I hadn't had much experience with prior to the MBA program. I met one of my biggest clients and best friends in the MBA program. He owns a construction company and invests in real estate in Tulsa.

As I was getting my MBA, I was COO for Citizens Security Bank in Bixby. I immediately moved into a bank president's position after completing the program and have served in this role ever since. I believe the MBA program had a lot to do with that. An MBA from OSU clearly gives you credibility and it helped me become a more complete banker and manager.

That's not to say I haven't had some stumbles that taught me the value of patience. At the ripe old age of 27, I was hired by a large Oklahoma bank as President of its sizeable Tulsa division. I thought I could do the same things I had done at CSB and we would automatically be successful. So here I come, this kid, into this position with very seasoned bankers and I'm going to tell them what to do. I've been gifted with very good interpersonal skills and emotional intelligence. I can typically read how people are feeling, address these feelings, and build rapport and trust with them. But in this instance, I just didn't have the knowledge or the experience needed to be respected by my direct reports and peers. These people were legitimately more knowledgeable bankers than I was. Ten years later, I can embrace this type of talent and use those strengths to my and the organization's benefit, but back then I was very insecure. I wanted control and I was just completely over my head. I shouldn't have been hired for the position, and I shouldn't have taken it because I just wasn't ready.

I was there for about a year and it could have been disastrous because I didn't produce at the level I was accustomed to producing or that they expected. I was feeling very vulnerable in the position. Thank goodness, my former bank called and asked me to come back to help with their expansion plans. I learned a lot and became a much better manager. I think I've been much more valuable to every organization I have been with since that experience. But that was a definite low point because I'd gotten into a position where I was over-promoted and didn't know how to get out of it. I didn't want to admit I'd made a mistake and I didn't want to be a failure, so it was very challenging.

In the spring of 2007, I got a call from the owners of Regent Bank asking if I would be interested in being their president. I wasn't, but knew that the bank had underperformed for an extended period of time. I also knew the chairman well, and knew that he was not passionate about banking. He had inherited the bank and was a fantastic guy, but just didn't fit the mold of the community banker. I asked if they would consider selling the bank. At the time, I had recently had friends and acquaintances who said they would be willing to invest if I ever wanted to "do my own thing." Initially the chairman wasn't interested in selling, but after some thought, changed his mind. For five or six months, we negotiated the purchase. It took forever with so many details. Because of my ethical duties to my former bank, we would negotiate at night on the telephone from 10 p.m. to 1 a.m. after I got my kids to sleep so that I could focus on my current job during the day. We actually made the deal at 3:42 a.m.

When we signed the agreement to purchase, I didn't have a single penny raised. I had my wife's and my investment amount, but still a long way to go. Ethically, I couldn't raise any money because I was working for another bank. I had my list of people and I was hoping they had meant what they said and I resigned from my former bank. Now I was unemployed with a contract to purchase a bank for $11.5 million. I sat down in my home office and stared at the number one name on my list. Finally, I picked up the phone and said "Tom, we've talked for years about maybe doing something and I wanted to call you first. The opportunity has arrived. Here's what it is and why I think it could be successful. Would you be interested in investing?"

There was silence on the other end. He finally asked, "What's your minimum investment?" And I said "$100,000." I needed much more, but I was too scared to ask! Fortunately he came back and said to count him in for a substantial investment, and that he had a couple of people he thought would also be interested. We actually raised almost $16 million in less than a month to allow for immediate growth. I have 72 investors that are all families, mostly from this area, and my wife, Angela, and I are principal shareholders. We have a board of twelve directors chosen from the investor group. We acquired Regent Bank, located in Nowata, OK, with the desire to expand back into Tulsa, and in August of 2008 we did. Tulsa is where my clientele is, where my influence base is, and I hand-picked my staff from banks I've worked at before.

My biggest challenge has been the fear of failure. My other career option was to stay a bank president working for somebody else, with a pretty limited chance of failure and a lot of security. It was somebody else's money. Regent was a very high risk situation. I knew how to be pretty successful in the business but it was a leap of faith, particularly given what has happened with the economy. As I remind our stockholders, I don't think anyone has faced the issues that we've had to manage since we bought Regent Bank. What I worry about is my 72 investors who are my friends and clients, and some are even family. I don't want to have to look in their eyes and have them say, "Sean, we put everything into this; we trusted you, and you let us down." That trust is what you cannot replace. Having an MBA gave me the knowledge, the contacts, and the experience to make that leap of faith.

I've also been fortunate enough to share what I've learned as an author and speaker. In 2007, I released *Out of the Blocks*, which is a guide to transitioning from college to career. It represents the relationship between a soon-to-be college grad and his mentor. It's all about developing a clear vision of where you want to go, holding yourself accountable to that vision and finding a mentor to help you along. For some reason people don't take advantage of mentors. I don't know if we're too proud or too embarrassed. But people will help you. If you just ask them, they will help. Rather than making up the steps as you go along, wouldn't it be a whole lot easier to find someone and ask "how did you do this"? *Out of the Blocks* has been tremendously successful, and I have performed speaking engagements all over the country.

On the personal side, I actually have a couple of more books to write per my publishing contract. The next outline's already complete. It's about a very different stage of life than what *Out of the Blocks* was, but I think it's even better. The next book will target someone later in life, who isn't exactly where he thought he'd be at this stage. I'm pretty excited about it and will hopefully impact people with what I've learned.

Professionally, I want people to look at Regent Bank and say, "That is such a quality organization. They grow but in the right way. They're good to their communities and to their clients and their employees." I believe that even if we aren't making the profits we want, we have a duty and an obligation to support the schools and the nonprofits and the community. Instead of Christmas gifts to clients we make dona-tions in their names to local food banks. I would like for us to be "the" small to medium-size business's bank of choice, but also to be viewed as compassionate about our clients and communities.

I would highlight several key factors that have been critical to my success: Perseverance, because you really underestimate some of the gut-checks that successful business people have gone through. We always see them at their best, but nobody sees those sleepless nights or trying times. Emotional intelligence, because the ability to sense and feel what your employees and clients are feeling is very important. Time management, because I could never have fathomed 200 phone calls and 400 to 500 emails a day—trying to decide the best way to spend THIS minute of time. And vision or optimism, because nobody wants to say "I will take responsibility and we can do this." My problem is just the opposite; I am blindly optimistic. My board will often say "Sean, we've got to be realistic here." As long as you keep doing your best, I believe you will succeed. You're never really finished until you give up.

Sean Kouplen
Contributed by Angela Kennedy

KEY SUCCESS FACTORS: Perseverance, Emotional Intelligence, Time Management, Vision/Optimism

WEBSITES: www.bankregent.com (bank);   www.outoftheblocks.net (book)

SOCIAL MEDIA: LinkedIn—Sean Kouplen; Twitter—seankouplen

EDITOR'S NOTES: Sean and his wife, Angela, live in Bixby, Oklahoma with their three children. In addition to being the President, CEO and owner of Regent Bank, he is President of Regent Capital Corporation and a top selling author. *Out of the Blocks* has been in the top 50 books on Amazon.com, peaking at number 37. Sean is also a highly-sought management and leadership consultant and public speaker, having spoken in 20 different states and to universities all over the country. He and Angela were fundamental in founding a local community church and Sean co-founded the nonprofit Bixby Community Outreach Center, which provides temporary assistance. The Center has served tens of thousands of people who are struggling financially. Sean personally raised over $100,000 to revamp the Bixby Chamber of Commerce, now recognized as one of the top Chambers in the state. Sean's other leadership positions and awards include serving as past president of the OSU National Alumni Association, Bixby Chamber of Commerce, and Rotary Club of Bixby; as Chairman of the Oklahoma Bankers Association, Intermediate School Board of Regents, International Trade Development Council, and Oklahoma Workforce Investment Board; on the board of directors of Tulsa Junior Achievement and Tulsa Chamber Small Business Council; and as the Bixby Chamber of Commerce "Citizen of the Year" and the Tulsa Metro Chamber Small Business Financial Services Champion 2010.

While it is well enough to leave footprints on the sands of time, it is even more important to make sure they point in a commendable direction.

—James Branch Cabell

RELATIONSHIPS BUILT ON TRUST

Joe Kreger—I was born and raised near Tonkawa, Oklahoma on a beef cattle and wheat ranch. Growing up on my family ranch in Oklahoma had a great impact on my life. I began working on the ranch at a very young age, allowing no time to play sports after school or weekends. I learned a lot of individual responsibility and a high degree of work ethic. I learned the value of physical labor and mental strength to form problem solving skills. These early lessons have been of great service to both my educational and professional careers. I also learned that I need to rely on the support of friends and neighbors to be successful. I learned perseverance and the importance of forming good relationships and gaining the loyalty and trust of people I care about.

My grandfather was a physician, and we were very close, so I considered medical school. However, I decided late in college that medical school was not for me. After completing my B.S. in animal science at OSU, I worked outside of Oklahoma for about three years doing ranch management consulting. In those years my interest in business management and finance started to grow. I eventually decided to pursue my MBA and began the process of selecting the business school I wanted to attend. My grandfather graduated from the University of Pennsylvania Medical School, so I considered Wharton and was accepted to the University of Texas and Duke. At that time, the MBA program at OSU ranked as a top 10 value-added program in the United States. I looked at costs, and since I wanted to be near my ranch and work in Oklahoma for the rest of my life and career, I decided to earn my MBA from OSU. I've always been very pleased with the decision.

When I was an undergraduate from 1990 to 1994, we hardly used personal computers in school. We did work on some software applications, but nobody really used computers extensively at that time for class work. When I started my MBA in the fall of 1997, there had been a technology revolution, and every professor had his/her own website and syllabus online. We could turn in our course work by email. It was great to get my MBA at that time because we really utilized a lot of new technology as a part of the learning process.

Another interesting aspect of my program was getting to know and work closely with many great international students. I made friends from Indonesia, Turkey, the UK, India, Kazakhstan, Sri Lanka, Uzbekistan, and China. I had not met many international students in my undergraduate years. Most of them were in graduate programs in CASNR, but not undergraduates. I really enjoyed the close interaction with all fellow students, working on group projects and assignments. I learned about a lot of different cultures in that dynamic environment of student diversity. I believe they learned a little about working with an Oklahoma cowboy as well.

There is no question that my education has been a huge asset to me. Graduate study in accounting, finance, management, leadership, and organizational theory has been of great value to me in starting and succeeding in my business. The knowledge of organizational culture, corporate financial policy, and corporate governance has guided me to a broader and more holistic perspective in understanding my clients' business challenges and opportunities.

During the summer following my first year in the MBA program, I interned at the OSU Food and Agricultural Products Research Center. That summer I went to Oklahoma City to meet with a family friend who was formerly a CEO of a $1 billion plus bank. I was interested in banking, and my plan was to ask for his thoughts about which Oklahoma banks I should be talking to. My friend had his own very successful financial planning practice. Over time he started painting a clear picture for me of his practice and how he served professionals, small businesses, and public corporations. I did not expect it, but I became attracted to this industry and began to see how I could be successful in that type of practice. Through most of my second year in the MBA program, it became really clear to me that I wanted to start my own financial and stewardship planning practice.

Upon graduation from business school, I established my Wealth Management Advisory practice, Kreger Financial. I eventually obtained the Certified Financial Planner™ designation. I currently serve genuine, motivated business owners and professionals who want financial security and want to leverage their financial resources to accomplish what is most important to them and their families. Mission Statement: *We completely understand the circumstances and goals of those who care deeply about their families and professional future so that through our mutual stewardship they are at peace with their financial security.*

It was not until I'd been in my current business a few years that I realized how important some of the experiences of my youth were to my professional skills. I was very active in Future Farmers of America and attribute a lot of my organizational and leadership skills to my experiences in this organization. Probably the most beneficial FFA experience I had was livestock judging and giving oral reasons for my placements. That arena of competition really taught me to make timely decisions with imperfect information, think on my feet, and not only justify those decisions but also describe the process I employed to arrive at them.

Some significant personal challenges that I experienced in my youth also shaped me both personally and professionally, such as my mother's severe long-term illness, my two sisters' accidental deaths, and economic downturns on the ranch. Before I started my MBA, I was diagnosed with multiple sclerosis. It's a neurological degenerative disease which affects mobility by slowing down nerve impulses. There were a lot of physical and emotional challenges to overcome, as it's a chronic disease with an uncertain future. One of the primary symptoms is fatigue, so I could not work at the pace I had been accustomed to all my life. I have certainly experienced other changes in my physical abilities. There were incredible insights I gained and positive relationships I formed through these challenges, which really had a beneficial impact for me in the long term. All these events had a huge influence in shaping who I am today.

Confidentiality is the most important professional discipline in my industry, so there are significant risk factors in utilizing information technology in my organization. People are very much concerned about identity theft and information security today. It continues to surprise me what people with the wrong motives can accomplish by misusing technology. But I can't imagine operating my business without Information Technology (IT). The long-term planning, financial forecasting, and modeling that we do today in my business are the direct result of advanced IT resources. We certainly rely on sophisticated financial planning and tax planning software. We also rely on other communication management and client database management software. Some of the forecasts and reports that we generate now for my clients would not have been possible even five or six years ago. These tools also help a great deal in managing and communicating my schedule. My office syncs my Blackberry wirelessly so my staff and I always know where I need to be and what I need to be doing. These are simple things but are of huge benefit to me.

I believe that in our businesses we should not focus only on ourselves. We should first focus on being a leader through service to both our internal and external customers. My primary value for success is wisdom that is paramount to understanding. We place special emphasis on seeking first to understand the circumstances and goals of our clients before we make recommendations or render service. We are stewards of relationships built on trust, expertise, confidentiality, and integrity. We earn the trust of others through strength of character. We are genuine, authentic, and highly competent. Finally we value personal and professional growth by developing new skills through continuing education that gives us larger and richer professional experiences. We can never stop learning and must constantly develop our skills to avoid mediocrity. We must always reach beyond our clients' and customers' expectations to provide more than they ever imagined they could experience.

My future career plans are to become better at my mission and grow my business through stewardship and service. I just want to get better at what I do to impact more genuine people in a more meaningful way. I also want to continue the progress of my family ranch in order to develop both an interest and an opportunity for the next generation as we strive to make a positive impact on the Oklahoma beef industry.

Joe Kreger
Contributed by Vamsi Krishna

KEY SUCCESS FACTORS: Foundation in Jesus Christ, Wisdom and Understanding, Stewardship, Trust, Personal and Professional Growth

WEBSITE: www.joekreger.com

EDITOR'S NOTES: Mr. Joe Kreger has been married to Traci for 13 years and has a daughter, Caroline, and a son, Landon. Joe's areas of expertise include financial planning, estate planning, business planning, investment and advisory services, risk management, asset and income protection, and retirement planning. He was a million dollar round table qualifying member for the years 2004-2010 and won the National Quality Award from 2002-2010.

If you are genuinely a good person and work hard at all you do, you can't fail.

—Michael D. Long

BANKER TURNED ENTREPRENEUR

Michael D. Long—After 19 years in the commercial banking business, I knew I needed a change and a new challenge. I was tired of sitting on the sidelines watching other people seek out business opportunities and succeed at them. Don't get me wrong; I enjoyed my time in commercial banking at NationsBank. I had the good fortune of meeting influential business leaders and making important connections. Moreover, my experience at NationsBank gave me a thorough understanding of the ins and outs of financing business ventures.

I had a great childhood and spent most of my youth growing up in Bartlesville, Oklahoma. The son and only child to a banker and a homemaker, I was raised with a strong set of values that continue to shape me today. Looking back, I learned the two keys to my success during those early years—be a good person and work hard. I believe both principles apply equally to your professional and personal lives.

After graduating from high school in 1970, I moved to Stillwater to attend Oklahoma State University. My interests led me to study business, and after four years of college I graduated with a Bachelor's of Science in finance and a minor in accounting. Not quite ready to enter the workforce just yet, I decided to stay in Stillwater to pursue a Master's of Business Administration. That decision proved to be a very good one for several reasons. First, it took my understanding of business from a conceptual level to an applications level. Secondly, when it came time to enter the workforce, I believe that having a graduate degree in business was a real differentiator. Lastly, I gained a lot of maturity from the experience and felt well prepared to take on the next challenge.

I entered the workforce at First National Bank in OKC in 1976, but moved to Republic Bank in Dallas (later becoming NationsBank) in early 1977. I had the privilege of working in several areas—including corporate, energy, syndication, and commercial banking groups. Along with a thorough understanding of business finance, the experience exposed me to a variety of business leaders. The most notable was Sam Walton, founder of Wal-Mart. On several occasions, I had the opportunity to listen to his business plans and was most impressed with Mr. Walton's focus, vision, and leadership. I can honestly say that he has been the only genius I have ever met.

Initially after leaving NationsBank in 1995, my business partner and I formed L&G Partners, a private equity partnership in which we bought two companies and started three others. I undertook an operations role in one of the firms as CEO of PAC Pizza, LLC. After three years at L&G, I joined CGW Southeast Partners in Atlanta, another private equity firm, as a partner. In 2007, I helped co-found MSouth Equity Partners with three others and we raised our first fund under the MSouth banner.

By definition, private equity investment firms focus on raising private capital to gain a controlling interest in businesses with growth potential. After 5-7 years of working with a company's management to improve efficiency and grow the cash flows of the company, the company is then sold, merged, or recapitalized. MSouth Equity Partners targets companies primarily in the southern US and in the lower middle market range of $25 to $150 million in transaction size. The principal business industries have tended to be business services, distribution, and specialty manufacturing. At times, our growth strategy has dictated the acquisition of companies complementary to our portfolio.

MSouth Equity Partners abides by a four-tiered investment philosophy. First, we seek to partner up with the current management of the company—creating a relationship of mutual interest in the success of their company. Second, we feel that growth is the best way to build shareholder value in the long run. Therefore, we pursue companies with future growth opportunities. Third on our list is an existing capital structure that supports our strategic plan for the company. Lastly, MSouth's partners personally invest in all company ventures. We believe this shows commitment and aligns our interests directly with those of our investors.

One of the ways we encourage growth in a company is through technological advances. We always engage IT specialists to evaluate newly acquired companies. The two key areas we strive to improve on are efficiency and customer satisfaction. We also use IT to create financial modeling for capital budgeting and predicting future cash flows. Each company we work with is different; therefore, we tailor the IT changes to match the company's needs. Sometimes there are few or none; sometimes, a lot!

Working in the private equity world requires a substantial amount of human interaction. You essentially become a working partner at the board of directors' level with several companies at any given time. Success is the result of having a vision of what needs to happen and how to get there. Leadership is the key to making everything happen. I believe that to be an effective leader, you must treat everyone with respect. You must be honest with your people. At times this means being firm, but you must always remain fair and consistent.

After working for 35+ years, I can tell you that life is a lot like a marathon. The average career lasts 40 to 50 years, so make sure it's something you are passionate about—or at a minimum something that you get tremendous satisfaction from. I believe that if you are genuinely a good person and work hard at all you do, you can't fail. At retirement, you'll look back and feel that you contributed in a positive way to your career and family. That's the most important advice I can give. Best wishes—Ride 'Em Cowboys!

Michael D. Long
Contributed by Edwin J. Patry

KEY SUCCESS FACTORS: Passion, Perseverance, Integrity, Empathy, Treating Everyone with Respect

WEBSITE: www.msouthequity.com

EDITOR'S NOTES: Mr. Long is a man of strong character and leadership ability. He and his wife, Joyce, have two children and he has one child from a previous marriage. The oldest, Morgan, 27, is a teacher in Houston, TX. Next is Spencer, 16, who is a junior in high school, plays football and basketball, and attends boarding school in Maine. The youngest, Sydney, 12, is in the 7th grade at a school in Atlanta and is competitively engaged in basketball and equestrian activities.

The difficult we do immediately; the impossible takes a little longer.

—Roger Lumley
(Motto of the U.S. Army Corps of Engineers during World War II)

(M) MOTIVATION (B) BUILDS (A) ACHIEVEMENT: AN MBA SUCCESS STORY

Roger Lumley—"The difficult we do immediately; the impossible takes a little longer." My father, as a World War II Veteran, exemplified the essence of this message. He inspired the drive in me that enabled me to earn my MBA at OSU and achieve the success I have enjoyed throughout my career. I grew up in Tulsa, Oklahoma, where my parents provided a stable foundation. However, my mother suffered from a long illness and passed away prior to my sophomore year at Thomas Edison High School. My two older sisters had already left home. As a bachelor with my Dad, I had to grow up very quickly at the age of 14. My father was my role model and inspiration. He was a man of character and strong work ethic. He aspired to instill those qualities in my sisters and me. He grew up raising cattle and farming outside Emporia, Kansas, and settled in Tulsa prior to WWII. While working full time, taking care of his children and a sick wife, he attended night school at The University of Tulsa and earned an accounting degree. It was a very sad day in October 2006, when Dad passed away.

Dad encouraged me to become an entrepreneur when I was 12 years old and I started my morning paper route. This was a real challenge as it required me to deliver papers at 5:00 a.m. on my bicycle. But, it was my first exposure to business. It generated revenue (selling papers), I built accounts receivable (money owed by my subscribers every month), and I had accounts payable (paid the *Tulsa World* for my papers). I opened my first checking account, which Dad taught me to balance to the penny. With this experience, I then started a successful lawn business. And to this day, I still balance my checkbook.

My dad was always encouraging me to be productive and maintain a positive attitude. Dad involved me in as many things as possible to develop character and discipline, and to keep me out of trouble. I became an Eagle Scout and was active in MYF at the Boston Avenue Methodist Church. I played baseball, wrestled, and ran track. Hunting with my father was when I felt closest to him. We were not wealthy, but he always provided opportunities for me to learn something. While I was in high school, I remember coming home one day and telling Dad that I had been chosen to go to Europe for a study abroad program at Cambridge University. I was expecting my dad to say that we couldn't afford for me to go on a trip like that, but to my surprise, Dad encouraged me to go. It was a culturally enlightening experience that changed my life.

I didn't begin my college years with much of a plan for my future or know what career path I would choose. I was a very average student in high school, so I wasn't really scholarship material. I chose Oklahoma State because I became familiar with the school by visiting my sister while she was there. I went through rush with three high school buddies and we all pledged Sigma Nu.

I enrolled in the business school because my dad was an accountant. With no real goals, I exploited fraternity life for my first two years. While working at Bank of Oklahoma in the summers, I noticed the bank preferred hiring MBAs. Wow! A light came on when it occurred to me that if I was going to be successful, I needed an MBA. I developed an interest in banking because of the diversity and exposure to different kinds of businesses and industries. However, my grades were not high enough at that time for acceptance into an MBA program. So my motivation to pursue an MBA began a two year trek of working hard to get my grades up to overcome a 2.5 GPA. This meant I had to ace the last two years of my undergraduate studies. I just kept driving toward my new objective to get a graduate degree and MBA. I thought that if I could become the best academic student possible, I would prove to others that I could do it. And I DID IT! I was accepted into OSU's MBA program in the summer of 1978. I knew that if I earned my MBA, I would get hired at a bank and make my dad proud. Completing the MBA was prestigious; I gained tremendous self-confidence that I could overcome the stigma of being an ordinary student and an "average" person.

The MBA program at OSU had small classes and strong interaction between the faculty and students. The professors were invested in the students and wanted them to be successful. The classes were engaging and interesting. I was awarded a graduate teaching assistantship and the MBA Scholar Award. I was also a member and an officer of the Financial Management Association. With an MBA under my belt at the end of 1979, I knew that I had achieved this goal because I was tenacious and capable of hard work. It was a great year!

After graduation, I immediately pursued a commercial banking career. I went to Dallas, where there were larger banks, to find a job in a new city without knowing anyone. While my first wife, Jan Nichols, accompanied me on the job quest, it took courage to go to a new place where I'd never lived before. Jan received her accounting degree from OSU and, since we'd made a joint decision to begin our careers in Dallas, she accepted a job offer from Ernst & Ernst in Dallas (the predecessor to Ernst & Young). Jan was very supportive of my career decision, and it did make it easier since she already had a job. After several unsuccessful interviews, my job search looked bleak. But I was relentless and was finally hired at First City Bank in Dallas. My MBA starting salary was approximately 20% higher than the salaries of employees with undergraduate degrees.

After completing the management training program, I was selected to become an oil and gas lender. I was thrust into oil and gas accounting classes and geology/petroleum engineering classes at UT in Dallas. This was a major hurdle for me! After three years, I was hired at The First National Bank of Boston's office in Dallas to lead a team of professionals as a senior lender in the energy group. The energy business plummeted in 1986 and catapulted me into leveraged buyout and structured finance lending. During the late 80's, leveraged buyouts were the rage, resulting from the junk bond market created by Michael Milken, and I was right in the middle of it.

As my career accelerated, I was grateful for my MBA. The critical thought and the analysis of business and financing situations were skill sets I developed to find solutions for my clients. I am a deal guy, and I enjoy creating wealth and raising capital for businesses. Bank of

Boston's new venture in Dallas was successful, and I built a team of professionals and the business model to achieve its goals.

Throughout my career, I often sought mentors. My dad inspired the work ethic in me, but other key people in my career helped me hone my business skills. At Bank of Boston, my first boss, a West Point graduate, was a tough and scary manager. His business acumen and analytical skills were acute and he was an aggressive negotiator. I gleaned the best from him, from learning to negotiate strategically to creatively structuring financing transactions.

After ten years with Bank of Boston, an executive recruiter introduced me to my next employer, Mercantile Bank, which was accompanied by a move to Kansas City, MO. While there, I created a new corporate lending business unit, hired 15 people, and developed a $200 million loan portfolio. This position required an MBA.

The banking business has not been without its ups and downs. In fact, it's been fraught with change. The tumultuous 80's resulted in surging Savings & Loan failures, the price of oil hit historic lows, and banking deregulation also translated into bank failures, mergers, and acquisitions. As the saying goes, "The only constant is change"; thus, adaptability became one of my strongest skills.

The CEO who hired me at Mercantile Bank left 18 months after I started there, due to an acquisition bringing in a new CEO. He was the mentor who had convinced me to relocate to Kansas City, and a few months later he was gone. I had to adjust to all this internal change as well as change throughout the industry. In my eight years at Mercantile Bank, I had five different bosses. I had to adapt to different management styles and to different goals and objectives, and I still built a successful business in my group. So my adaptability certainly helped me survive all those changes.

In 1999, I decided that I'd had enough of the acquisitions and adapting to all the change and I left the banking industry entirely. I yearned to try something different and to seek improvement in my career. I left my profitable business unit for an entrepreneurial venture as Director of Finance with Dunn Construction Co., one of the largest commercial contractors in the U.S. I moved from this position into a merger and acquisitions unit at a regional accounting firm in Kansas City, BKD, LLP. However, after the 9/11 disaster in 2001, the global M&A business came to a screeching halt . . . and so did my business at BKD.

These were tough years, but I wouldn't give them back. Working in non-banking businesses for four years gave me a unique perspective on what it's like to be on the other side of the table, and in other types of businesses. But while it was a great experience, I returned to my original passion, commercial finance and corporate banking. The networking skills that I'd developed during the first part of my career enabled me to reach out to professionals I knew in the banking industry in Kansas City. From these contacts, I secured a position as a Senior Vice President and Team Leader at Gold Bank in Kansas City, subsequently acquired by M&I Bank of Milwaukee, WI. Once again, more change and the need to adapt.

Six years later, another executive recruiter called on me, and I did it again. With a colleague, I joined Bank of the West, headquartered in San Francisco, to develop a new corporate lending unit in Kansas City. BNP Paribas, a global French bank is the parent company; it is very solid and one of the largest banks in the world. I am a Senior Relationship Manager in the National Banking Division and our team has created a profitable business with assets exceeding $350 million and deposits of more than $200 million. In just three years, we constructed a business unit that generates $6 million in annual operating earnings, and we're still growing!

The drive that possessed me to earn my MBA also enabled me to do my very best and to shine in my career. As a top performer in our division for the past two years, I was privileged to be selected for the President's Club and Outstanding Relationship Manager awards. I consider myself a self-starter in terms of making things happen. Through all the career changes—from going to find a job in Dallas and a new environment, to being recruited to Kansas City and building a successful business unit in a bank—the MBA gave me the opportunity and ability to build my credibility. What I discovered along this path are several critical elements and factors which enabled me to become successful:

- Passion—you have to love what you do; you need that internal drive to reach your goals;

- Intellectual growth—you have to be mentally challenged to succeed; ask lots of questions;

- Adaptability—develop a thick skin; manage and adapt to a changing environment;

- Tenacity/Perseverance—stand fast and never give up; keep on trying no matter how much adversity you face;

- Networking—more often than not, it's who you know, not what you know; and

- Civic Responsibility—never forget those who enabled you to get where you are and give back to your community.

The foundation for my achievement has been the unconditional love of my family—my wife, Suzanne, and my children—and those people who believed in me at Oklahoma State. This "base camp" of support has provided much of the inspiration for my success. In the 20-year old kid who got a late start, the pilot light was ignited to become the over-achieving MBA graduate student and the enlightened professional. As they say, "The rest is history."

While I am passionate about my business and providing depth of service to my clients, I also feel very passionately about giving back to the community to which I owe my success. This includes my commitment to The Spears School of Business at OSU. In my opinion, giving of your time, energy, and talents adds more value than just writing a check. As a member of the Spears School Alumni Board, I sincerely want to make a difference. I desire to serve as a mentor for MBA students and, with my experience, help bridge the gap between the business world, students, and the faculty.

Additionally, I am a board member of The Hope House in Kansas City, an organization that provides shelter for domestic violence victims. I am also an event co-chair (with my wife) and a fundraiser for the Parkinson Foundation in Kansas City. This organization is dear to our hearts, as my brother-in-law suffers from Parkinson's disease. Our family sponsors the Dramatic Truth School of the Arts Ballet Academy, also in Kansas City, and I am a former board member of the Don Bosco Centers in Kansas City, serving the elderly and underprivileged.

Achieving my MBA gave me the maturity, the life skills, the ability to adapt, a thick skin, and the intellectual confidence to succeed. I have learned enormously from my mistakes and have become very adept at asking for help. Many of the best lessons have been learned from making mistakes and overcoming challenges. Think of all the entrepreneurs out there that failed time and time again, but they finally got it right. Remember, "The difficult we do immediately; the impossible takes a little longer."

Roger Lumley
Contributed by Elissa Malone

KEY SUCCESS FACTORS: Integrity, Prudence, Passion, Perseverance, Tenacity, Adaptability, Intellectual Growth, Networking

WEBSITE: www.bankofthewest.com

SOCIAL MEDIA: Facebook—Roger Lumley; LinkedIn—Roger Lumley

EDITOR'S NOTES: Roger Lumley's first priority is his family. He is a proud husband and devoted father of four. His wife, Suzanne Dimmel, is a Broker, Senior Vice President, and Principal, in the national real estate brokerage firm of Cassidy Turley in Kansas City, MO. When Roger and his wife set their goals as a team, their children describe them as "unstoppable." This is especially true when it comes to their family and philanthropic endeavors. Roger and Suzanne are inspired fundraisers for many organizations.

Roger is very proud of his family and he loves each of his children dearly. Kathryn Glass, Roger's stepdaughter and the oldest, is a reporter and producer for the Fox Business Channel in New York; his daughter Catherine Lumley is a second-year medical student at Wayne State University in Detroit; his daughter Bonnie Lumley is a senior in the School of Journalism at the University of Missouri in Columbia; and his stepson Scott Glass, is going to junior college and working full time.

Roger considers himself an eclectic and adventurous guy, with a lengthy "bucket list" and many interests.   His hobbies include golf, motorcycle riding, boating, hunting, skiing, and visiting exotic places. He traveled to South Africa in 2008 on a big game safari and in 2011 he will visit a client in Australia.   He enjoyed riding in a NASCAR this year and concluded the summer with a motorcycle road trip to Sturgis, SD—interesting pursuits for the traditional commercial banker.

You only get one chance at life, so pursue your dreams and be responsible.

—Bob McCormick

THE EFFECT OF ONE PERSON

Bob McCormick—One event has stuck with me: the man who stood up against the tanks in Tiananmen Square in China. I ask myself, "Why didn't the tanks just run over him?" More importantly, I realize that one person can do so much good and bad. This is a lesson that has been repeated my entire life.

I am a native Oklahoman. I grew up in Tulsa and have lived my entire life in Oklahoma with the exception of four years immediately following college. I came from a divorced family, which taught me the importance of managing money, and in high school my dad was involved in real estate; however, my passion for money management wasn't established until college.

In 1981, I graduated from Oklahoma State University with a degree in business administration majoring in finance and economics. A week later I married my wife, Julia. I knew I wanted an advanced degree: an undergraduate degree is a preliminary degree and there is definitely a competitive advantage to obtaining a Master's in Business Administration. In addition, the 1981 job market was poor and my new bride had two years of instruction to complete at OSU. Therefore I decided to stay and get my MBA at Oklahoma State University.

During my time as an MBA student I focused on finance much like I had in my undergraduate years. My advisor recognized this pattern and reminded me that I wasn't getting a Master's in Finance. He recommended I look into studying marketing to become a well-rounded business professional. My MBA program did just that; it helped me become a well-rounded professional outside of finance.

As an MBA candidate, I enjoyed two professors in particular, Dr. Simpson and Dr. Kaminski. Dr. Simpson was teaching his first Financial Futures class when I was a student. That was a great class, especially since it was a subject I loved. I also enjoyed being Dr. Kaminski's graduate assistant during his time as a doctoral student. One of my early MBA memories is being caught in the technology change from punch cards to computers. By using the word "computers," I mean terminals tied into a main computer. This is a memory that links to my term as an Adjunct Professor for Portfolio Management. Excel was unheard of when I got my MBA. It's almost inconceivable how in-depth a person can go with analysis these days. However, my most important experience was my work experience.

As a student I was extremely proactive and focused on continually learning. My first job was at First National Bank. Later, I decided to change jobs and began knocking on doors. One of those doors was the Edward Jones Stillwater office run by Steve and Judy Hull. When I came knocking, Steve gave me an opportunity that got my foot in the door.

That job at the Stillwater Edward Jones office gave me real life experience in addition to my class work, and it was the real world experience that I found very satisfying. That experience and my MBA were critical to obtaining my first position after graduation.

Immediately after obtaining my MBA degree I accepted an Internal Auditor position for Edward Jones at the St. Louis home office—a little disappointing because it was not the west coast location I wanted or specifically in the investment profession I was striving for. It was a good opportunity though, especially as many of my fellow students were not getting job offers. As an MBA, I had a huge advantage; when recruiters came to campus they would interview MBAs over undergraduates. I realized that these were minor setbacks. I learned to understand the importance of patience and to keep the right attitude.

The Internal Auditing position was a management trainee position. I, however, was more interested in investment research. An additional challenge came from one of the partners directly. On my first day at Edward Jones, he told me, *"Bob, I don't know what department you will end up in but it is not the research department."* I viewed this statement as a challenge to begin pursuing the Chartered Financial Analyst (CFA) designation on my own. I never became a broker; instead, after two years as an Internal Auditor, I moved to the research department where I focused on securities analysis.

I stayed at Edward Jones for an additional two years before taking an Investment Manager position with the Trust Investments Department at First National Bank of Tulsa. I worked for First National Bank from 1987 to 1992 before taking my current position at Trust Company of Oklahoma as a portfolio manager and Chief Operating Officer. My position as COO has increased my involvement. Not only am I involved with management decisions and the direction of the company, I am also an owner of the Trust Company of Oklahoma, a company with sixty-five employees and four offices, so I am never bored.

I have learned through my experience that a good work ethic, atti-tude, and ethics are important for success. To be a better profes-sional, you must always work hard and constantly learn. To have a healthy life, it is necessary to have a positive attitude. When serving customers, it is important to be empathetic with your customers' point of view and never lose sight of your ethical code. It comes down to whether or not you can look at yourself in the mirror. Success essen-tially boils down to the golden rule: do unto others as you would have them do unto you.

I've been blessed that I have a career that I can keep doing for a very long time and I plan to keep serving my customers at the Trust Company of Oklahoma. There is always a challenge in my career. It keeps me mentally alert and it never gets boring. My advice is this: you only get one chance at life, so pursue your dreams and be responsi-ble. Don't let others dictate your dreams but sometimes in life you must make the responsible choice. Treat everyone with respect, and keep an open mind because you're not always right. Be humble because every day teaches you something new.

Bob McCormick
Contributed by Katie Nicholas

KEY SUCCESS FACTORS: Work Ethic, Positive Attitude, Ethics, Empathy, Intelligence

WEBSITE: http://trustok.com/

EDITOR'S NOTES: Bob McCormick is the proud husband of 1983 OSU graduate Julia. They have three children; two call OSU their

Alma Mater and one is completing high school. Bob and his brother-in-law are proud graduates of the OSU MBA program. He lives in Tulsa and on November 22, 2010 was featured in the *Tulsa Business Journal.* He enjoys bicycling and woodworking.

Choose a job you love and you will never have to work a day in your life.

—Robin Wantland from an old Chinese Proverb

WITH THE HELP OF OTHERS

Robin Wantland—I spent the majority of my childhood in Oklahoma, five early years of which were in Edmond. My father was a pilot in the Air Force, so my family moved around quite a bit. I was born in California, but my family moved back to Norman, Oklahoma, where we eventually settled. I went to Norman High School, where I was a three-sport letterman in football, track, and golf. My family has a long line of athletes dating back to my granddad, who was a four-sport letterman at the University of Oklahoma, and my dad, who also ran track.

With my success as an athlete, I had it all planned out; I was going to eventually take my skills and walk on to a football team in college. That's when one of the most humbling experiences of my life occurred. I suffered a season-ending injury in my junior year, preventing me from playing the rest of the year. The injury gave me a lot of time to think and understand the world around me and the importance that social popularity and position had played in my early years growing up. I quickly realized that my reliance on my athleticism could only take me so far. This event was quite eye-opening for me and helped strengthen my relationship with God, a spiritual awareness which I have used as my anchor and base throughout my life.

Luckily I had other activities in high school to keep me busy and grounded. I was an Eagle Scout and at one point held a position as a class officer. I also was a leader in Norman's YoungLife Club and the McFarlin Church Youth group. The combination of such activities has helped me become a better leader and a better human being. Most of my summers were spent either working construction or as a counselor at various Boy Scout camps.

Now came the time for me to select a college to attend. This decision, which was largely influenced by my father, was quite an easy one.

Growing up in Norman, Oklahoma, one would think the choice was obvious. Not with my father; I recollect him saying, "As long as we live in Norman, you are not going to school at OU." So I went with the other somewhat obvious choice, "the other school"—Oklahoma State University.

So here I am, a young adult at a new school, looking to make new friends, experience new things, and I run into my first obstacle: choosing a major. One thing I knew for sure was that I wanted to be in a promoting and selling environment. I chose marketing as my major; I figured it would give me the best opportunity to develop my social and leadership skills. Another thing I did as an undergrad was join the Beta Theta Pi social fraternity. With this organization, I was fortunate to hold multiple officer/leadership roles and honors as an "All-Fraternity" athlete in both football and track. My goal at OSU was to get involved as much as possible and to take advantage of every opportunity that came my way.

One of the first significant opportunities for me at OSU came about as a result of meeting a professor of mine, Dr. Bob Hamm, as a sophomore; he was the professor of my marketing class and one which I really enjoyed. One day, he invited me to hear him speak, an opportunity which I could not pass up and was quite thrilled about. After his speech, I approached him and asked, "Dr. Hamm, what was the gist of your speech? I could not follow it"…to which Bob started laughing. I followed that up with "I just didn't get it." And that conversation— I think it was my honesty and initiative—was how my relationship and friendship with Bob started.

Bob was a great influence on me throughout my life. He was a great professor, a great mentor, and a great man. At the time I met him, he was a professor in his 50's who was known to take 3-4 young sophomores/juniors like me under his wing and act as a mentor for each of them. He had a passion for teaching and wanted to share his knowledge and experiences with others. Bob was, and continues to be, very involved not only in the community and his school, but more importantly, the world. He is a very well-traveled man who has a love for international students and making an impact on their lives. Bob has been mentoring young students for as long as I've known him, close to

35 years. With the other people he's mentored, I always joke that it's as if he has over 120 sons and daughters.

During my sophomore year in college, I did what every other student at the time was doing—I began searching for an internship. I set my sights high; IBM was where I wanted to work, and at the time that was the place to be. This is where Bob chimed in and gave me some advice. He didn't think that I would enjoy this sort of career and felt that banking was the way for me to go. He put me in contact with a friend of his who worked for IBM in Tulsa and had me shadow him for a couple of days. After I'd spent some time with the guy on the job, he drove me nuts. He was so driven and was convinced he was going to make a million dollars by the age of 27. He worked 90 hours a week with reckless abandon, and it became clear that this career would not be for me. I later found out that a friend of mine took the IBM route and burned out in four years.

So I took Bob's advice: I pursued a career in banking. I took on two different internships during the summers at OSU, both with local banks and both with Bob's help. The first internship was with Stockyard's Bank and the second with Bank of Oklahoma, where my responsibilities were to build a call list for commercial bankers. During these internships, you don't really learn much about the business, but you get an idea of what bankers do and the type of people that are in the business. At times during my internships, I was taken to lunch and got to better understand the social aspect of the banking industry and how the bankers spend their days.

I graduated from Oklahoma State University with a Bachelor's in Marketing in May of 1977. Upon graduation, I contemplated going to graduate school, with one of my top choices being the University of Texas in Austin. That's when Bob came in and offered me a deal I couldn't refuse. He said if I came to do my MBA at OSU, he would offer me a graduate assistantship to help him write a bank marketing textbook. The assistantship, which helped me pay for the 36-hour graduate program, also allowed me to develop a stronger relationship with Dr. Bob Hamm.

The MBA program at OSU benefited my career more than I can put into words. My transition from the undergraduate to the graduate program was a memorable one. I was quickly immersed in what seemed to me like a new school. The new friendships, the new friends, the people I had never met made the MBA experience much different than the one I had as an undergraduate. The MBA gave me two things: a better understanding of finance/accounting and the extra maturity that I gained through interactions with students and professors. The finance and accounting classes, something I lacked as an undergraduate, helped me a lot in the banking business.

I concluded my MBA degree in 1978. The combination of my degree along with my two internships helped me land a premier banking job in Dallas. The jobs in those days were very competitive, so having an MBA not only put me above the rest, but gave me a higher starting salary. In all honesty, I'm not sure I would've landed that first job without the internship experience and graduate degree. Initially, I had three cities I wanted to work in: Kansas City, Houston, or Dallas. I wanted the big city experience and I wanted to learn from the best training programs available at that time. I always liked the Tulsa area and figured I would eventually move there, but after interviewing in the bigger banks in other areas, Dallas seemed to be the perfect fit.

When I accepted my first job with First National Bank in Dallas after my graduation in May of 1978, I had not yet completed my thesis, which was on the efficiency of advertising in the banking industry, so I asked not to start until September. I took the next few months to complete my thesis and also spend two months at Camp Kanakuk as a counselor. I felt I needed these few months to gather my thoughts, contribute my time to the community, and have some fun before I started my career. At First National Bank, I started as a management trainee, training as a commercial and real estate banker, and joined the Metropolitan Lending Group in 1979. I was the top producing commercial banker in 1981 and 1982, when I was promoted to district manager of Metropolitan Banking.

In August of 1983, I began my 17 year career at Mercantile Bank in Dallas. Throughout that time I was fortunate to hold a variety of roles: President of Mercantile Bank Lincoln Centre, Chairman of Mercantile Bank—Dallas Community Banking Group, and Executive Vice President—Metropolitan Lending Group. Also during this time, I had the pleasure of meeting the person I consider my third mentor. He was the Chairman of Mercantile Bank at the time and his impact on my life was so large that I feel it defines who I am today. He taught me about work ethics and what it means to have integrity, and more importantly, he taught me about leadership skills and the importance of building relationships with the people who surround you. He demonstrated to me that building relationships isn't just about spending time with your employees but also about rolling up your sleeves and working alongside them.

The majority of my career was spent under the Bank One name (which bought out Mercantile Bank and would later merge with J P Morgan/Chase), where I spent most of my time doing something I love: building new organizations. Under the new ownership, I was allowed to start a pilot for the small business banking line of business. I was able to build the program from one commercial banker to over two hundred commercial bankers in 6 states (Texas, Oklahoma, Louisiana, Arizona, Colorado, and Utah) over a ten year period. We built a state-of-the-art, centralized loan center in Dallas for loan processing, decision making, and monitoring (which is the national platform that Chase Bank still uses today).

During my time at the bank, we were able to develop two channels for revenue production. One channel used the branch system to focus on managing small business production, cross sales, and retention, where the target client generally had annual revenues of less than 3 million dollars. The second channel was a traditional commercial banking strategy that targeted clients with revenues of $3 million to $25 million. The commercial bankers were located in our larger branches in the larger metropolitan markets to be convenient to their clients and prospect base. I was responsible for the Sales/Service staff and the Underwriting Center, and had a coordination role with staff in Credit Administration, Marketing, Finance, Product Management, Treasury Management, Retail, Human Resources, Operations/IT and Investments. With the success of these two channels, I eventually became President of the Business Banking Division for Bank One.

In January 2002, I joined Compass Bank as a National Director of Business Banking. My role was to coordinate a national platform of 200 bankers and design products, policies, and processes to sell and service middle market, privately-held businesses in the major metropolitan markets in five states (Alabama, Texas, Florida, Arizona, and Colorado). Here I met my fourth mentor; he was the Vice Chairman of Compass Bank and he made it real clear to me: "Don't be too serious about your job and have fun with it." It was during this time that I improved my leadership skills, by spending more time creating relationships with the people I worked with. These relationships taught me the significance of collaboration. In my position as a leader, I had a number of direct reports, managing close to 15-20 at a time. It was crucial to have open communication and to work together to achieve our goals. Another thing I learned from him was the work/life balance. Although he took his job seriously, it was from him that I learned that family comes first; the relationship you have with your family leads to the successful environment that you create at work.

In April of 2007, I joined The Highlands Bank, a commercially oriented boutique bank in Dallas started by four very experienced commercial bankers. I joined as the Managing Director of the Commercial Banking Group, which had not yet been created. The bank was able to grow from $60 million in loans and $125 million in deposits to $300 million in loans and $450 million in deposits in just three short years. With the retirement of one of the original partners in 2008, my role expanded into being the President. We have 83 employees in 5 different locations, and were able to achieve profitability in just 14 months of operation. We have seen continued success with the raising of additional capital ($30 million) to expand our operations into the Dallas/Fort Worth area.

Although I've enjoyed much success in my long career in banking, I owe much of it to my experience as a student at Oklahoma State University, from my early encounters as an undergraduate to the long-lasting relationships I was able to build during my time in the MBA program. The things I learned at OSU have guided me through many of the decisions I have made throughout my life.

My decision to go to Oklahoma State University was one of the best I made as a high school graduate. It was the first time I entered an atmosphere where I didn't know a soul (with the exception of my cousin). I was exposed and forced out of my comfort zone. This encouraged me to meet new people, and over a four-to-five year period create long-lasting friendships that I would never have made had I gone to the University of Oklahoma. That is one of the strengths of OSU: the ability to accept individuals from all walks of life and offer them opportunities that are not available anywhere else. After completion of the MBA degree, I quickly realized that the program is every bit as good as, and in some cases better than, the programs that my friends went to. The MBA curriculum gave students the ability to run a business as a team. In 1978, I had a chance to start a bank, take different responsibilities, and run that bank over a 12-quarter period, well ahead of when I would actually use those skills in the business world.

The other thing I would highlight during my time as an MBA student at OSU was the opportunity to assist Dr. Bob Hamm with writing a bank marketing textbook. An additional highlight was my Master's thesis, which was to analyze the banking industry and to better understand the effectiveness of advertising in that industry. My project was to perform a comparative analysis for a local bank named "The Bank," and to study the efficiency/effectiveness of three different advertising techniques: statement stuffers, ads in the paper, or radio ads. With this assignment, I was not only able to help Bob write his book, but better understand the industry and how it works—skills I later applied in my career. The analysis which I performed, I could not have done without my knowledge of computer modeling—which I learned in my courses as an MBA student. My experience with this project, along with cutting edge computer capabilities, set me above the rest of my competition and launched me early on in my career. I can't brag enough about Oklahoma State and the opportunities it's given me: from a great mentor in Dr. Bob Hamm, to the technical skills that I picked up in my classes and, most importantly, the relationships that I have built and grown.

As of today, I am retired and still living in Dallas with my wife of 30 years, Diane. I enjoy golfing, mentoring young couples, and spending time at our lake house. I have accomplished a lot in my life; but to me, success isn't about how much money you've made or what kind of house you have. To me, it's about significance and what kind of impact you've had on other people. I'm grateful to have had six mentors throughout my life, my dad being the first, who have taught me to share my experiences with others. These men have been mentors socially, spiritually, and in business. I think having a mentor is absolutely critical. Each one of my mentors has been about 15-20 years ahead of me and has been able to give me insight and help me think through decisions. Having these men as an inspiration, I have made it my purpose to become a mentor for other young individuals and to make the same impact on their lives as my mentors have made on mine.

I've been in banking for 32 years; and although I am retired now, there is no way I will stay retired. If I stay retired for another 3-4 months, I'll go crazy. These days, I am still looking for opportunities, something I've done throughout my career. Every time I left a bank, the bank was well positioned and run by good people, and I was ready for new opportunities. At the end of the day, I really want to build things. I'm not a maintainer, I'm a builder. I was able to do this successfully at every bank I've worked for and want to continue. Some other things I want to do in my spare time are to get involved within the community and to take part in mentoring disadvantaged students. One thing I told my team throughout my years as a leader was to select one activity and to get involved, find something that they're passionate about and donate their time to make a difference.

In my career in banking, and my various leadership positions, I've learned one thing: to be an effective leader, one must give time to their organization and their community. That is why I have dedicated my time to business organizations such as the American Bankers Association, the Consumer Bankers Association, and local organizations such as Northwest Bible Church and The Salesmanship Club. There are a few key factors that I attribute my success to: truth/integrity, passion/empathy, and servant leadership. Honesty and integrity are the most critical character traits to have as a leader. With just passion, you may alienate everyone around you, but if you have both passion and empathy, the whole team will succeed as opposed to just the individual leader. With servant leadership, the leader takes a behind-the-scenes approach and leaves it to the team to achieve their goals, supporting them along the way. The group achievements lead to the leader's achieving his/her goals. It's a very powerful model and is very tough to accomplish; however, it can lead to the best results for the entire group.

The advice I would give to future MBA students comes from an old Chinese proverb:

"Choose a job you love, and you'll never have to work a day in your life."

Find something that you're passionate about, discover your skills and abilities and find where you can put them into use in the marketplace. Know what your passions are and find a place where you can make a difference.

The next piece of advice comes from a trip I made to Israel in March of 2001. The trip made a huge difference for my kids, and was an eye opener for my whole family. The neat thing about the trip was we got to see the Jordan River. The river, which flows out of Mt. Hermon and continues into the Sea of Galilee, is beautiful, full of wildlife and plant life, and just full of activity. The Jordan River continues south and drops into the Dead Sea, which is quite the opposite of the Sea of Galilee and the Jordan River. Although it is the same water, there is nothing living in the Dead Sea, no trees, no wildlife, and nothing flowing out of it. The one 'Word Picture':

The only way that a person can survive and grow is to give themselves away.

I don't ever want to be the Dead Sea.

Robin Wantland
Contributed by Maciej Pietrus

KEY SUCCESS FACTORS: Truth and Integrity, Passion and Empathy, Servant Leadership

EDITOR'S NOTES: Mr. Wantland has had a long and successful career in the banking industry, starting out as an intern and going on to hold positions including Executive Vice President, President, and Chairman. Even though Robin is currently retired, he is still seeking new and exciting opportunities. Robin resides in Dallas, Texas with his wife, Diane. In his free time, he enjoys playing 18 holes of golf.

Knowing how important his mentors were in shaping the course of his life and career, he takes great pleasure in opportunities to mentor others. Robin is an active member of his community with involvement in both banking associations and his local church.

CHAPTER NINE

THE ENTREPRENEURIAL SPIRIT

The world of entrepreneurship is one of excitement, challenges, and rewards, with three out of four Americans aspiring to be entrepreneurs at some point in their lives. The stories brought to life by the entrepreneurial spirit of the alumni featured in this chapter will inspire, educate, and empower.

It takes a determined and well-rounded man to invest completely in both his business and his family.

—Barry C. Blades

I STARTED IN A SWIMSUIT
AND FINISHED IN A BUSINESS SUIT

Barry C. Blades—I embarked on my first career path at age ten, and I kept at it for eleven years. It was all consuming: long hours and tough physical labor. The money simply wasn't there, but it paid enormous dividends in skills that aided me in becoming a successful business-man. When I was twenty-one, my life focus changed. As I began to pursue new avenues and ambitions, my first years as an aquatic athlete had prepared me well.

Many of the habits that I applied in school and subsequently in busi-ness, I learned in the pool. Swimming tutored me in discipline, work ethic, and commitment to schedule. Five days a week, my teammates and I dove into the Phillips Petroleum pool in Bartlesville, Oklahoma, at 6 a.m. Every day after school I joined the rest of the team for a second workout. My teammates taught me how to relate to my peers and to work well with others. The other kids' parents looked after all of us, instilling in us strong values and respect for authority.

Our coaches worked tirelessly, pushing each of us to our limits and demanding our very best. I remember one high school coach in partic-ular, Pete Payne. "Barry, you don't seem to have a killer instinct in the pool," he told me.

"I'm trying, Coach," I promised, "I'm just not sure that I can be any better." "You've got more, Barry. The best man wins in a race. I need you to be committed to winning, to being the best guy in the pool." Mr. Payne's drive and confidence stirred my sense of rivalry and made me a better athlete. Many times since then and to this day I have replayed his words in my head. I'm not going to win at any cost, but I work to focus my killer instinct and aggressively pursue my goals.

At home my parents modeled the values that they expected to see in my brother, sister, and me. They established the norm of high expectations. I never considered turning in my homework late or defaulting on my word.

Both of my parents worked hard. Mom stayed home to raise us when we were young. Then when I was in third grade, she returned to the work force in order to save money for her children's college education.

I remember helping Mom prepare for an interview. I lay on my stomach on the living room carpet. A few feet away, Mom sat erect at her writing table by the window. I had been appointed to help her practice her shorthand skills. I read aloud at the pace of two words per second while she scribbled furiously. She got the job as administrative assistant at Arnold Moore Funeral Home.

When I graduated from high school, Oklahoma State was an easy choice for my college education. I barely considered an out-of-state school because of the cost. OSU had a reputation for strong academics and offered me a modest swimming scholarship to offset my tuition. I had friends on campus, including my roommate and future brother-in-law and several of my high school swimming mates.

I worked through general education classes my freshman year. My first marketing class was taught by Bob Hamm. One afternoon, Dr. Hamm put a tough question to the class. Proudly, I called the answer. He grinned and tossed me a large cardboard Tootsie Roll full of candy. Dr. Hamm took a shine to me and eventually became my academic adviser. He was influential in my declaration of a marketing major in my sophomore year.

I raced through my undergraduate degree in three-and-a-half years, even squeezing in enough hours for an accounting minor. Eighteen hours of credit through CLEP had given me a good head start on the program. I graduated as one of the top ten seniors at OSU that year.

I made the decision to pursue my MBA at OSU in the spring of 1976. Briefly, I entertained the idea of going to the University of Texas for my Master's degree. However, several reasons compelled me to stay, not the least of which was that I was anxious to propose to my girlfriend, who still had two semesters left in her Bachelor's degree at Oklahoma State. We wedged a December wedding between my graduation with a Bachelor's degree and beginning my Master's program.

I finished my MBA quickly and walked proudly across the stage in the spring of 1977. Thirteen companies had extended job offers as I came out of school.

I chose to join the consulting division of Arthur Andersen & Co. at the encouragement of another one of my professors. "You can go to work for them without being an accountant," Professor Bruce Collier told me as I sat in his office, anxiously worrying my thumbs. "There are numerous divisions within the company and in the consulting division there are a lot of people like you with MBAs."

My first day at Arthur Andersen was June 1, 1977, and I stayed with them for nine and a half years. The years with Arthur Andersen were stimulating. I often characterize the company like the Army's old motto, "A great place to start." However, at the end of my time there I faced one of the most difficult setbacks along my career path.

Arthur Andersen is considered an up-or-out organization. I had progressed quickly through the ranks and was on track to make partner. It was essential to have people willing to advocate on one's behalf. The consulting partners in Tulsa, Steve Barnett and Neil Kidwell, were both in my corner. The head of the Tulsa office, Dick Kristinik and his superior, Dave Ewing, were on my side as well. Stars were aligning and it looked like I was going to make partner.

Suddenly, the year I would have come up for partner, Dave Ewing died unexpectedly. Shuffling quickly ensued to cover Dave's spot and the resulting vacancies. All of my advocates, Neil, Steve, and Dick, were transferred to different offices. I had no history with their replacements.

"We know you were told that it was time for you to make partner," the new leadership told me. "But we don't know you and personally have no reason to recommend you for partner. It's time you moved on."

Leaving Arthur Andersen was a huge blow. I remember lying awake at night wondering if I had done something wrong and what to do next. I wrote a letter that I never mailed. But God had a plan for my job future.

It was an unspoken truth at Arthur Andersen that you would make a lot of money, but your first obligation was to the firm and your family came second. Ultimately, that would have never worked.

My next step was a big risk. I recalled my dad's encouragement when I was young, "Strive to someday own your business, Barry. The best scenario is to work for yourself." So, I gathered my wits, my skills, and my nerve and ventured into the arena of independent consulting.

My dad had been right. Over time, through hard work, good connections and loyal clients, I built the business I own today, SixthSenze, Inc.

Networking is a big part of establishing a prosperous business. Many of my peers utilize trend-setting means of marketing such as Facebook, Twitter, and LinkedIn. However, I have found that face-to-face communication and verbal recommendations by trusted sources are the most profitable. Through such methods, I acquired my current clients and have reached beyond my farthest dreams as an independent consultant.

I worked steadily to build my business. I spoke to everyone I knew and reinforced old connections. It paid off. George Dotson, of Helmerich & Payne International Drilling Co., called me out of the blue. "Barry, I got your name from Ed Malzahn. He says I should talk to you about improving our manufacturing processes here at H & P. I'd like to fly down, pick you up and take you to Houston for a meeting and to get your proposal. What do you think?"

The proposal sold. Trust and relationships flourished. What began as 90 days of work turned into a significant ongoing project. SixthSenze, Inc. has proven more profitable than any point of my career so far.

My work continues to grow through networking and making contacts. It has been affirmed over and over through the confident praise and recommendations of satisfied clients. George Dotson once told me, "Barry, we are making good progress, and again I credit much of it to your willingness to align your work with us. Hiring your services was a major success for us."

Barry C. Blades
Contributed by Abby D. Kelly

KEY SUCCESS FACTORS: Work Ethic, Integrity, Perseverance, Networking, Passion

WEBSITE: www.sixthsenze.com

EDITOR'S NOTES: While pursuing a successful, independent career as a businessman, Barry and his wife, Janis, raised four daughters. Barry made sure that his daughters enjoyed a wide variety of experiences including horseback riding, water skiing, snow skiing, softball, and play acting.

All of Barry's girls have attended college. The oldest, Abby, graduated from OSU, while Kelsey graduated from Wichita State University. Jennifer completed her undergrad at OU and earned her M.D. from the University of Kansas Medical School. She is now serving in the Navy. Rachelle, will graduate next year with her teaching degree from Wichita State.

It takes a determined and well-rounded man to invest completely in both his business and his family. Barry has balanced the two expertly.

Mentoring is a brain to pick, an ear to listen, and a push in the right direction.

—*John C. Crosby*

MENTORED AND MOTIVATED

Paul De La Cerda—The first 10 years of my life were very different from my last 26. I was born in an urban, low-income area in the heart of Los Angeles in a town called Pacoima, CA. I came from a family of labor workers and farmers. The area, at the time, was growing both in population and in gangs. In fact, the boys I played with next door were aspiring gang members. As you can imagine, my young childhood environment was quite challenging.

When I was 11, my parents decided it was time to move to a safer city with better schools. Santa Clarita, CA was well known for its superb education system. My parents may not have known this at the time, but moving us into Santa Clarita is what really changed my life. If we had not moved, I do not know where I would be today. This move inspired me to become a straight "A" student, be a great athlete, and find success in serving others.

My dad has always been someone I have looked up to. He is the person who influenced me to take the path I am on today. As a Vietnam veteran and firefighter, my father has always been a hero. His dedication to public service and saving lives is what instilled in me my ethics of public service.

I started out my collegiate career at Adams State College in Colorado as a scholarship cross-country runner. After winning an NCAA Championship and All-American status, I decided to go on a road show of universities to look into transferring to a college that had the major I wanted to pursue. I knew that I wanted to do more than be a successful cross-country runner. At a young age, if my parents wondered where I'd slipped off to, they only had to look in the garage where I was tinkering and inventing things—as engineers famously do. So it was no surprise that while touring universities, I was very impressed by the Stillwater community and the prestigious engineering program at OSU. That is where I ended up—and it didn't hurt that I received a full athletic scholarship.

My entrepreneurial spirit sparked when I was an undergraduate student in OSU's College of Engineering, Architecture and Technology. During my studies as a Civil and Environmental Engineer at OSU, I started to discover my calling and joined many leadership clubs on campus. As regional vice president of the Society of Hispanic Professional Engineers during my junior year, I and several other engineering students raised the funds to travel to a national inventors competition in Florida where we entered my idea for an electronically operated doggy door called the "Pooch Pass." We won 1st place over Stanford, MIT, and Harvard. After we won the competition, the story was featured on the front page of the *Daily Oklahoman* and the *Tulsa World*. It was then when I realized that I had a potentially marketable product that I could patent and sell for a profit, but one thing was holding me back. I didn't know much about business! After I was featured on the morning news in Tulsa, an OSU alumnus, Frank Hart, tracked me down to assist me in patenting my idea. A year later, I became the first undergraduate at OSU to acquire a United States patent.

Naturally, after graduating as a Louis Stokes OKAMP Engineering Scholar, OSU Leadership Legacy honoree and OSU Alumni Association Top 10 Senior, I decided to continue my education with an MBA so that I could learn more about business and entrepreneurship.

I was fortunate when I started my MBA program in 2000 that I already knew what I wanted to do and focused on building my own business. After landing a top academic scholarship for Hispanic MBA students, I took every opportunity available to learn from faculty and staff about how I could get my high-tech business off the ground. Two of the most important relationships I developed at OSU were with Dr. Earl Mitchell and Dr. Ken Eastman. At the time, Dr. Mitchell was the Vice President for Multicultural Affairs and Dr. Eastman was the Director of the MBA program. Their mentorship and advice helped me achieve something I never thought was possible. I wrote and submitted a business plan for my "Pooch Pass" patented invention to the U.S. Department of Commerce Minority Business Development Agency Business Plan competition. I walked away with top honors at the competition and a full scholarship to the Darden School of Business Administration's Executive Management program. Later that year, I was invited by the Governor's Office to help establish Oklahoma's first Hispanic Chamber of Commerce, which exists today to help serve Oklahoma's Hispanic business owners. I could not have accomplished any of these things without the guidance and support of the OSU MBA faculty and Dr. Ken Eastman.

I was now at the height of my academic career, but one special thing changed my focus—having twin daughters, little girl "Pokes" who were born at Stillwater Medical Center. If you remember, 2002 was not a good time to be entering the job market because of the dot-com crash. Even though I had established a business and had a good product to sell, I could not overcome the forces of the economy. At this point, we decided to sell my business and move back home to California, where I entered the realm of public service. I was excited to get back to my roots and do what my dad had instilled in me at a young age—serve your community.

The first job I held after returning to California was as a Director for Homeland Security and Public Safety in the Mayor of Los Angeles' office. This is where I got my first hands-on experience in politics and public administration, and it seems to have stuck with me. From there, I went on to hold a couple of jobs in the areas of development, non-profit management, marketing, and operations with several different companies. In 2005, the Dean of Economic Development of my hometown community college recruited me to launch an exciting new program. My experiences at OSU in the MBA program and as a small business owner gave me an advantage as the Founding Director of the Small Business Development Center (SBDC) at the College of the Canyons in Santa Clarita. The program has assisted thousands of entrepreneurs in learning to profit from and grow their small businesses while creating new jobs. I also took the opportunity to serve as an adjunct business instructor on campus.

After dabbling in the business community and working for other people, I decided to open my own consulting business. While I was working at the College of the Canyons, I started to realize that I had life-changing business experiences and advice that could be useful to entrepreneurs in the community. This led to the opening of De La Cerda &

Associates, a firm that focuses on public and government relations, marketing and business development, and access to capital for small to medium-sized businesses. In my role as CEO and President, our work has resulted in empowering the local economy in the region.

At the age of 30, I was elected to the local school board as the first Hispanic school board member of the district and the youngest elected official in my hometown. When I recount the path I have taken since graduating with an MBA from OSU, I realize that all the leadership tools and resources that OSU provided were essential in helping me make the decision to serve others in this public office.

I came to OSU as an NCAA All-American athlete intending to run cross-country and win titles for the athletic department. Along with being a Big 8 and Big 12 conference and district champion, I also ran away with academic scholarships and leadership awards and founded my first technology company. My relationships with the OSU faculty and advisors were vitally important factors to my success. If I could give one piece of advice to students, it would be to always continue to seek mentorship. Mentorship guided me at OSU, assisted me through the business development process and continues to inspire my career. Mentorship will continue to play an important role in my future.

Paul De La Cerda
Contributed by Michael Rogers

KEY SUCCESS FACTORS: Mentorship, Motivation, Focus

WEBSITE: www.pauldelacerda.com

SOCIAL MEDIA: Facebook—pauldelacerda; Twitter—PaulDLC; LinkedIn—pauldelacerda

EDITOR'S NOTES: Paul is a proud father of identical twin girls, a successful business owner, and a community leader in his hometown of Santa Clarita, CA (North Los Angeles).

Community leadership roles include:

- Saugus Union School District, Current Board President, LA County School Trustees Association

- Santa Clarita Valley Chamber of Commerce, Hispanic Business Committee, Founder; Government and Public Relations Committee, Member

- Society for Marketing Professional Services/American Marketing Association, Member

- City of Santa Clarita Enterprise Zone Advisory Committee, Member

- Los Angeles YMCA-North LA, Board Member, Development, Communications and Marketing Committee

- SCV Green Energy and Sustainable Development Committee, Past-President

- Michael Hoefflin Children's Cancer Foundation, Co-Chair; Gala, Advisory Board Member

Honors and awards include:

- San Fernando and Santa Clarita Valley Business Journal 40-under-40 Leadership Award

- Top 50 Most Influential Professionals Award, Santa Clarita Valley

- National Society of Hispanic MBAs, Past-Director, Top MBA Scholars Award

- OSU MBA Ambassador / OSU Alumni Association Top 10 Senior

- Tulsa Hispanic Chamber of Commerce, Founding Past-Director

- OSU Leadership Legacy Award

- OSU Lew Wentz Scholar / OSU Mercedier Cunningham Scholar

- US Hispanic Engineering National Achievement Award, "Engineer of the Year" (1998)

- OSU Multicultural Engineering Programs "Engineer of the Year" (1999)

Find your passion and pursue it relentlessly.

—Scott Householder

LIFE ON THE EDGE

Scott Householder—I can remember the first time I hiked the Grand Canyon from rim to rim. The mental and physical challenge was enthralling. Standing on the edge, looking out over the immense landscape I had just conquered was such an amazing experience; the view was breathtaking. As I stood there, so small, in comparison to the massive valley I had just crossed, I was humbled by the beauty and vastness of God's creation but also encouraged and empowered by doing the seemingly impossible. As I reflect on my personal and professional life thus far, in many ways it parallels a Grand Canyon rim to rim hike, as I am both humbled and amazed by my journey.

My journey began in 1958 in Oklahoma City, Oklahoma. My mother raised me in a small town outside of Oklahoma City: Bethany, Oklahoma. My mom is a wonderful person and I am thankful for the values that she instilled in me. She raised me with strong Christian morals and taught me the importance of stewardship over God-given talents. She demonstrated a good work ethic and taught me to have the same. My mom encouraged me to help others and contribute to society, teaching me the impact it can have on the world. My life was blessed from the beginning by being raised by my mother. I was also blessed to have a great church youth group—it also had a significant impact on forming my values. I cannot discuss my upbringing without also mentioning my Boy Scout Troup 84, fearlessly led by Scout Master Tom Yarborough. I learned many useful skills in Boy Scouts and further discovered the importance of service.

As I was looking at my future and deciding on my education, I chose to stay in Oklahoma and attend Oklahoma State University. My older brother followed in my footsteps and also attended and graduated from OSU. I majored in marketing and earned a minor in economics, thoroughly enjoying my undergraduate experience. At the time I was getting my Bachelor's degree, Dr. Manzer, a faculty member whom I am still in contact with and have a lot of respect for, was the head of the MBA Association. He encouraged me to continue at OSU to earn my Master's in Business Administration. Taking Dr. Manzer's advice—and having earned graduate credits as an undergraduate honors student as well as loving the school—I decided to remain at OSU for my MBA.

My time at OSU was an awesome experience. I have very fond memories of the program. I spent a lot of time in the library but also visited Theta Pond one day when my fraternity brothers threw me in! You just don't forget things like that! One project that especially stands out in my mind was "Derby Days." As a Sigma Chi I chaired the event and helped come up with fun contests such as the "Yard of Cloth." We had a blast raising money for troubled children. As an MBA student, I served as the President of the MBA Association and had the opportunity to work with the faculty on many projects. The MBA program was a great time of my life, and I learned so much that has been valuable to me throughout my career.

Upon completion of the MBA program, I was immediately hired by Exxon Mobile in Houston, Texas. I served as a Zone Supervisor for gas stations, car care centers, and motor fueling stations. My zone included 13 units, or stores, and 122 employees. My zone had lost money for ten years when I took over. I used the MBA case analysis approach for each store and within twelve months, we built the #1 profit zone in the nation. We remained #1 in the nation for three consecutive years. Exxon was a great place to get my feet wet in management, and having an MBA was critical; in fact, it was a job requirement. Having an MBA also made a significant impact on my income: in 1981 I was making about $40,000 more than the average college graduate. This put me at such a financial advantage that in 1984, I was able to leave Exxon Corporation and buy into a college tour company, where I became the Vice President of Sales. As part owner in the company, I used the knowledge gained in the MBA program in all aspects of the business. As an entrepreneur, I had the confidence and competence to join a restaurant acquisition company in Baton Rouge, Louisiana because my experience in the MBA program left me well rounded in business.

When I joined American Express Financial Advisors in 1986, my MBA helped me build a retail client base for investments and estate planning. I was the #1 first year advisor and the #1 second year advisor and built the #1 district in the U.S.—and was then promoted to Divisional Vice President in Phoenix, Arizona. The MBA knowledge was important in all roles I held with American Express, especially the Vice President's role because of my involvement in management, marketing, and all business components. This knowledge helped me improve the Phoenix office from 172nd out of 176 branches to #1 in the country. I gained much experience during my time at American Express Financial Advisors—learning best practices and gaining a command of the business—and built on that which I had learned from the MBA program.   In 1996 I founded Householder Group Estate and Retirement Specialists in Scottsdale, Arizona, where I am currently CEO, and we now have 50 offices across the country. My vision for Householder Group is to grow to 175 offices across the nation.

As I reflect on my business experience leading to the startup of Householder Group, I must reach back to my childhood. Most would say that this is my first company, but my uncle and I would say otherwise. When I was seven years old, I had my first business—selling mistletoe at Christmas time. My uncle would take me to pick it and I would put it in little baggies and tie bows on them with red Christmas ribbon. I made $20 that first year in the 1960s. I believe the entrepreneur in me was born with this venture. Early on I was also given great advice to always work for the biggest and the best company around and then opportunities would open up. When I was with American Express Financial Advisors, I saw a need and in that need, I saw an opportunity. I now offer high-quality, independent estate planning to a niche group of clients who would otherwise be underserved. I did a nationwide search of independent firms to see if there was a firm that fulfilled my ideas. None existed with a nationwide expansion model that suited me. So I developed a business plan, and implementation started at my dining room table with a group of about half a dozen like-minded individuals.

The startup of Householder Group was such an exciting time; and as I was being presented with various opportunities to build, it was a challenge to turn down opportunities that did not focus on our core competencies. But as I had learned in the MBA program, I stayed true to our core, allowing us to build a unique company. I am so thankful for all that I learned in the OSU MBA program as that knowledge has assisted me in reaching my current professional position. I am also very thankful for the people along the way who have taught me valuable lessons in life and in business. As I mentioned, Dr. Manzer has mentored me since before my career began, encouraging me to earn my MBA. When I was at Exxon, Glendall Rand taught me how to lead the managers and how to work *with* people rather than through people. Bob Holt, at American Express Financial, taught me sales leadership and business operations for financial advising.

My personal mission statement is "Have Fun. Help People. Make Money." Although I believe that to be successful you have to enjoy what you are doing in life, I think it is essential to find what your passion is. My passion is to help advisors create $1 million practices while providing our investment clients financial security. I have fun doing it! I believe that whatever you do, you have to impact the world in a positive fashion and make the world a better place by helping others. There is a strong correlation between the number of people helped and the amount of money made. It is a win-win situation. If I could give one piece of advice, I would say to find your passion and pursue it relentlessly. We at Householder Group have been able to help hundreds of thousands of people and have done so with honesty and integrity. This is a very important aspect of our business.

It is also important to remember to give back to your community and help others. At Householder Group, we donate to the Leukemia and Lymphoma Society. We chose the Society because my son, Davis, who is now 17 (and doing great!), had leukemia when he was 2½ years old. We appreciate what the Leukemia and Lymphoma Society does and hope to help others who are battling cancer. I have also had the opportunity to serve on several boards and have coached 24 soccer and basketball teams. I believe that community involvement and giving back to the community in which you live is essential to make the world around you a better place. I am so thankful for all that I have been given and all that I have been able to give. Earning my MBA has no doubt enhanced my career and helped me reach where I am today and has allowed me to help more people. Thus far I have achieved that which may have seemed impossible, much like my rim-to-rim hike, and the amazing journey continues!

Scott Householder
Contributed by Elizabeth DeWitt

KEY SUCCESS FACTORS: Have Fun, Help People, Make Money

WEBSITE: www.householdergroup.com

SOCIAL MEDIA: LinkedIn—scott-householder

EDITOR'S NOTES: Scott is a distinguished member of the financial services industry and is recognized as an expert in sales and marketing. Since its inception, Householder Group has been named the fastest growing investment advisory firm in the nation. It is often sought by major financial news networks for financial advice and opinions. Householder Group is frequently quoted on CNBC, the Squawk Box, and in the *Wall Street Journal*. It is a highly respected organization, and Scott's leadership and vision will guide its growth far into the future.

Scott is not only an exceptional businessman; he is a wonderful family man. He and his wife of 25 years, Debby, have three children: Megan, Davis, and Caroline. Scott remains very involved in their extracurricular activities. He also enjoys kayaking, mountain biking and cycling, water and snow skiing, and hiking: he has climbed twelve 14,000 foot peaks in his lifetime.

Taking on challenges in order to better yourself is always achievable.

—*Daniel G. Howard*

NOT A GAME SHOW, THIS IS REAL LIFE

Daniel G. Howard—300lbs. That is what I weighed before I decided to change and take on what was the most significant challenge of my life. Once I was able to set my mind on truly becoming a different person, my "Biggest Loser" metamorphosis was complete. I ended up losing one hundred pounds in just over three months. It was far from easy, but doing so forever changed me and my understanding of what can be achieved if you focus on a goal. My transformation enabled me to realize that challenges taken on in order to better yourself are always achievable. Deciding to change was a major hurdle, physically but even more mentally. It was not my last moment of mental clarity. I had many more on my journey as an Oklahoma State University (OSU) MBA graduate. I hope that my story will encourage others to reach similar goals and that they can incorporate my suggestions into their life to experience the same fulfillment I have been fortunate to achieve.

I was born Daniel G. Howard and my life journey began in the small town of Mankato, Minnesota. I moved to Texas for a brief period in my youth and ultimately ended up in Oklahoma where I graduated from Union High School in Tulsa. According to my father, when I was 6 or 7 years old, I proclaimed to all present, "I am going to get my MBA!" I have no recollection of making this prophetic announcement, but he remembered and reminded me the day I walked across the stage in Gallagher-Iba Arena to accept a hearty "Congratulations" from Dr. Ramesh Sharda. To my mind, my MBA journey began soon after completing my undergraduate degree in Computing and Information Sciences at OSU.

While in Stillwater, I was able to secure employment with the OSU Foundation, managing the alumni database and working with development staff as the Coordinator of Computer Services. Although working for the Foundation was a great experience, it quickly became apparent that I needed a better understanding of the business world, particularly in the areas of finance, accounting, and marketing. I could see through my daily interactions with the various directors that if I wanted to achieve true success outside of the technology field, I would need to understand how to communicate in the language of business.

The Foundation was very accommodating and allowed me to continue working part time while attending classes for my MBA. Today, I still marvel at the support I received from my mentor at the Foundation and appreciate how she understood that further development of my business skills would benefit both of us. With this support, I completed my studies and received my MBA in 1994. Reflecting on the MBA program with fellow graduates, we often remember Executive Interaction or specific instructors, but I am lucky enough to have a much more special memory. As part of a class project in one of my MBA classes, I along with four other students co-authored and published a book entitled *OAMC to OSU, A Postcard History*. I understand, and am proud to say, that this was the first time that a group of students started a company for class credit—truly the first "entrepreneurial" class project in the history of the program. This project helped me gain significant and valuable knowledge in business plan development, raising investment capital, and marketing—skills I carry with me to this day.

Upon completing my MBA, I was fortunate enough to secure an interview with a leading developer of healthcare information systems, Cerner Corporation, and accepted a business analyst position at their world headquarters in Kansas City. On my first day of work at Cerner, I actually sold the postcard history book I'd co-authored at OSU to founder/CEO Neal Patterson, also an OSU MBA alumnus. I believe it made an impression on him that lasted throughout my career there. During my six years at Cerner, I gained tremendous experience in various product groups, ultimately heading up the company's supply chain management division. With hard work and the skills I gained in graduate school, I was recognized by management and placed into a Cerner leadership development program—*Top Gun*. Identified as one of the top fifty future leaders of the company, I was immersed in an intense and challenging program alongside other associates from more nationally recognized schools such as Harvard, Yale, and MIT. Upon being nominated for the program, it was clear to me that my graduate degree had more than prepared me to compete against individuals from America's most celebrated programs. I eventually was promoted to Managing Director of the supply chain software division and continued sharpening my business skills by implementing systems for the largest healthcare companies in Oklahoma and Missouri and the Mayo Clinic in Jacksonville. Looking back on the opportunities presented at Cerner, I am sure my MBA was a critical element of my success.

After leaving Cerner, I accepted a position with H&R Block, where I was Group Manager of the Information Systems Division at the company's world headquarters in Kansas City. At H&R Block, I was charged with leading the team to develop the first web-based retail accounting system for the company. The goal was to improve the flow of disparate sales information from the 5,000 stores disbursed throughout the country into the centralized headquarters. It was 1999. Broadband access was still in its infancy and costly. We were charged with transferring the information via dial-up telephone lines from each retail outlet—without a dedicated line. Nonetheless, my team created and deployed a working implementation that allowed the company to achieve the desired information turnaround and save millions of dollars in manual accounting.

During my year at H&R Block, my wife, Tiffany (also an MBA alumnus), had an opportunity to work for her family's business. The opportunity and challenges were too good to pass up, so we moved back to Oklahoma where I embraced the chance to further develop my business skills by entering the classroom once again.

I am a firm believer in making yourself fully present to embrace learning opportunities. Our return to Oklahoma was just such a chance. I applied and was accepted to the Oklahoma City University School of Law. Three years later, I successfully accomplished another new life goal, graduating *magna cum laude*. Before graduating, I had accepted an associate attorney position with the business litigation department at McKinney & Stringer, P.C. At the time, McKinney & Stringer was the second largest law firm in Oklahoma. This position provided a very rich and rewarding work experience as well as the opportunity to develop many business relationships which I rely on today. Six years ago, I decided to strike out on my own and opened a solo practice—Daniel Howard & Associates, PLC—and after a year, joined some friends from McKinney & Stringer and Rubenstein, McCormick & Pitts, PLLC, where I currently am *of counsel.*

Tiffany and I are strong believers in the value of our business educations and see mentoring of OSU's young, up-and-coming leaders and entrepreneurs as both a benefit and an obligation of being Spears School of Business MBA graduates. The knowledge I obtained in the program, and the subsequent opportunities and successes, is something I am very grateful for. While I cannot say for certain where my journey would have led me without my MBA, I am certain it would not have been as fulfilling.

If I were to make some suggestions for the next generation of business leaders at OSU, they would be to embrace learning opportunities that are thrown your direction—they always pay dividends; never be afraid of taking risks and stepping out of your comfort zone; take advantage of opportunities that arise, in particular international study or business opportunities abroad; and finally, be as outgoing with others as you can within your own capacity. Embrace the challenge of meeting new people no matter how shy you are, as it will pay you dividends.

I am very proud to say that in 2010 I now find myself a father of eight-month-old twins. I look forward to this next challenge of teaching my son and daughter some of the lessons I have learned. I hope my story has been inspiring for those who took the time to read, and best of luck in your journey.

Daniel G. Howard
Contributed by Noé Duran

KEY SUCCESS FACTORS: Embrace Learning Opportunities, Take Risks and Be Adventurous, Be Social, Be Open to Other Cultures

WEBSITE: www.oklawpartners.com

EDITOR'S NOTES: Mr. Howard is married to Tiffany, whom he met at OSU and who is an MBA alumnus as well. Meeting and getting married to Tiffany is something that Dan felt was also a major life transformation during his time obtaining his MBA. Dan is chair of the steering committee for Edmond's Young Professionals (EYP) and takes pleasure in passing on his experiences and learning to the next generation of professionals as an Adjunct Professor. He is definitely most interested in continuing to develop leaders and entrepreneurs, and he and Tiffany love to contribute to OSU whenever they have the opportunity. Dan is a member of the American Bar Association's sub-committees on Cyberspace Law, Internet Law, and Cyber Security. Dan is also a member of the Oklahoma, Oklahoma County, and American Bar Associations.

Find ways to make those around you better at what they do.

—Sam R. Lloyd

EDUCATION TO ENTREPRENEUR

Sam R. Lloyd—I was born and raised in Poteau, on the east side of Oklahoma. Being from a small town had its benefits and its shortcomings, but ultimately it was the incredible education I received in this near-village of four thousand that laid the groundwork for the successes of a lifetime. It's hard to believe that the mentorship and teaching of one small town teacher has been so instrumental to the course my life has taken, but my middle school and high school English teacher, Mrs. Cherokee Rose Carter gave me an excellent foundation in the mastery of the English language and writing skills and, more importantly, taught me the value of a high quality education.

After graduating from high school, I followed in my parents' footsteps and attended Oklahoma State University in Stillwater. I arrived in Stillwater every bit the intimidated teenager from a small town, but was relieved to find that the quality education I'd received in that small town gave me a competitive edge in the classroom. My confidence grew and I relished my time as a student at OSU. While an undergraduate, I spent much of my time preparing myself for the world of business as the president of the insurance fraternity, Beta Gamma Sigma, honor society. I also flexed my entrepreneurial muscle by incorporating the Volkswagen Club of Oklahoma. I received my Bachelor's degree in business administration with a concentration in insurance and decided it was time to get to work in the real world.

I moved to Oklahoma City and began my work in insurance. After two years in OKC, I moved with my wife and two sons to my hometown, Poteau, OK. To my surprise, when you're a 22-year-old recent college graduate, it's not easy to act as a financial advisor in a small town of four thousand people who knew you in high school. I decided to go back to OSU and earn my MBA, but I did not have the money to get there on my own. I contacted Dean Swearingen, and he was instrumental in getting me on the path of financial aid and a fellowship from Continental Oil that opened the doors of the MBA program to me.

In 1965 I moved back to Stillwater to begin my MBA study. I found my graduate studies to be challenging and fulfilling and enjoyed being back at the University. In addition to my own studies, I became a member of the business school faculty and taught two insurance courses each semester. I also served as a faculty advisor for the insurance fraternity. I truly enjoyed spending time with the students. This experience would greatly influence the rest of my career as an instructor and businessman.

In 1967 I graduated from OSU with my MBA and stayed on the faculty of OSU for another year teaching marketing and insurance classes before I moved to St. Louis, Missouri where I began work on my doctorate degree at Washington University. Afterward I began work at the University of Missouri—St. Louis and stayed there for seven years as the Assistant Dean for Continuing Education for the School of Business Administration and a member of the marketing faculty. Then I moved to Dallas, TX where I worked for a year as the Director of the Management Development Center at Southern Methodist University.

Twelve years after completing my MBA at Oklahoma State University I decided to branch out and start my own business. After ten years of experience devoted to educating future leaders and managers, it was a smooth transition into consulting and training. In 1977 I launched SuccessSystems, Inc. and continued to create management development programs to train future and current business leaders. We offered a variety of training programs in partnership with university continuing education departments throughout the United Sates. While the transition was a relatively easy one based on the network of contacts and professional relationships I had developed over a decade, it was not always a smooth road once I was in business for myself. In 1985 one of my clients that marketed our one-day seminars declared Chapter Seven bankruptcy and left my company holding the bag for a $90,000 loss. Working through that hardship was one of the toughest challenges in my company's history. We had to find a new source of revenue to replace the lost income and we had to develop a strategy to pay our own employees and subcontractors while staying afloat. This challenge taught me an important lesson about diversifying my sources of revenue.

Fast forward 33 years from when I started my business and I'm still here as the President of SuccessSystems, Inc. I've published six books and spent my career developing business leaders and executives. I've learned a few valuable lessons along the way that have helped me become successful and that I've passed on to others to help in their success.

I credit my BS and MBA education from OSU with giving me a solid educational foundation on which to build with my experiences. Without this broad understanding of the workings of businesses, organizations, and interpersonal relationships, I would not be where I am today. I often find people's knowledge is limited to their specific area of expertise and they don't see how their part adds to the whole. This ability to see the sum total of multiple interdependent units is a skill that the MBA program gave me. Without this fundamental understanding, many business leaders fail.

A basic lesson that is sometimes not taught effectively in business school is goal setting. I believe it is fundamentally important for leaders to be strategic thinkers and set effective goals for their organizations. This goal setting requires another critical fundamental: effective communication. Without successful relationships built on effective communication, goals cannot be communicated, shared, or achieved.

Finally, marketing is vitally important to the success of any business venture. Many new business ventures fail, and poor marketing is often the cause.

At 70 years old I continue to provide my management development seminars and coaching sessions, but I have reduced the business side of my life and now devote more time to recreation and travel. I serve as a volunteer for the Boulder County Sheriff's office, as a facilitator in the "Restorative Justice" program and a mediator for conflict resolution. I also serve on the Colorado State Council for the Society for Human Resource Management. I encourage you to find ways to make those around you better at what they do. This is what I have devoted my business and my life to, and it is a truly rewarding calling.

Sam R. Lloyd
Contributed By Jason Zumwalt

KEY SUCCESS FACTORS: Marketing, Networking, Perseverance

WEBSITE: www.trainingforsuccess.com

SOCIAL MEDIA: LinkedIn—Samrlloyd

EDITOR'S NOTES: Mr. Lloyd lives in Boulder, CO with his wife, Tina Berthelot. Mr. Lloyd's parents attended Oklahoma A&M (neither graduated) and his maternal grandmother earned a B.A. degree from Oklahoma A&M when few women had college degrees. She was the principal of the elementary school on South Lowry Street in Stillwater, and her husband built most of the houses in the 1300 block of S. Lowry. They had made the run when Oklahoma Territory was opened to settlers and stopped in what is now Stillwater.

Sam Lloyd is a highly lauded trainer and coach of executive and business leaders. He is the author of numerous articles in business journals and six books: *Developing Positive Assertiveness, Self Empowerment, Leading Teams: The Skills for Success, Accountability: Managing for Maximum Results, Achieving Life Balance,* and *Coaching Skills for Leaders.*

Surround yourself with the best and brightest people and take pride in their success.

—Herman Luffman

WORDS TO LIVE BY:
CHARACTER, CONFIDENCE,
CONSISTENCY, COMMITMENT

Herman Luffman—Born and raised in Enid, Oklahoma, I grew up with great mentors—my parents. My parents had strong discipline and an incredible work ethic. They taught my siblings and me to always work hard and believe in ourselves. Because of their humble backgrounds and their example, we knew we could accomplish anything we wanted. After graduation from Enid High School in 1953, realizing I was not quite ready for college, I enlisted in the Air Force. I was trained as a Russian linguist and served four years in the Air Force Security Service. At the end of my enlistment, I returned to Oklahoma, where I attended the University of Oklahoma in Norman for three years and then transferred to Phillips University in Enid to finish my undergraduate degree in economics.

Phillips University did not have a placement program for graduates at that time, and I was convinced I needed to further my education. Oklahoma State University had just started a Master's of Business Administration (MBA) program that replicated that of the Harvard Business School, including using many of the same case-study textbooks. So in 1961, I enrolled at OSU and began driving back and forth daily from Enid to Stillwater working on my MBA. I graduated in 1962, a member of only the second class to graduate under what was then a new program. As an aside, because I was a daily commuter student working two jobs—one in Enid and one in Stillwater—the pressures on my time did not always allow me to find legal parking on campus. This created one last obligation before receiving my degree—I had to pay the bursar a sizeable sum for all the parking tickets I had accumulated in the back seat of my worn out car!

Upon graduation from OSU, I was recruited by Conoco Pipeline Company's Management Training Program and began my training in Artesia, NM. Thirteen transfers and six years later, I became Conoco's Manager of Pipeline Operations in Ponca City, OK. Later, I left to join the former Executive Vice President of Conoco to form Lovett C. Peters and Associates in Boston, MA and became involved in a number of energy-related ventures and positions including Acting President of Aryshire Collieries in Indianapolis, President of Outerbridge Terminal Company in the New York Harbor area, and President of Queen City Terminals in Cincinnati, OH. After leaving that association, I became President of Gulf Interstate Engineering Company and Senior Vice President of its parent company, Gulf Interstate Company, headquartered in Houston, TX. This was an opportunity for a turnaround of a formerly successful firm which was experiencing some management challenges. I was fortunate in being able to recruit many of my former Conoco associates, and we successfully turned the company around, greatly increasing its market value, and through stock option incentives, establishing some meaningful personal assets. Much of this success was based on expanding operations into the Middle East (Saudi Arabia, Abu Dhabi, Egypt), Europe (England and Italy), Central and South America, and Alaska. The financial results of this successful turnaround enabled us to pursue our dream of founding our own energy-related company. We formed Independent Terminal & Pipeline Company (ITAPCO) with the goal of purchasing underutilized petroleum distribution assets from the major oil companies which were, at that time, facing major capital expenditures to meet rapidly expanding environmental requirements.

Among the successes in which I take a great deal of pride are the creation and building of ITAPCO and acquiring my pilot's license, enabling me to fly my own personal airplane. ITAPCO became a resounding success and I became a pretty fair pilot. Our timing was good. Over a period of 20 years, we acquired 26 petroleum terminals and pipelines from major oil companies and established operations in 13 states. Through the use of innovative information technology and computer-based operations, we were able to store and distribute the petroleum products (gasoline, diesel fuel, heating oil, kerosene, military and civilian jet fuel, etc.) of several major oil marketers through a single facility. At first the concept of the major companies—the

Exxon's, Shells, Chevrons, etc. of the world—outsourcing this segment of their distribution pattern was a very difficult sell. But after demonstrating the improvement in logistics management resulting from several companies using a common comingled inventory source, it made too much sense for them to ignore. It also relieved these firms of much of their historic environmental, safety, and human relations exposure while allowing them to preserve their individual marketing presence. Our technology enabled us to preserve the individuality of each shipper's products by injecting the customer's specific additive into an otherwise non-specific fungible product. The process improvement, like most great ideas, was simple but provided a major breakthrough in productivity and, hopefully, cost savings to the consumer.

I had a personal setback in 1998 when I was diagnosed with a brain tumor. This led to the very difficult decision to sell ITAPCO companies in 1999 and to let my pilot's license lapse. Personally and professionally, this was the most trying time in my life. After many tests, surgery, and immeasurable lost sleep, the doctors determined the tumor was an Acoustic Neuroma and benign. Praise God!

Today, I remain a very active 75-year-old who enjoys Tai Chi, running, fishing, and hunting. I also enjoy entertaining friends and former colleagues at our West Texas lodge and our South Padre home. I have been married to my lovely wife, the former Miss Patricia Ann Holloway of Enid, Oklahoma, for over 50 years. We returned to reside in Enid in 2007, where we spend most of our time with our family. I am and always have been committed to working hard and achieving goals, personally and professionally. The traits I live my life by are character, confidence, consistency, and most of all, commitment. I believe in being charitable and taking care of others. In business, I try to surround myself with the best and brightest people and I take pride in their success. As President of ITAPCO, I insisted our employees be allowed to own shares of our company stock. The "silver lining" to having health issues that forced me to sell the company, was to watch as some of our employees became millionaires from the sale of those shares. This could not have made me happier.

Because of the strong upbringing by my parents that drove my resolve and commitment, and of course, my OSU MBA, I have found great success. I am truly a blessed man.

Herman Luffman
Contributed by Patty Tyson

KEY SUCCESS FACTORS: Character, Confidence, Consistency, Commitment

EDITOR'S NOTES: Mr. Luffman's many charitable contributions include gifts to the Nature Conservancy, the Acoustic Neuroma Association, the Northwest Oklahoma Blood Institute, the United Way, and the Aircraft Owners & Pilots Association. He is a member of Phi Eta Sigma Fraternity at the University of Oklahoma, a graduate of the Army School of Languages (Russian), and a former student and instructor of the School of Pipeline Technology at the University of Texas. He studied Spanish at Rice University Extension School and is a member of the First Presbyterian Church in Enid.

Work hard and find something you believe in, something you're passionate about, and something you love to do each and every day.

—*Monica Mamica Mezezi-Pino*

WALKING THE DOG

Monica Mamica Mezezi-Pino—As I walk down the streets of Guelph, I look down at Wizard happily trotting along. The jingling of her collar breaks the silence of another brisk night in the Ontario province. As I continue walking, I realize it took quite a chain of events to end up settling down in a place like this. It wasn't exactly what I had in mind while growing up in Albania. Don't get me wrong; working in the medical field was always a dream of mine, but the journey here was about as unlikely as Wizard finally finding a place to do her business. As the small Lhasa-Pekenese continues sniffing around, I look back to my time in Albania.

Growing up I knew the field of medicine was for me. I longed for the opportunity to help others in need of care. Albania's education system didn't provide the best platform for making this dream come true however. The quality of education was good, but the Albanian government chooses your field of study after high school. I finished top in my class through the 12th grade and received the Gold Medal Award for straight A's all four years. This award normally allows you to choose your field of study. The Albanian government, however, chose trade economics as my focus after high school instead of medicine. This was one of my life's biggest disappointments. It wasn't long until I was off to the University of Tirana in our nation's capital. Upon graduation I became a teacher's assistant at the University and later became one of the first instructors to ever teach marketing at that university. About six years after I graduated, I was presented with a life changing opportunity: I was awarded the Alexander Hamilton Fulbright exchange scholarship, a full scholarship to Oklahoma State University's marketing department for one year. I was ecstatic.

In 1992 my husband and 3-year-old son, Aami, moved to the United States with me so I could continue my journey in higher education. In

Stillwater, Oklahoma, I was introduced to a great program. The classes, case studies, and—most importantly—the department staff are my favorite memories of OSU. I viewed Dr. Larkin Warner and Dr. Steve Miller in particular as great mentors and advisors. They made my trip to America a smooth transition and helped me feel welcomed into the OSU family.

Wizard made a hard tug at the leash, snapping me out of my daze. She is startled as snowflakes begin to fall on her. Her caution quickly turns to jubilation, though, as she eagerly snaps at every flake she can. As if I needed anything else to distract her.

After getting my MBA, I was ready to take on the world. I'd been studying and working hard for 20 years just to get to where I was that day in 1995. I actively began looking for work in the Tulsa area. It wasn't easy. Companies seemed reluctant to hire. During my job search in Oklahoma, an opportunity presented itself in the Northeast, where my aunt owned a restaurant called the Gold Coast Grille. My family and I moved to Connecticut, where I applied the skills I'd learned at OSU, taking concepts from my marketing classes and putting them into action. It was during this time that I met Michael Cecchi and Dr. Jacques Cohen. Little did I know they would become my business partners for many years to date.

We founded genX International; our primary focus is to bring the most advanced technologies, products, and services to the market to help improve embryo and cell culture. Times were difficult at first. When starting a medical company, initial overhead costs are always high. In time though, genX began to grow and we were able to move our company from our basements to real office buildings. Before long, business was good and finding money for overhead costs was no longer a problem. Time seemed to fly and before I knew it, genX International gave life to other companies such as IVFonline, LLC and LifeGlobal, LLC. It didn't take long for our companies to go international with offices in Canada and Belgium. None of this would've been possible without my MBA.

If it hadn't been for my marketing classes and meeting great minds in business and innovative people like my partners, I would never have been able to help grow a small business from a basement to a real international company. Furthermore, these classes helped me target a relatively small, but necessary, market when it came to embryo culture. At OSU I also learned how to give a brief and effective presentation. In the field of medicine, no one has much free time; everyone is on the run. Being able to give a powerful presentation in a short time has done wonders in my business career. And the numerous case studies I completed in Stillwater gave me the social skills to interact with business men and women in the medical field. Oklahoma State's MBA program truly paid off for me.

As Wizard finishes what she set out to do, I smile and begin leading her back home. My journey from Albania, to Stillwater, to Connecticut, and now Guelph has been a blessed one. It wasn't always easy, though. Mentorship has played a large role. It helped me when I was a student at OSU and continues at my offices today. While money was tough to come by at times, money was never my main focus. It's about taking pleasure in what I do. I wake up in the morning looking forward to new challenges every day. While my degree from OSU has helped greatly, you can't rely solely on your diploma to carry you through life. You have to continue to work hard. Luckily I found something I believe in, something I'm passionate about, and something I love to do each and every day. As Wizard shakes the snow from her fur, the loud clanking of her collar snaps me out of my daydream of reliving my story and being thankful for the path on which it has taken me. "What do you know, Wizard; we're home."

Monica Mamica Mezezi-Pino
Contributed by Alexander D. Pannone

KEY SUCCESS FACTORS: Persistence, Determination, Perseverance, Self-belief

WEBSITE: www.ivfonline.com

EDITOR'S NOTES: Monica Mamica Mezezi-Pino resides in Guelph, Ontario, Canada. She enjoys working out daily, which usually includes walks with Wizard. She is married with a son who is currently studying bioscience at the University of Guelph. She is the chief editor of *Fertility Magazine*, a magazine that informs and offers the best new products to increase female fertility. She is a member of the American

Society for Reproductive Medicine and The American Association of Biocatalysts and was nominated for the RBC Canadian Woman Entrepreneur Award in August 2009.

Business, more than any other occupation, is a continual dealing with the future; it is a continual calculation, an instinctive exercise in foresight.

—Henry R. Luce

PERSISTENT DEDICATION

John Wilcha—I was born August 31, 1942, in Yonkers, New York. My parents were both immigrants from Eastern Europe; my mother came from Czechoslovakia and my father from Ukraine. I was raised in a railroad flat, which could be described as a shotgun apartment. In order to heat the apartment, coal had to be gathered to fuel the furnace. The urban environment I grew up in was relatively poor, but the neighborhood was tight knit and people always helped one another. My father was a factory worker and my mother was a maid. As a child, my parents instilled a lasting realization of the necessity of hard work and educational attainment as the foundation for success. With little extra money, my parents sent me to a private elementary school. While in grade school, I was always employed with jobs varying from delivering newspapers to selling watermelons.

Because of my good grades, I was awarded a scholarship at Manhattan prep school in the Bronx, which was a stepping stone into Fordham University, where I majored in finance and philosophy. While at Fordham, I worked for the Gerber Food Company and joined Alpha Kappa Psi, offering an opportunity to build many relationships. After graduation in 1964, I married my wife and we felt adventurous, so I applied to various MBA programs outside of New York. My wife and I wanted to see how the "other" part of the country lived, so I aimed to attend graduate school in the Midwest. Oklahoma State University was appealing because of its offer of an assistantship and a job for my wife in the Agronomy Department. I had a very good experience in Oklahoma and realized that people in the Midwest aren't too different from those on the East Coast. I graduated from OSU in August 1965.

After graduation in 1965, I began searching to start my career in marketing and product management. I had a 1A classification for the

Vietnam draft, which meant I had a high probability of being drafted, so many companies were leery of offering positions. My initial job offers were generally in retail and did not fit my desire to work in marketing or product management. Luckily, I was never drafted, patience paid off, and in 1966 I secured a position in marketing with Standard Brands. In my 11 years at Standard Brands, I rose from Assistant Product Manager to Vice President. However, in 1976, I was let go due to a political situation with the new president, which was traumatic to the family and a learning experience for me. Searching for employment without a current job was a lesson learned, but about one month later I took a position as VP for the Gallo Winery in California. Because the business was family owned, the job at Gallo did not provide the level of responsibility I desired, so I moved back east to work as the VP of Marketing and Sales at Drake Bakeries, a decision which was not received well by my family, who were enjoying life in California. However, at Drake I had direct authority over the sales force, which was exhilarating and very rewarding.

At Drake, I acted on a personal philosophy of not allowing issues to get channeled up to the President, a policy which required plenty of time and energy to achieve. The president I worked with for a few years was very close to me, but got sick and a new president was appointed who had a radically different personality and leadership style, so I quit for a short time. After being asked by the President to return, I did, but this second term did not last, as issues remained. However, I was able to search for jobs while still being employed.

Next, I joined Arnold Bakers in 1981 and rose to President in a short time. While I was president, we conducted major restructuring and were able to increase profits dramatically in 3 years. Arnold Bakers was sold to CPC International at a large gain to the shareholders (18 to 1 return on investment). The experience gained during the acquisition was very beneficial in my next undertaking, which was purchasing Wilos Baking Company and shortly after selling out to Merrill Lynch. In 1988, I became CEO of Amerifoods, Inc., which over a few years integrated 23 separate corporations into one company. Seeing an opportunity in 1997, I along with Michael Dubilier purchased Old London Foods, where I served as Chairman, President, and CEO. After eight years, we sold Old London Foods to Nonni, Inc. After the sale in 2005,

I joined Dubilier and Co. as Chairman and have since purchased many companies for the private equity firm. Presently, I also serve as Chairman for three companies: Blue Grass Dairy and Food, Inc., DC Safety Co, and Perfecta Products Co. Today, I focus on overseeing planning and execution.

John Wilcha
Contributed by Kevin Lahn

KEY SUCCESS FACTORS: Taking Action, Passion, Delegation, Responsibility, Communication, Attention to Detail

WEBSITE: www.dubilier.com

SOCIAL MEDIA: LinkedIn—John Wilcha

EDITOR'S NOTES: John Wilcha has been married to the former Patricia Swift since 1964. They have two children, Jennifer and Christopher, both of whom reside in the New York metropolitan area. Over the years, John has completed a few adventure vacations in his spare time such as visiting the North Pole, Burma, Mongolia, Cambodia, and Nepal. He has an interest in mountain climbing and has completed climbs at Mount Kilimanjaro, Mount Fuji, the Himalayas, and Northern Karakoram. He has completed 200 scuba dives in various places such as Palau, Truck, and the Great Barrier Reef. Mr. Wilcha enjoys staying active, having participated in marathons, playing golf, and fishing as often as possible. John has served as Past Chairman of Fordham University Alumni Board of Governors and eight years as trustee and Past Vice Chairman of the Baker's Association in addition to serving on numerous Fordham University committees, outside charities, and other boards. He is the recipient of several awards including Fordham College Business Administration Man of the Year, New York Bakery Executive Man of the Year, and the Ellis Island Medal of Freedom.

CHAPTER TEN
THE LEADER WITHIN

An MBA is a coveted degree that signifies management and leadership training. If effective leadership is measured by results, then all of the following individuals have proven themselves as great leaders.

A good objective of leadership is to help those who are doing poorly to do well and to help those who are doing well to do even better.

—Jim Rohn

LEADING THE LEADERS

Ron Crossland—"The biggest problem with leadership is the communication between a leader and a constituent," John W. Gardner had answered without hesitation to my "Stump the expert question." Gardner's response altered my career and the career of my late partner, Boyd Clarke. John Gardner was not simply our mentor for a short time. He was a trained psychologist who worked with the CIA on intelligence testing and personality measures. A well-known figure in public leadership, Mr. Gardner was the recipient of the Medal of Freedom—the civilian equivalent to a Medal of Honor in the military. Sitting in his office chair in Washington D.C., Mr. Gardner paused, reflected, repositioned himself, and said, "We know great communication when we experience it, but we do not understand it." I realized there was much to learn about leadership communication, which excited my dual, and often competing, interests—science and art.

Born in 1951 in Sherman, Texas, I was the product of a blended family—eight children from three marriages. My father, a skilled typewriter repairman, rescued my mother from starvation while raising 3 children with no child support. Coming from humble origins with parents of a low socioeconomic status, I learned the value of a dollar. My childhood was spent moving around Texas, Oklahoma, and New Mexico, totaling 27 different homes and 13 public schools by the time I finished high school. Military children seldom experience as much movement.

I was essentially the perpetual new kid in school. The asset behind the deficit of not having long-lasting childhood friendships was my skills at observing human nature from a young age. I developed "survival social skills" at school that made it possible for me to read the room and work the crowd. While searching for answers, I understood that education was the road to economic and social stability.

Two male family members served as role models for me. One of my older brothers, who died before his time, joined the Navy with a focus on electronics and was stationed on a nuclear submarine. He would come home on leave and dazzle my imagination with his stories of life under the ocean and helping keep the sub alive, almost as if he was its personal trainer. By age 15, I dreamed of becoming a Navy pilot and attending Annapolis, perhaps the only ambition I ever had that impressed my father. I remember watching my dad tear down a typewriter with very small gears and screws. He could disassemble and reassemble a typewriter of several hundred parts in 2 hours. He was always tackling some impossible customer problem and was able to fix nearly all of them. He taught me that there's a difference between knowing something and being able to use the knowledge towards something practical.

There were stringent requirements to becoming a Navy pilot. I worked hard and campaigned well and received nomination letters from both Oklahoma Senators and my national congressman. At the time, I worried that asthma would keep me from being accepted into the training program. However, to my dismay, the physicians confirmed my colorblindness, a problem that had created a great deal of childhood teasing and frustrated art instruction. The Navy had waived the asthma, but there is no correction for colorblindness. I was devastated, but determined. I worked 40 hours/week during high school sacking groceries and stocking shelves, as I knew my college education would now have to be self-funded. Graduating from Enid High School in 1970 ranked 44th of 612 led me to Stillwater, OK.

I attended Oklahoma State University to pursue a degree in electronic engineering technology, graduating in 1975. Science had always been a passion; however, I realized my energy interests were purely intellectual, not vocational. I also had a constant interest in human behavior. During my undergraduate years, I had a roommate who took business classes. Realizing the aspect of human behavior in business, in my junior year at OSU, I decided to pursue an MBA degree while finishing my undergraduate degree. During my time at the OSU College of Business (later renamed Spears School of Business), an organizational behavior class solidified my keen interest in human behavior. Interestingly, during both undergraduate and graduate years, I maintained a job working 40 hours/week. In 1977, I graduated to the workforce with an MBA degree.

After completing my MBA, I worked in a copy shop near OSU's campus, basically a smaller version of what Kinko's became. I created a business plan for scaling the business to a franchise type of operation, but the owner and I could never raise enough capital to make the idea a go, so I turned towards larger corporations to seek my fortune. My entrepreneurship lay dormant for a while.

NCR was the first corporation to ever train a professional sales staff, and human development was in their work ethic. At NCR, I was selected as 1 of 19 employees to enter a fast-track management-training program. This program lasted 9 months and incorporated training equivalent to 5 years of work experience. Unfortunately the company abandoned its program before it had a chance to prove its merits. Disappointed, I looked for more fertile pastures and went to work for AT&T. A successful sales career led me to increasing managerial opportunities during my seven years there. Working during and after the telecom deregulation years, I saw what happens to organizations that lack inspired leadership. As AT&T recoiled from wave after wave of reductions, right-sizing's, and reorganizations, I became more fervent in my efforts to develop leaders to deal with these difficulties. In my last job there, I was able to study leadership and proposed a methodology for leadership development that would not only create better leaders for AT&T, but would help AT&T become the benchmark destination for other companies who wanted to develop leaders. My proposal was turned down and my entrepreneurship woke from its hibernation.

In 1987 Boyd Clarke and I started International Leadership Associates. I sold my house to bankroll the start-up and moved into an apartment. It took one year before the company started making a profit. Over the next decade, International Leadership Associates (ILA) grew in reach and profitability. During this time, we maintained a close alliance with the Tom Peters Company, a management consulting leadership training company. In 1997, Tom Peters invited Boyd and me to take over management of his company. We sold ILA to our partners and Boyd became CEO and I became Vice-Chairman of the Tom Peters Company. We had a number of terrific years together until a series of misfortunes struck—the post 9/11 recession, Boyd's untimely death, and Tom's own health problems. Layoffs and restructuring are emotionally draining and challenging—but a common part of small business operations. However, those dynamics coupled with losing a partner through death and major career reconsiderations is extremely hard.

In 2004 Tom took his nameplate and restructured his business, and I had to help lead the rebranding of the organization left behind. Naming a company is far harder than naming a baby. I turned to science once again. The hottest part of a flame is the blue point. The color blue is associated with the hottest stars in the universe. We became Bluepoint Leadership Development. I wanted to ignite people's passion, their greatness, their blue point of leadership. My partners at the time honored me with the chairmanship, which I held until 2007, when I stepped down to spend more time with my family and turn my attention to other business and personal interests.

I have enjoyed developing leaders around the world. I have served over half the Fortune 500 at one time or another, worked in 18 different companies and had offices on 3 continents. I have co-authored 2 books: *The Leader's Voice* and *The Leadership Experience.* Numerous individuals have inspired me, including Boyd Clarke, Tom Peters, Jim Kouzes, Steve Coats, Steve Houchin, Ken Silvia, and of course the man who paid it forward early in my career, John W. Gardner.

I also do pro bono work with school systems as well as with inner city business development programs. I offer all these hungry individuals the advice that has sustained me: work hard, remain a lifelong learner, and hold close the partners you can trust.

Ron Crossland Leadership Development in Mason, OH is my current business. My primary focus is leadership communication and I offer seminars on the topic and work with a number of past employees who have gone on to start their own businesses. I am proud that all the leadership development businesses I have started or been an executive for are still in vibrant operation.

As a lifelong learner, I am finding ways to broker my basic message via multimedia digital experiences. Greening my business is best done through reductions in travel and paper. I am on a mission to find the best ways to do this without lowering the quality of the developmental experience. Science and art are converging in the digital world and I am as excited as ever.

I'm glad I chose to spend more time with my family, as the kids are now into their own lives. I have returned to a lifelong ambition to write and have finished the first in a trilogy of novels that are perhaps best described as the *Da Vinci Code* meets the Catholics and Mormons in Mexico City.

Passion is a fuel ignited by opportunity. Taking full credit for an achievement is dishonest because randomness and luck play a role in our lives. Some call this providence. I call it simply good fortune. Either way, preparedness and passion are the catalysts for molding opportunity into success.

Ron Crossland
Contributed by Jonathan Weaver

KEY SUCCESS FACTORS: Staying Current with Ideas and Technology in your Field, Passion, Integrity, Creating Opportunity

WEBSITE: www.roncrossland.com

SOCIAL MEDIA: LinkedIn—Ronald Crossland

EDITOR'S NOTES: Ron is a writer, an intuitionist, a factoid junkie, and a research synthesizer. He exudes a contagious energy and is a continuing source of optimism. Ron has co-authored *The Leader's Voice* and *The Leadership Experience*. He enjoys writing poetry and short stories, and has just finished his first novel, *Eve's Bones*.

Getting to the top is easy . . . staying there is the hard part!

—*Luciano Cunha*

GETTING TO THE TOP— AND STAYING THERE

Luciano Cunha—In recent years there has been a renewed push by American business schools to prepare students for the international business environment. My own international experience started well before I enrolled at Oklahoma State as an undergraduate in the fall of 1998. I was born and raised in Santa Rita do Sapucaí, Brazil, a city with a strong electronics and telecommunications industry. At the age of 16, I earned a technical degree from Escola Técnica de Eletrônica and accepted an analyst position with IBM Brazil. Although my time there was brief (lasting some ten months), it proved to be an enriching experience that would change the course of my professional career.

Despite my age and relative inexperience, IBM Brazil's vice president of operations gave me the keys to several different divisions within the organization, charging me with the task of leveraging information technology to streamline our operations and improve operating margins. Many of the mid-level managers I worked with had been with the organization longer than I had been alive. They greeted me with a great deal of skepticism, but what I lacked in age and experience, I made up for with hard work and intensity. I gained valuable experience in supply chain management and purchasing with IBM Brazil before accepting a transfer to the United States.

Soon after my arrival in America, I set my sights on furthering my education, and I enrolled as an undergraduate at Oklahoma State University. I worked 2-3 jobs at a time while pursuing my degree in computer sciences with a minor in mathematics, all while honing my English skills and adjusting to American culture.

As graduation approached, I began to plan the next phase of my development as a business professional. Armed with the knowledge and experience I had gained at IBM and backed by a degree from OSU, I had little doubt I could land a successful job in the private sector. Nevertheless, I sensed a need to expand my business repertoire and began considering where I might pursue an MBA. Although I considered a number of other programs, I ultimately chose to remain at the Spears School of Business. Familiarity factored into the equation, but more importantly, the MBA program at Oklahoma State offered what I perceived to be the greatest potential return on my investment, delivering a high-quality education at a reasonable cost.

During my time with IBM, I had had the opportunity to work with all but one of our departments: Marketing. Since I viewed my graduate program as a chance to move away from my technical, math-heavy background and broaden my horizons, I elected to emphasize marketing in my MBA coursework. My two years in the program proved to be an excellent opportunity to expand my so-called "soft skills."

Some of my most beneficial experiences and fondest memories as an MBA student occurred as a result of the program's emphasis on group projects. I keenly recall one group project on which all six of our team members were from different countries! My job today relies on a number of remote team members working from several countries to accomplish a common goal, and I can truly say I was prepared to manage them as a result of my experiences at OSU. Several of my professors structured their classes in such a way that it felt like we were operating in a business environment while we were still in school, and this, too, was valuable. Everything I do today I did in some form or fashion during my final semester as an MBA student thanks to comprehensive projects and scenarios like Dr. Dooley's final, a simulation project in which we essentially ran an automotive manufacturer.

Following graduation I worked as a product manager, first for One Light Corporation of Redmond, Washington, and then for RealeStudios of Arvada, Colorado. Both were small, entrepreneurial software companies, and I was actively engaged in product design, development, and marketing, which allowed me to integrate my technical expertise with the business acumen I acquired as part of my MBA.

In April 2004, I accepted a position as an operations analyst with Penloyd, LLC, of Tulsa, Oklahoma, a manufacturing company that had recently been purchased out of bankruptcy by a small group of investors. As part of the turn-around effort, I spearheaded and directed the firm's information technology and research and development efforts, leveraging them to boost the firm's profitability. I was also actively involved with our finance, accounting, and human resources departments. Personnel issues were rampant. Ultimately, we laid off a majority of the 850 employees, rehired most of them, and then trimmed the ranks to 350 in an effort to become a leaner, more efficient organization. After three years we had boosted annual revenues from a mere $15 million to over $85 million. Leading the turnaround at Penloyd was a valuable experience because it required the application of many of the basic business fundamentals I learned as an MBA student at OSU.

Opportunity knocked again in July 2007, and I accepted a position with To-Increase, an independent software vendor (ISV) headquartered in The Netherlands and specializing in enterprise resource planning (ERP). As a senior solutions consultant, I worked one-on-one with potential clients to understand the nature of their business and subsequently develop products uniquely tailored to fit their industry's specific needs. Our products are commonly used to manage sales and engineering processes, projects, and distribution and support channels.

Today, I am the Global Industry Director working with To-Increase's clients and employees all over the world. I retain many of the responsibilities that went with my previous position, but I also manage the sales and consulting personnel for my industry verticals world-wide. Preferring to conduct business in person, I regularly travel to Europe and across the Americas to meet with my clients, superiors, and subordinates. I am constantly striving to further understand the challenges confronting our firm from all angles, and I feel like my efforts have contributed to our organization's success. Our success is reflected by the fact that we have received Microsoft's top award for ISVs in each of the last two years.

In the final analysis, all business boils down to one thing: People. The business I'm in now is a people business. I realized long ago that the math will only take you so far. We can show our clients calculations, and we do, but when it comes down to it, it's an emotional decision—

a gut instinct, really. They are asking themselves, "Do I trust this guy?" We are in a people business. Sometimes it becomes too profit-focused, but I strive each day to remain committed to the strong values and ethics that have led me to where I am today.

I attribute a great deal of my success to the education I received at Oklahoma State, particularly what I learned in the MBA program, but I refuse to rest on my laurels. To that end, I continue to invest in myself by pursuing other educational opportunities such as the Kellogg School of Management's Executive Scholar Program. A mentor doesn't have to be your boss; a mentor just needs to be someone with whom you can exchange ideas. And so I meet other people at Kellogg and learn from them. I encourage young business people and MBA students to continue to invest in themselves following graduation. Salaries and titles can be taken away, but knowledge will take you to the next level. Getting to the top is easy…staying there is the hard part!

Luciano Cunha
Contributed by Holt Tripp

KEY SUCCESS FACTORS: Passion, Values, Investing in Yourself, People

WEBSITE: www.lucianocunha.com; www.to-increase.com

SOCIAL MEDIA: LinkedIn—Luciano Cunha; Twitter—lucianocunha

EDITOR'S NOTES: Luciano resides in Broken Arrow, Oklahoma, with his wife, Terisa, and their two children. He attributes all of his success in business to the love and support of Terisa, who holds a degree in psychology from Oklahoma State. In his spare time, Luciano enjoys spending time with his wife and children and pursuing his passion: Work!

A strong work ethic will take you to places you want to be.

—James Dobson

OVERCOMING THE ODDS

James Dobson—I was born in Stillwater, OK and raised 22 miles down the road in the small town of Coyle. My family owned a small farm outside of town where I was taught to live off the land. I grew up realizing the true meaning of a good work ethic. Though I have a great appreciation for that experience, I concluded that manual labor would not be one of my lifelong goals. I was determined to work hard and climb my way to the life I desired.

Growing up on a farm, joining the local 4-H club was a natural fit. My first taste of success occurred when I received a national 4-H scholarship that gave me the opportunity to start college. I chose to obtain a Bachelor's degree in mathematics, and Oklahoma State University was an obvious choice for me. Aside from the fact that it was so close to my home, my uncle had been the captain of the great Henry Iba's first basketball team in 1933. This connection gave me an opportunity to work for the OSU Athletic Department while attending school.

My job at the athletic department continued after I finished my Bachelor's degree. After being told that I could remain in that position for two more years, I decided to pursue a Master's degree. Since mathematics was the prerequisite to business, the MBA program was an obvious choice. While in the program, I was blessed with the opportunity to be a teaching assistant and shared an office with other graduate assistants. Some of my most fond memories from that period are of times with future professors Dr. Lee Manzer and Dr. Pat Dorr.

My MBA degree first became helpful when I was in the Air Force. After finishing the MBA in 1971, I was sent to Vance Air Force Base in Enid, OK. There, I was enrolled in one year of undergraduate pilot training and then became the pilot of a B-52 Bomber. Because of my MBA degree, I was promoted more quickly than others in the air field.

The opportunities continued after leaving the Air Force. I applied for three civilian jobs, received three interviews, was offered all three positions—and began working for Kerr-McGee Corporation in Oklahoma City. Within five years, I was reporting to the Chief Financial Officer (CFO). Seeing the control and responsibility offered by that position, I was determined to become a CFO some day and decided that becoming a Certified Public Accountant (CPA) would be a necessary stepping stone in reaching that goal faster. So I attended night classes for four years.

After several years of climbing upwards, I experienced the toughest time in my life. It began when the founder of Kerr-McGee passed away and the CFO of the company retired. Dean McGee, the founder, was one of my sponsors as I worked my way up through the organization. Marvin Hambrick, the CFO, was my closest mentor, as I worked closely with him in the financial sector of the business. Marvin taught me the ins and outs of the financial world because of the potential that he saw in me.

Around this time the company decided to "streamline" operations through a labor reduction. Since neither of the men who knew me best was working any longer, my work and impact on the company seemed to go unnoticed and I was left without a job. This example should serve as proof to anyone of how important a mentor is on a person's career path.

Though times seemed gloomy, I realized that I would have to perse-vere to reach my goal of one day being a CFO. Little did I know that a year later I would receive an offer from Bauer Audio Visual in Dallas to serve as their CFO. Losing what I thought was a secure job gave me the opportunity to jump to the position that I desired. Although Bauer was a much smaller company, it offered a chance for me to gain expe-rience and grow as a leader in the CFO position.

After much experience at the top of a few small and mid-sized corpo-rations, I now serve as Vice President and CFO of Explorer Pipeline in Tulsa, OK. Explorer is a major interstate pipeline company which oper-ates a 1,900-mile petroleum pipeline system that runs from the Gulf Coast to Chicago. This is the job I always dreamed of. I have the responsibility and control to make this organization run as smoothly as possible even during tough economic times. I plan to continue working in this position for a few more years. Furthermore, I currently serve as an adjunct professor of Finance for a night class at a nearby university. This experience is proving to be one I enjoy, and I look forward to pursuing teaching as a position in my future.

People sometimes ask me what internal struggles I have faced during the pursuit of my career goals. I am an introvert. Many times I have had to force myself to be more outgoing. Working definitely appeals to me more than attending social events. With that said, I do take time to serve and give back to my community. For example, I serve on the board for Youth Services of Tulsa and am chairman of the finance committee. Also, Explorer Pipeline supports the local United Way and is very charitable in the Tulsa community.

My small farm roots have now flourished into something that is more fruitful. I just needed nourishment along the way, and the MBA program at Oklahoma State definitely was that. Along the way, I have realized the importance of good friends, solid connections, and honest mentors. I have been able to fulfill my life's desires and am so thankful for the blessings received. My strong work ethic stuck with me even after I left the family farm, and with perseverance, I continue to climb to the places I want to be.

James Dobson
Contributed by Michael Vance

KEY SUCCESS FACTORS: Honesty, Integrity, Hard Work. Do the Right Thing, Never Talk Bad about Your Employer, Always Value the Importance of Mentors and Sponsors

WEBSITE: www.expl.com

SOCIAL MEDIA: Facebook—James Dobson; LinkedIn—James Dobson

EDITOR'S NOTES: James Dobson is a former airman of the United States Air Force. He now holds his dream job as Vice President and CFO of Explorer Pipeline. James resides in Tulsa, Oklahoma with his family, who is very dear to him. In his spare time, he enjoys hunting, fishing, snow skiing, and shooting sporting clays. He strongly believes in giving back to his community. He serves on a board for Goodwill and through his company, participates in charities such as the United Way.

Leadership is the capacity to translate vision into reality.

—Warren G. Bennis

YOU NEVER KNOW WHERE YOU'LL END UP

Timothy Dooley—It's been a long, hot, midsummer's day. Your east-bound road trip has taken you through plains, swamps, and forests. As the sun sets, you find yourself on a long and lonely highway some-where among the cotton fields between Alabama and Georgia. The long day has taken its toll on your resilience, particularly that of your stomach. Eying a Wendy's, you swerve across two lanes of traffic to grab your favorite Spicy Chicken Club sandwich. You secretly shiver with delight as your mouth begins to water.

Does this sound familiar? If you've experienced a similar situation in the southeastern US or on the west coast, chances are you've eaten my chicken. My name is Timothy Dooley and I am Vice President of Engineering at O.K. Industries of Fort Smith, Arkansas. An umbrella organization, I hold the same position for each of several divisions, including O.K. Foods, O.K. Farms, and O.K. Transportation; I'm also the Executive Vice President of Ecology Management, Inc. We are the 10th largest poultry supplier in the United States, processing 3,000,000 birds each week and providing jobs for over 4,000 people across the country. I am responsible for many areas of the company including engineering project design and management, all environmental matters, wastewater management, protein recovery operations, risk management, governmental relations, and utility matters. As a member of the board of directors and the executive committee, I consider myself among the top seven executives and regularly confront decisions that impact animal, human, and environmental wellbeing.

Though I humbly acknowledge that the opportunities and benefits that accompany my position are significant, looking back on my career, I recognize that it has not always been a smooth ascent to the top.

As I approached my senior year as a chemical engineering undergraduate and hopeful MBA student at OSU, the career opportunities abounded. Anxious to ply my trade in the real world, I decided to forego my MBA degree, despite the 33 hours of prerequisites I had amassed, and upon graduating took a position at Williams Brothers Engineering. It was an exciting job: I was a member of a large consulting firm which took me all over the globe, most notably, Libya. In fact, we began our project in the midst of the now infamous 1981 Gulf of Sidra incident in which US planes shot down two Libyan aircraft in return fire over their own waters. Though we were working in the desert and so escaped much of the anti-US hostility rampant in the cities, the actions by the military leader Muammar al-Gaddafi prompted then-President Ronald Reagan to deem him the "mad dog of the Middle East." By December of that year, US passports were invalidated for Libyan travel, calling all US personnel out of the country…including our team. Three weeks after returning home, exhilarated by the challenges and successes of our project, I was laid off.

The economy is cyclical. The environment in the early 1980s was similar to that of today—high-level jobs are few and qualified college graduates are many. Williams Brothers was in a severe economic pinch, and two-thirds of my colleagues in the consulting firm had to be let go. This was an emotionally challenging time for me, as I was confident in my abilities, had produced quality results, and had just purchased my first home. Rather than succumb to these pressures and settle for something less, I decided to make lemonade of lemons and went back for my MBA.

It's important to remember that some things happen for a reason, and were it not for the MBA program, I would never have met my wife, Satina, who received her BA degree in business at OSU and later received her Master's in Education. Because of all the courses I'd taken in my undergraduate career, I only needed one year to complete my degree. Yet in that single year I had some great experiences. Most notably, as an MBA graduate assistant for the Office of Academic Research, I worked to develop a quarterly reporting system using the first personal computer ever on OSU's campus. Prior to that we worked on the campus computer, which took up the whole room and required me to feed it thousands of paper cards in order for it to analyze data. So the opportunity to do basic programming on such a small computer was like using Star Wars technology. Needless to say, we've come a long way since then.

Thanks to the formalized, advanced business training that my OSU MBA provided, I had a unique skill set. Combining the MBA with my undergraduate and professional experiences made me an ideal fit for several large corporations, and upon graduation I took a position in the financial division of Kansas City Power and Light. While there, I was fortunate to receive a very broad-based business perspective through the application of both engineering and business techniques I had learned at OSU, while creating and maintaining a corporate financial modeling system for use in long-range planning and budgeting.

They say that the one thing constant in life is change. As an aspiring chemical engineering student in high school, were you to have told me that I would spend most of my professional career working to produce better chicken, I would have thought you were crazy. But life does throw us these curve balls. When my wife and I tired of the commotion of Kansas City and desired to move closer to our Oklahoma roots, I applied for jobs in an unconventional way: I made cold calls. Though the success rate from using this technique is typically dismal, I soon got a reply from O.K. Foods, Inc. requesting an interview. I was so shocked and excited that I realized I had neglected to research what exactly O.K. Foods did, though the stationary did have a blue and red seal guarded by two toy soldiers. Maybe it was a toy company? I'm embarrassed to say that I had to make inquiries of the corporate secretary as to the company's product and the significance of the toy soldiers in the logo (which represents our motto "Quality Guarded," not toy-making) before my interview began. Despite my inauspicious start, the company created a unique position to make the best use of my abilities: Corporate Engineer. Looking back on it, my unique experiences, coupled with my MBA training, opened the door for this career.

I have been fortunate to have had senior members take an interest in me and believe in what I was trying to accomplish. Mr. Lou Rasmussen at Kansas City Power and Light and Mr. Collier Wenderoth, Jr. at O.K. Industries were such individuals. They helped further my technical and leadership abilities. To this day, I remain truly grateful to these individuals for their guidance and interest in me. In fact, their efforts have made such an indelible impression that today I strive to do the same for promising youth in my company, with the hope that they will continue this mentorship tradition in a cycle of continuous giving.

Apart from my professional pursuits, I am an avid bowler and have been involved in the sport since my undergraduate days, participating on the OSU Varsity team. I believe that the same principles that have brought me success in the business world have also brought me great success in the sport of bowling. I am proud to be a member of the Professional Bowlers Association and to have had many successes at both amateur and professional levels. Though I like to play, I have also served on the boards of several local, state, and national bowling associations. I even met my wife in the sport of bowling—on the OSU Varsity squad. In addition to her high school teaching responsibilities, she is the bowling coach—and from time to time I enjoy coaching as her assistant. Aside from bowling, I believe that communities need strong leaders and as a result, I have chosen to devote my time and resources to Leadership Fort Smith, an organization that targets 20 promising individuals annually and develops their leadership skills through an intensive, year-long program.

To offer advice to you who will one day shape the world, above all I believe that success comes from one's integrity, concentration, and ability to manage stress. As Alan Simpson once said, "If you have integrity, nothing else matters. If you don't have integrity, nothing else matters." When the inevitable problems arise, trusting those around you is critical, and I strive to serve as a model for this at O.K. Industries. At the same time, success does not come without hard work. Thus the ability to focus all of one's efforts in order to see a goal through to its fruition is equally important to taking steps forward as an individual and a company. Finally, to achieve balance in one's life and achieve maximum productivity, I believe that work needs to be left at work. I can say for sure that my wife appreciates this last one.

I look forward to the many challenges that will come with my work and anticipate many more productive years at O.K. Industries.

Timothy Dooley
Contributed by Kip Kelley

KEY SUCCESS FACTORS: Integrity, Concentration, Stress Management

WEBSITE: www.okfoods.com

SOCIAL MEDIA: Facebook—Tim Dooley; LinkedIn—Tim Dooley

EDITOR'S NOTES: Mr. Dooley is the Vice President of Engineering at O.K. Industries. He lives in Fort Smith, Arkansas with his wife, Satina, who also graduated from OSU. Tim is an avid bowler and is very involved in his community. Aside from his wife, numerous family members have also graduated from OSU. Both of his brothers, his father, and several in-laws attended OSU. In addition, his step-father has an OSU MBA from the early years and also played on the football team in the 1950's. The Dooley family enjoys giving him a hard time for playing in the "leather helmet" days.

Value the impact you have on your community and those around you.

—Lana Ivy

NONPROFIT:
A NON-TYPICAL CAREER PATH

Lana Ivy—I was born and raised in Eastern Arkansas in a small town of about 15,000 people. Although I did not work on the farm as a child, we lived in a rice farm area where hard work was instilled in my four sisters and me from an early age. The small-town roots and my large family gave me a solid foundation on which to grow. Early on I learned the importance of compromise, hard work, and contributing back to the community. These qualities have served me well and have played an integral part in my career over the past twenty-six years.

I first traveled to OSU in 1978 to pursue an undergraduate degree in management. My undergraduate instructors were very motivational and encouraged pursuing an MBA after graduation. After deliberating on my options, starting the MBA program in the College of Business (later renamed the Spears School of Business) seemed like the best choice. A poor job market in 1982 and the fact that my husband was working at OSU at the time also factored into my decision. The MBA program offered a strong faculty committed to the students. Many of the courses were team oriented, which gave me the opportunity to hone my interpersonal skills while collaborating on team projects. The program was challenging, yet rewarding, and the devoted faculty members made the experience enjoyable.

Since graduation from the MBA program in 1984, my career has followed a somewhat different path than that of a standard MBA graduate. My work has been exclusively in the nonprofit sector with an emphasis in development. Money is not the be-all and end-all for me; rather I am interested in giving back and having an impact on the community around me.

Upon graduating, I started work at Oklahoma State University for the College of Business in the Business Extension office. While there, I was in charge of marketing professional development to the local community. This gave me the opportunity to grow roots into the community and put to use the interpersonal skills I obtained during my graduate degree. After two years in the office, I started work for the OSU Foundation where my main job was to raise private funds. I began networking with OSU alumni and learned how to develop relationships with potential donors. My work for the OSU Foundation was where I got my start in the development profession and learned the basic skill sets which would carry me through the rest of my career.

Since leaving OSU I have worked for several nonprofit organizations, and to each new position, I brought a specialization in development. A development career is comprehensive in that it includes the areas of management, board development, strategic planning, marketing, fundraising, and public relations. After leaving the OSU Foundation, I worked for the University of Oklahoma Health Sciences Center in Oklahoma City and from there, I moved to the National Cowboy & Western Heritage Museum. While at the Cowboy Museum, I started a planned giving program with the donors to help sustain a more steady flow of contributions. When I took a position with the Oklahoma Zoological Society as the Executive Director with a staff to manage, I was able to put into practice concepts learned during the MBA program at OSU. This position allowed me to exercise leadership and management skill sets that had not been previously applicable.

In my current position as Vice President of Development at the Dean McGee Eye Institute, I have the opportunity to work with patient care, vision research, and education, all areas that are extremely important to me and the community. I am responsible for working with the board, community partners, donors, and our physicians to increase the level of support for DMEI. This includes fundraising for a capital campaign, an endowment fund, and various programs such as indigent care, education, patient care, research, and special projects. Additionally, I provide oversight and direction for the development and community relations departments. DMEI is a nonprofit institution and giving back is part of our mission statement. We do not turn down any patient because of an inability to pay for services. We have established a partnership with Harding Charter Preparatory High School in Oklahoma City to offer eye screenings and follow-up appointments for disadvantaged students. We offer these patients glasses if needed and for those cases where surgery is required, we provide that as well. We make available free glaucoma screenings in Oklahoma City and are actively involved in local health fairs.

Throughout my career I have grown personally and professionally, but this growth has not come without setbacks. The event that had the largest impact in my life was when my son was diagnosed with Type 1 diabetes at age 11. There was a significant change in my family dynamic, and the diagnosis did limit possibilities on the career horizon. Even with this realization, however, I feel I have been able to find opportunities to give back to the community and make an impact on those around me. I have sought to become a mentor in my field, especially to young women starting in development. Having a mentor was very important for me when I started in the 1980's. Even though women in development were scarce, the male mentors I had were extremely inspiring and helped me become the professional I am today.

Along the way I have had the opportunity to meet some amazing individuals. The most inspiring have been many of the donors I have developed relationships with over the past 26 years. Building relationships is extremely important in development, so the teamwork and interpersonal interaction that I experienced during the MBA program have been very beneficial. Sincerity is a must when it comes to building lasting relationships and will make a difference in your success, especially in the development profession.

Many may wonder how well the MBA program prepared me for work in the nonprofit sector. In overall structure, a nonprofit is similar to traditional organizations, with the main difference being in how individuals are developed: a lot of the focus is on mentorship and professional development, while pedigree and level of education take a secondary role. Although the end-goal is different, the nonprofit sector needs MBA graduates to work in and manage their organizations. Many nonprofits are starting to recognize the benefits of an MBA and now, more than ever before, MBA graduates are in demand.

What does my future hold? No matter where I end up, I definitely want to stay active in nonprofit organizations. I think I would like to work overseas before I retire, so I may have to leave the great state of Oklahoma before too long. Social justice issues interest me, so I may look at opportunities in that field next. Like I said, money is not a be-all end-all for me; the impact I have on the community and those around me is what I value. As long as I'm working towards accomplishing that, I will be in the right place.

Lana Ivy
Contributed by Branden Felker

KEY SUCCESS FACTORS: Integrity, Perseverance, Networking, Work Ethic, Sincerity

WEBSITE: www.dmei.org

EDITOR'S NOTES: Ms. Ivy has been extremely successful in the nonprofit arena in terms of securing management positions, earning awards, and most importantly, having a tremendous impact on the community. In addition to DMEI receiving the 2010 George Kaiser Family Foundation Award at the Oklahoma Nonprofit Excellent Awards, Lana has received several individual accolades:

- Graduate, Leadership Oklahoma City, Class XXII, 2004

- Organizational award for best Newsletter, *ZooSounds*, Society of Professional Journalists, Oklahoma Chapter, PR category, 2003

- Awarded the *Silver Level Achievement Award for Outstanding Performance*, National Cowboy Hall of Fame Walk to Cure Diabetes Team, June, 2000

- Awarded the *"OU Fundraising Achievement Award"* for 1996-97, selected and given by the Vice President for Development, University of Oklahoma

- Received *"Special Award"* for Success in Fundraising by the Council for Advancement and Support of Education (CASE) Southwest District IV, 1989

As mentioned, Lana is very dedicated and involved in the Oklahoma City Community. The following is a list of activities she participates in:

- Rotary Club 29 (Downtown) OKC—since 2001, serves on various committees and as a mentor

- Leadership Oklahoma City Alumni organization—member and serves as a mentor

- OKC Youth Leadership Exchange—board member and officer; served as a mentor and treasurer

- LOYAL Oklahoma City—young professional group; serves as a mentor

- Association of Fundraising Professionals—board member and serves on various committees

- Oklahoma Center for Nonprofits—serves on the Alliance Networking committee

- Oklahoma City Public Schools Foundation—serves on the scholarship committee

- Juvenile Diabetes Research Foundation, Central Oklahoma chapter—past volunteer

- Beta Gamma Sigma (National Business Honor Society)

- Oklahoma State University Alumni Association—life member

Ms. Ivy has one son, Andrew, who is 22 and a senior at Southwestern University in Georgetown, Texas. Her interests include reading, traveling, exercising, dancing, listening to music, watching sports, volunteering for good causes, growing in her faith, and spending time with her dogs, family, and friends. She enjoys traveling, both for personal and professional reasons. She likes history and learning about different cultures. She has traveled extensively in the U.S. and abroad, including England, Scotland, Mexico, Africa, Russia, Poland, Denmark, Norway, Sweden, Finland, Iceland, and Estonia. Currently, the top of her "bucket list" includes visiting Israel and Italy.

Expand your borders and learn from every experience, both good and bad. You will have opportunities you never expected and you will prosper both personally and professionally.

—Toby Joplin

FROM SETBACKS TO SUCCESS

Toby Joplin—I grew up in the small town of Owasso, Oklahoma, with my parents and my brother. My childhood was a lot like a movie you may have seen, *The Sandlot.* I did the normal things like school and chores, but whenever possible, my friends and I would play baseball and basketball as much as we could. My parents were my role models and instilled in me the belief that I could accomplish anything I set my mind to. That underlying belief has guided me throughout my life and kept me focused, whether I was experiencing frustrating setbacks or amazing success. But no matter the circumstances, I have been blessed with a good life and great family and wouldn't change any of my experiences for the world.

I was the first one in my family to attend college, which was a struggle since I had no role models to learn from and no one to pay for it. I worked hard and paid for my education by managing a pizza restaurant, which gave me my first taste of the business world. I was good at math so guess what I majored in? That's right—accounting. After graduation I started working for a retail chain called OTASCO. Life was good for a couple of years and things were starting to happen. I had just purchased my first home and my wife was pregnant with our first child when the bottom fell out. OTASCO filed for bankruptcy and suddenly my world was thrown into disarray. It was a very stressful time, but a time that also allowed tremendous growth for me both personally and professionally. I came out of the ordeal intact and after working for several more years, I decided to round out my accounting degree and get my MBA from OSU. I did most of my work through OSU-Tulsa and enjoyed every second of it. The faculty was top notch and I enjoyed working and struggling with other students to achieve our goals. After graduating with my MBA, I worked for a small software company and experienced yet another setback. The company was sold to Intuit and in order to keep employment with them, I would be required to move to Texas or California. I wasn't excited about moving my family around, so I didn't take the offer. After working elsewhere for a bit, I finally decided to go back to Intuit; it turned out to be one of the best decisions I ever made.

At Intuit, I started as a Senior Product Manager and was responsible for a particular software product. This job allowed me to use my MBA in a variety of ways including marketing, management, and information systems, and to interact with subject matter experts in those areas to accomplish my work. While at Intuit I was tasked with creating a website where people could have their tax questions answered, and that is how TaxAlmanac was born.

TaxAlmanac is a website along the same lines as Wikipedia in that it is a user contribution system where people can go to get answers to their tax questions. Initially I was given 30 days to develop a site like this, and while the task was daunting, my team and I finished in around 33 days. The website was such a success that I was interviewed by *Time* magazine; and *Business Week* called it one of the Top 50 Uses of the web in 2005. It was also written up by *Forbes*, the Stanford University Graduate School, and the *Harvard Business Review*. Obviously I was very pleased with my decision to join Intuit and was on cloud nine! Despite all the success and accolades though, things were changing in my life and I was about to make a very difficult decision. I left Intuit and my somewhat celebrity status and did what was best for my family— moved back to Oklahoma.

I took a job as CFO of Impact Productions, a small film production company that makes Christian and family values films. This challenge was one that took me out of my element but also allowed me to pursue something I felt very strongly about: family-friendly movies. Despite helping with the production and marketing of one successful theatrical film, *One Night With The King,* which starred Omar Sharif and Peter O'Toole, an unsuccessful venture with the Weinstein Company led to the business struggling and I had to do something I hope to never have to do again: fire myself. The company didn't need me and couldn't afford me, so in the best interest of the company I walked away and into the position where I am currently: Vice President and CFO of R.L. Hudson & Company.

I arrived at R.L. Hudson in 2008 with a hope of better things to come and looking forward to a new challenge. Then—surprise—the economic downturn came along! Almost immediately I was thrust into a situation where the very existence of the company depended on our ability to restructure and become profitable again. Talk about "out of the frying pan and into the fire"! Fortunately we were able to consolidate some of our facilities around the world and renegotiate leases and lines of credit to keep the company solvent. I am proud to say that 2010 may be our most profitable and successful year in the past 10! I am very happy with my current position and can easily see myself continuing to work towards expanding the success of R.L Hudson.

As I look forward to the next 10-15 years and what challenges it holds, I am excited. I am contemplating getting my PhD and at some point would like to scratch a lifelong itch of teaching and giving something back. I have always gained great satisfaction from seeing employees prosper and become successful, and I think teaching would just be an extension of that experience. If it never happens, I am ok with that, but it is definitely something on my "bucket list."

As I look back, I realize that I have learned a lot over my lifetime and some things were key to my success. Hard work, determination, and the ability to deal with setbacks have helped me achieve the success and become the person that I am today. I encourage all new graduates, both undergrads and those with advanced degrees, to keep a broad perspective and be open to different opportunities. I never wanted to be thought of as "just an accountant," and if you expand your borders and learn from every experience, both good and bad, you will have opportunities you never expected and you will prosper both personally and professionally.

Toby Joplin
Contributed by Matthew Gorsuch

KEY SUCCESS FACTORS: Surrounding Myself with Talented People, Working to Solve Other People's Problems, Not Being Afraid to Start Over

WEBSITE: www.RLHudson.com

SOCIAL MEDIA: Facebook—Toby Joplin; LinkedIn—Toby Joplin; Twitter—SmokeyOkie

EDITOR'S NOTES: Toby Joplin, CPA, has been successfully helping organizations with strategic and financial plans for over twenty years. He is the Vice President and CFO of a $30 million dollar company serving many of the largest and most well-known companies around the world. Toby has his BS and MBA from Oklahoma State University and is certified to practice public accounting in Oklahoma. He serves on the Advisory Board for the Oklahoma State University School of Accounting and the board of directors for Impact Productions. He also volunteers, teaching individuals and organizations about finances and business through Financial Peace University, Crown Financial Ministries, and Business by the Book curricula. He is married to his wife of 30 years and has two grown children. In his spare time, he enjoys distance running, cycling, reading, and attending sporting events.

Deflect as much praise as you can to others on your team when things are going good, and take responsibility when improvements are needed.

—John Killam

VICE PRESIDENT OF EVERYTHING!

John Killam—When I was a senior at Putnam City High School, I had a younger girlfriend. She was the studious type and without knowing it, she inspired me to reevaluate my own study habits. That year I earned a 4.0 GPA for the first time in my life and was actually excited about the possibility of attending college. I decided to go to college at Central State University so that I would be close to my girlfriend. It turned out to be one of the better life decisions that I ever made, even though we broke up before that fall term even began. Not only was I having the time of my life, I was in a place that had me excited to learn. After that first year, I knew that I wanted to continue my education— and during a trip to Stillwater realized where I wanted to continue. It was 1976, and I found myself at *Streakers Night* (the Thursday night before Spring Break when people ran naked up and down the Strip in Stillwater); I was soon convinced that Stillwater was the college town for me. That summer I transferred to Oklahoma State University and a few very short years later graduated with my undergraduate degree in accounting.

My success as a student changed my aspirations considerably. At OSU I had the chance to meet and interact with businessmen and entrepreneurs who were willing to share their knowledge and offer advice. Having the drive to be the first in my direct family to graduate from college, get an MBA, and ultimately a CPA, I realized that I had the tools to find success in business.

I wanted to continue my education after my undergraduate degree but wasn't quite sure of the program that would fit me best. Although I enjoyed accounting, I hated the perception that accountants were all stuffy professionals who lived boring lives and spent 8 hours a day in cubicles. I simply wasn't sure that having a Master's in Accounting would give me the tools to do what I wanted to do as a professional. I decided that an MBA would provide a broader curriculum and the foundation I would need to attain my professional goals. After an extremely productive meeting with Dr. Manzer (the head of the MBA program at that time), I was convinced that the MBA program at OSU would be a good fit for me.

When I graduated in 1981, the economy in Oklahoma was about to see a big change with the demise of the S&L industry and the crash in oil and gas prices. It took me 5 months to get my first job—as a Financial Analyst at Getty Oil Company in Oklahoma City. I was extremely well prepared for the responsibilities, which focused on budgeting, variances, and evaluating new exploratory wells. After a year and a half, I was promoted to a Senior Financial Analyst position at Getty's Division Office in Tulsa, OK. Getty was purchased by Texaco in 1985 and I was asked to move to Denver—with no possibility of a raise and the distinct possibility of not having a job after 2 years. I took the severance and started considering my next move.

When I first started hanging out at Eskimo Joe's, I really liked the service philosophy the employees always had—be friendly, make customers happy, and show everyone a good time—which was in complete contrast to what I thought an accountant would be doing, and I envied those who were having so much fun in their jobs. Stan Clark and I were good friends and I had been a sounding board for him for several years. When I was at Getty, Stan and I used our finance department's financial software to create *pro forma* statements for him to get financing for a new restaurant concept, Stillwater Bay Oyster Company. This concept was very exciting to me—actually making a difference in a business. Working with Stan in such a high energy environment could really jazz a guy up. Several months after Stan opened Stillwater Bay Oyster Company, I was in Stillwater trying to figure out what to do with my life, when Stan asked me to work for him.

I had been reviewing Stan's financial statements for about a year and I told him that although I wasn't making a lot, he couldn't afford me. He said he couldn't afford not to hire me. So I became the first administrative employee Stan hired. At that time, I had no idea how great a decision I'd just made.

I'm currently the Vice President of Everything for Stan Clark Companies (we have several corporations, thus the VP of Everything) in Stillwater, Oklahoma. I participate with our overall corporate governance, emphasize management of our retail clothing business, and provide needed support for our other operations. I'm not a big "title" person, and being part of a small business has given me the luxury to create my own job titles. Other than the positions I held with Getty, I've been a Business Manager and Vice President of Everything!

My association with Stan Clark has done more to mold me than anything else. I have never met someone so positive in everything he does. I came from a very demanding family, where positive words were rarely spoken. When I met Stan, I couldn't believe his ability to cut through the drama of an event and positively work towards a good outcome. It's extremely unusual to see him upset about something, and if it does occur, it's for a very short time. Stan likes to call this positive feeling "being energetic in everything you do."

The most difficult transition I had to make at Stan Clark Companies was going from a "doer" to a manager. When employees first started coming to me for help with issues, I was too busy doing my work to give them the attention they deserved. It took me several months to figure out they *were* my work and that helping them was the most important job I would have.

Giving back to the community is one key principle at Stan Clark Companies. Everyone in management is required to be active in our communities—we are blessed to serve great people and it is imperative to not only be a part of improving the lives of those we serve, but being leaders in the movement. Our company is the title sponsor of the two biggest United Way fundraisers in Stillwater (Juke Joint Jog and the Three Amigos Golf Classic), and we are big contributors to the marketing efforts of numerous causes (Special Olympics, Susan Komen Foundation, OSU College of Education, and Stillwater Public Education Foundation, along with the athletic department at OSU).

My career plans are to continue to keep the Eskimo Joe's family of businesses relevant to our customers. We have an unbelievable culture and reputation, and it is a great responsibility to advance our reputation in the face of challenges from the economy, competition, and a lackadaisical attitude of "we've made it." We will never be where we want to be; we must make continuous improvements to succeed.

As cliché as it may sound, always do the best you can and realize only you can choose the attitude you will have through the journey of life. Blaming others for your inadequacies is a huge mistake—no learning happens when we don't take responsibility for our own actions and results. I have strived to live by and teach my children the following principles.

1. Honesty and integrity are the basic elements needed for any relationship—whether it's personal or professional. I need to know that you mean what you say and that you'll do what's right when nobody else is looking. If we don't have this, we can't work together.

2. A good work ethic is critical to leading any group. If you aren't willing to pull your weight, others will eventually stop following you. Having a good work ethic is part of being energetic in everything you do—people notice folks with energy, especially positive energy, and will be drawn to follow them.

3. Continue your education because professions and management theories are evolving constantly. By taking seminars and reading, you can stay current with new trends and ways to improve your business.

4. Show humility in your success, as you will only be as successful as those around you. Deflect as much praise as you can to others on your team when things are going good, and take responsibility when improvements are needed.

John Killam
Contributed by Annie B. Hedges

KEY SUCCESS FACTORS: Integrity, Work Ethic, Education, Humility

WEBSITE: www.eskimojoes.com

SOCIAL MEDIA: Facebook—Eskimo Joe's

EDITOR'S NOTES: John lives in Stillwater, Oklahoma with his family. He is married to Kelli Jones, the girl he met at Eskimo Joe's 23 years ago. He has 3 sons he is very proud of, and he loves watching them grow in their life journeys. John admires his sons for really getting the honesty and integrity idea that is so very important for success. Kelli teaches aerobics, and John enjoys playing golf several times a week. The entire family enjoys watching and supporting OSU sporting events, especially men's basketball. John is also a big believer in the private sector being the stewards of our society. He has been active in the Executive Committees of the Stillwater United Way and the Stillwater Conventions and Visitors Bureau and is currently on the CASA Board and the President of the Pioneer Booster Club.

Without passion, you will never be truly happy with your job and more than likely not be as successful. You have to love what you do in order to do great things.

—Linda Livingstone

LIVING MY DREAM

Linda Livingstone—I was born in Norman, OK but was raised in Perkins, south of Stillwater. My father was a basketball coach for the University of Oklahoma when I was born but later returned to Oklahoma State to coach with Mr. Iba, having played for Mr. Iba on the 1945 National Championship basketball team. Our whole family has always been OSU fans, and my decision to attend OSU was made at a very early age. My parents shaped the person who I am today. My introduction to sports at an early age by my father created a passion that has never left me. My mother was a grade school teacher who thrived on serving others. This is where my affection for education and service was really born.

When I first entered OSU, I planned on going to law school, so naturally I chose an undergraduate degree program that would line up well with that. I was told that economics would be a good starting point for a law degree. But soon after enrolling, I realized something just didn't feel right about the law school path I was following. I was really enjoying my business classes, and my passion for athletics was as strong as ever. It was then that I started thinking with my heart. I wanted to do something that I would love to do day in and day out; therefore, I decided that I wanted to become an Athletic Administrator, and a business degree seemed to be the ideal path. After just 3 ½ years, I graduated from OSU with a double major in economics and management.

Even though I graduated early, I was still playing basketball for OSU. I could have taken additional undergraduate classes to stay eligible, but I wanted to use the time I had more fruitfully. I took the unconventional route to an MBA and enrolled just 3 ½ years after I started my undergraduate degree. My years as an MBA student at OSU ultimately led me to the position that I hold today. It was during my MBA that a professor, Dr. John Mowen, planted the seed for obtaining my

PhD and educating others. He was both a very demanding Consumer Behavior professor and an extremely helpful mentor. I also worked very closely with another mentor, Dr. Steve Miller. He and I worked on a marketing research study focused on opening a campus in Tulsa, OK. This campus is now thriving.

In 1983, I graduated from the MBA program and married Brad Livingstone, who also played basketball at OSU. Shortly after graduation, I became the director of the recreation program, Kids Inc., in Woodward, Oklahoma. This position was both rich and challenging. Working directly with the city, the organization's board of directors, and hundreds of volunteers provided a challenging and rewarding starting point for my career. This experience also re-ignited the education flame and led me towards the path that I am on today. From Woodward we moved to Enid for a year, where I worked as an administrator in the local hospital. I did not enjoy this position at all and was motivated to get back into the realm of education. I wanted to do something that I loved to do, not something that would result in the best salary or title. So, in 1987 I returned to OSU to obtain my PhD.

Back at OSU, I found two more mentors, Dr. Debra Nelson and Dr. Margaret White. It was Dr. Nelson who suggested I consider Baylor for my first faculty position. She knew me well and thought it would be a great fit. I followed Dr. Nelson's advice, and in the fall of 1991, we moved to Waco, Texas, where I became an Assistant Professor in the Management Department at Baylor University. Here my passion for higher education was confirmed, and I loved every minute of my experience at Baylor. I was at Baylor for 11 years, the last four as the Associate Dean for Graduate Programs at the Hankamer School of Business. In 2002, I was fortunate enough to receive an offer from Pepperdine University to become the first female dean of the Graziado School of Business. This is the position that I hold today, and it really is my dream job.

Looking back on my own career, I can honestly say that there are four key factors to a successful and rewarding career.

1. Passion—Without passion, you will never be truly happy with your job and more than likely not be as successful. You have to love what you do in order to do great things. This may not

be the highest paying job you are qualified for, but if you are happy doing what you do, your career will flourish and you will have no regrets.

2. Integrity—This is most crucial. You must act with a sense of integrity to be successful. Nobody is perfect, but it is that striving to always act with a sense of integrity that can be admired and contagious.

3. Humility—You must take a humble approach to everything that you do. There is nothing wrong with being successful; just don't let yourself get caught up in your own hype.

4. Courage—This goes hand in hand with integrity. Without courage, integrity does not have the impact it should. You have to have the courage to make those tough decisions when you know they are right.

Take advantage of opportunities when they present themselves. These may be projects that are outside of your traditional role, or just networking opportunities. It will make you a better-rounded person and more well known. Plus, you never know where such opportunities will lead you. Also, having mentors is a must. Having multiple mentors, not just one, is vital to being successful. With a handful of mentors, you get the knowledge and experience from different viewpoints and you have the luxury of picking and choosing what works best for you. You also become a great mentor yourself and can pass on all the knowledge you have learned to the next generation.

Here at Pepperdine I am doing what I have dreamed of doing since college, and I couldn't be happier. Someday I might like to be a Provost or President, but until then I am happy being where I have always wanted to be.

Linda Livingstone
Contributed by Jacob Lusson

KEY SUCCESS FACTORS: Passion, Integrity, Humility, Courage

WEBSITE: www.bschool.pepperdine.edu

SOCIAL MEDIA: Facebook—pepperdine

EDITOR'S NOTES: Dr. Livingstone worked for over a decade at Baylor University and served as Associate Dean for Graduate Programs at the Hankamer School of Business for 4 years. She currently serves as Dean of the Graziado School of Business at Pepperdine University, the first female to ever hold this position. In 2009, Dr. Livingstone was elected to the Board of Directors of AACSB International, the association responsible for accrediting business schools. She has also served on the Board of Directors for the Graduate Management Admission Council. Dr. Livingstone was awarded the IABC-LA SUCCESS Award, which is given out each year to an outstanding business leader in the Los Angeles area. Throughout her professional career, Dr. Livingstone has authored multiple business textbooks and has been published in distinguished business journals.

Dr. Livingstone resides in Malibu, California. She and her husband, Brad, have been married for almost 30 years and have a daughter. Dr. Livingstone enjoys spending time with her family whether it's just a day at home or a day in the mountains or at the beach.

Don't let personal conflicts get in the way of good judgment. Build trust in yourself that helps you build your character.

—Matt O'Brien

KEEP KNOCKING ON THE DOOR

Matt O'Brien—I was born in Brooklyn, New York, and raised in St. Louis, Missouri. My dad, Vincent O'Brien, a World War II Navy veteran and father of six children, always encouraged me to reach for my goals and to "keep knocking on the door" of opportunity. This leadership and mentorship that my dad provided for me and my siblings was tremendous. It instilled in me the discipline and yearning for knowledge that I carry with me today.

During my youth in Missouri, I recall what a great team my mom and dad formed for raising six children. My father travelled nearly every week with his job, and my mom provided the weekly guidance, tutoring, and structure for our growing family. Both my mom and dad instilled in all of us a high need for achievement; my three sisters are doctors and PhDs (one attended OSU and one is an OSU PhD graduate) and my two brothers are corporate executives, each at the top of his field. Education and a sense of family were hallmarks of my upbringing.

Upon graduation from high school, I chose to attend the University of Missouri in Columbia to pursue my bachelor's degree in education. Completing my degree in late 1978, I headed west and got as far as Stillwater, where my sisters Pat and Edna lived. A massive December ice storm "extended" my stay in Stillwater, which led to a short career as a substitute teacher in the Stillwater Public Schools. While I love teaching, this did not seem like the right path at the time. Subsequently, I went to work for Bradley Mechanical, Inc., a local Stillwater mechanical contractor, and helped build National Standard, Mercury Marine, and several new constructions and remodels on the OSU campus. Then, the oil boom went bust, Oklahoma hunkered down, and the construction business dried up.

By that time I had met my wife, Debry, a future OSU graduate who at the time was living down the hall from my sister Edna in Murray Hall. University life still appealed to me and a graduate degree was on my list.   I enrolled in Dr. Mike Hitt's graduate level Organizational Behavior class and due to my interest, success in the class, and Mike's encouragement, I went on to the MBA program. Looking back on a 30-year career, this was a point of decision that has made all the difference.   I consider the MBA degree and the OSU program in particular to have played a pivotal role in my life. Recalling my father's reaction to my graduate school plans, I think he said, "Wait until I tell the nuns at St. Elizabeth's (my grade school back in Missouri)!" He was quite proud.

The experiences and relationships established during this time are priceless. I was Dr. Ramesh Sharda's first graduate assistant and from Ramesh learned the discipline of quantitative research. Drs. Mike Hitt and Duane Ireland encouraged me to teach again, and I was allowed to teach two semesters of Introduction to Management. Another highlight was that our team won the Executive Interaction competition in 1981—the business case we presented was on the application of the Phased Lock Loop, a key cell phone technology component, before cell phones! Finally, the experience of writing and defending a rigorous thesis was as difficult as it was liberating. While completing my MBA in late 1982, I recall that in my last semester, a professor mentioned how terrible the economy was for us as Master's degree graduates.   The early 1980's was the second greatest recessionary period since the Great Depression; mortgage interest was 16% and finding a job would be difficult.

My wife and I had a preference to live in Colorado; thus my job search was targeted there using the "internet" of the 80's, the Sunday *Denver Post*! I can still recall the moment I received the phone call offer from Martin Marietta (now Lockheed Martin) Aerospace Systems unit in Colorado. Accepting this job offer and relocating to Colorado was one of the most exciting moments for my wife and me, as our family and my career began to take hold.

After six years of serving in various business positions, I advanced in 1988 to a management role in the independent cost evaluation department for the Information Systems Group in Bethesda, Maryland. Returning to Denver in 1992, I became the Senior Finance Manager for the Ground Systems business area, and in 1997 I was selected as the director of business operations for the Energy and Environmental Sector in Oak Ridge, Tennessee. In 2001, I became the Senior Business Operations Manager in Boulder, Colorado, and remained in that position until 2004, when I was appointed to the position of Director of Independent Cost Evaluation for Lockheed Martin Integrated Systems and Solutions. At the end of 2006, I became the Director of Finance and Business Operations for Lockheed Martin Information Systems and Global Services in Colorado Springs with responsibility for leading all business operations functions for a division with $700M of annual revenue. In 2007 I was named Vice President of Business Operations and CFO of Sandia Corporation, a wholly owned subsidiary of Lockheed Martin Corporation that manages and operates Sandia National Laboratories, a multi-program Department of Energy research and development laboratory with 8500 employees and annual revenues of $2.5B. I am responsible for the leadership and laboratory-wide management of finance, accounting, procurement, property and logistics, business systems and services, pension and savings funds, contracts, work for other federal agencies, and policy management services at Sandia. As a member of Sandia's senior executive leadership team, I hold responsibility for developing and executing financial strategies, building relationships with key customers, cultivating and developing new business, and providing reach-back to Lockheed Martin corporate resources.

My mom and dad have demonstrated leadership to me throughout my life. One way that I lead is through service opportunities. I am currently serving as a board member and treasurer for Leadership New Mexico, a non-profit company dedicated to leadership development in New Mexico, and am a 2009 graduate of the program. I also serve on the Albuquerque Hispano Chamber of Commerce Board of Directors and as advisor to the Corporate Cornerstone Council for United Way. I have previously served as a national vice president and local chapter president of the Society of Cost Estimating and Analysis (SCEA) and am a member of the International Society of Parametric Analysts.

At Sandia, I am the Executive Sponsor for the Sandia National Laboratories American Indian Outreach Committee and serve as the Sandia Campus Executive to Oklahoma State University for Business Operations. Sandia National Laboratories was created by President Truman in 1949 to "Provide exceptional service in the national interest." In addition to our national security service commitment, Sandia takes its local community service responsibility seriously and contributes over $4 million annually to service groups, organizations, and charities in Albuquerque and the New Mexico area; and our employees, through United Way giving, contribute another $4 million as well as 124,000 volunteer hours!

I believe mentoring is critical to the development of leaders today. When possible, I urge companies to not necessarily institutionalize mentoring programs, where funding is required to keep it alive. As leaders, mentoring and coaching are part of our responsibility. I have adopted and encourage the use of "roundtable mentoring," where small groups of leaders at various levels of responsibility meet with a senior leader to discuss leadership and its development and practice. I like and recommend the book *Courage: The Backbone of Leadership* by Gus Lee with Diane Elliott-Lee. The book was given to me by someone who once worked for me with this sage advice: "Sometimes you could use a little more of this." He certainly had courage!

In addition to being a good practical book to read, it has provided me with three guiding principles for my leadership model: Courage, Integrity, and Character. Courage is facing the river of fear and crossing over to address those issues that are uncomfortable and easier left undone. Integrity is acting for what is right, no matter what. Finally, as Gus states in his book, Character is simply "the result of sustained courage and integrity." I have found that keeping these three principles in mind on a daily basis helps me frame what I want to be as a leader. As you can imagine, not every day can be counted as a success, but that's the great thing about life and business: each day you can try again.

It is amazing how life just passes us by so fast. In my career, I have reached—and at some point in your career you will reach—a stage where a personal or professional challenge will seem unsolvable and unrecoverable. I have found that this is not the time to make a drastic change in your course. You have to have the courage to cross that river of fear and maybe then make a change. It might be that this change is for the wrong reason and could bring about unintended consequences. Repair your relationships. Don't let personal conflicts get in the way of good judgment. Build trust in yourself that helps you build your character.

I plan to continue to work at Sandia Corporation. I would like to find an opportunity to serve on the board of directors of a "for profit" organization and possibly in future retirement as an executive director for a non-profit charitable foundation. Finally, I look forward the most to spending more time with my family, including my wife, Debry, my children, Nick and Lauren, their spouses, Amber and Arjun, and my first grandchild, Jamieson.

Matt O'Brien
Contributed by Brian Price

KEY SUCCESS FACTORS: Courage, Integrity, Character, Good Judgment

WEBSITE: www.sandia.gov

EDITOR'S NOTES: Matt O'Brien is the Vice President of Business Operations and CFO of Sandia Corporation. He lives in Littleton, Colorado, with his family, who are his dearest friends. His wife, Debry, has a zoology and medical technology degree from OSU, and his sister, Pat Darlington, has a PhD in Psychology, also from OSU.

Education is not the filling of a pail but the lighting of a fire.

—William Butler Yeats

IT PROFESSOR AND EXECUTIVE: THE BEST OF BOTH WORLDS

Brad Wheeler—My story is one that connects the values of a small-town-Oklahoma education to becoming an advanced technology professor and executive who travels the world. I was born in Weatherford, Oklahoma and was raised not far from there in the small farming community of Hinton. It was in this community of not more than 1,300 where I gained values and a work ethic that would steer my life in many unexpected directions.

Learning to work at an early age on a farm instilled essential skills and confidence. There is a lot to be learned through a good day's labor and I enjoyed the work thoroughly. Certain lessons in life can only be learned through experience. For one, if you are out plowing the field and the tractor stops working, you grab your tools and do all you can to fix the problem and keep going. Out on the farm I learned how to depend on my resourcefulness to complete a task—how to really dive into a problem, take it apart (sometimes literally), and put it back together with a useful solution. To learn early in life the ability to dissect a problem, solve it, and feel the satisfaction of doing so was invaluable.

My family also owned a General Motors car dealership. When I was in 6th grade, I was old enough to start helping out, and this was my first real taste of business. I started out by working in the Parts Department after school and on weekends, and eventually did about every job in the dealership from changing oil and washing cars to ultimately taking on business responsibilities. At the car dealership I learned about managing a brand, inventory, accounting, and working with customers.

It was also at the car dealership where I was introduced to my first computer—a Wang. This was before the first IBM PC and in the days of the hobbyist TRS-80 models. In 9th grade I taught myself to program a Wang computer and wrote a system that saved hours in preparing the weekly payroll. Thus began my fascination with technology, and little did I know that those experiences would lead to a career as a globe-trotting professor and university Chief Information Officer.

When it came time for me to go to college, Oklahoma State University was truly the only consideration. After five visits there for 4-H Roundup workshops, I was very excited to attend OSU even though OU was the hometown favorite. I was the first one in my family to attend one of the state's major universities. However, tragedy struck Oklahoma when I had barely started my sophomore year. Oklahoma plunged into a recession that threatened the livelihoods of many of its citizens. Bank failures rippled through the economy, and my family feared that they might lose everything. I put my education on hold and returned to help the family make it through the recession. This was a period of rapid growing up and lots of responsibility. As the Oklahoma economy imploded after the boom years of expansion, seeing those hard times and the collapse that harmed so many Oklahomans and altered their lives forever left an indelible impression.

A year and a half later, in 1987, I returned to college and obtained a degree in Business Management Information Systems. During my junior and senior year, I started to see the appeal in being a professor as I observed that college towns seem forever young and faculty can often be quite entrepreneurial in their topics of interest. Several professors, notably Drs. Kletke, Meinhart, Nelson, Nord, and White, were influential in sparking that interest.

After graduating I took a job at the Radio Shack Computer Center to pay the bills and to stay in Stillwater with friends. Seven months later I was offered a position as a TA in the MBA program at OSU. There, I met my first graduate mentor. Dr. Ramesh Sharda was an accomplished professor in the MBA program and excellent researcher. He pushed me hard and gave me early experiences in grant-funded research, publication, and doctoral courses.

After becoming a member of the OSU MBA graduate class of 1990, I sought entry to a PhD program and thought it might be at the University of Texas at Austin, but got that disappointing rejection letter. I'd applied to several other programs also and ultimately was accepted at

Indiana University. A few years later I did find special delight in being invited to the University of Texas twice to speak to the faculty and deans regarding advanced uses of IT for university education.

I didn't waste any time at Indiana. I completed the four-year program in 35 months, and had the good fortune to be the first doctoral student of Joe Valacich—a very successful junior professor who was also a farm boy from Montana. I graduated in 1993, just in time to hit another national recession. Prior to 1993, students were literally being chased down the hall by prospective employers with buckets of money. All of those jobs disappeared with the recession, but I was very fortunate to get a good job that year at a research university. It was a good fit for me to teach in the MBA program at the University of Maryland at College Park.

Quite unexpectedly, in 1996, I was invited to return to my doctoral alma mater and jumped at the opportunity to return to Bloomington, Indiana, where I remain to this day. It is a classic college town, much like Stillwater, but somewhat larger with a campus enrollment of 40,000. The remainder of the decade was consumed with research, teaching in a highly competitive MBA program, and eventually earning tenure and promotion to Associate Professor.

My research and teaching launched me into working with companies and teaching executive education programs all over the world. From my days in Hinton, OK, I never imagined teaching on six continents and in over 30 countries. In the busiest years, I'd sometimes travel 35 hours to Singapore to teach for two days and then zoom back.

I was quite happy in my work with MBA students and companies all over the world, but that path changed in 2001 when I was asked to take, on a part-time basis, a university-wide—all eight IU campuses—position as the first Associate Dean for Teaching and Learning IT. I had the great fortune of working for an excellent leader, Dr. Michael McRobbie, who was hired from Australia to be IU's first Vice President for IT and Chief Information Officer (CIO). As he grew in responsibility, he moved me through five different responsibilities in six years including directing IU's highly advanced supercomputing and research systems. Along the way, I co-founded the Sakai and Kuali open source software projects that ultimately grew into over $50M of shared investment among higher ed and commercial firms with a world-wide reach. These systems are dramatically reducing the cost of big systems for universities and have created new models for collaboration. Always the professor, I was also able to publish many articles that proposed how this new ecosystem could work out for open source software for universities.

By 2007, I was promoted to the academic rank of Professor at IU, and in that year Michael McRobbie became IU's 18th President. He appointed me CIO and VP for IT, and I took the helm of IU's $125M IT budget and 1,000-person staff. It has been exciting and challenging as an executive at the forefront of Information Technology for IU's 109,000 students, with an almost $3B budget and IT partnerships that span the performing arts and humanities to the sciences, medicine, and hospitals.

I still find some time to stay engaged with leading international companies through executive education and also work with universities around the world. As I reflect on the journey, I deeply value learning those early skills of hard work and problem solving with great support from my family and important programs like 4-H. OSU provided an excellent foundation through its undergraduate and MBA degrees, and I know my path would have been quite different without the faculty at OSU who provided me with considerable coaching that brought my true passions to light.

Brad Wheeler
Contributed by Anthony Zerwig

KEY SUCCESS FACTORS: Tenacity, Boldness, Vision, Judgment

WEBSITE: http://ovpit.iu.edu/bios/bwheeler.html

SOCIAL MEDIA: LinkedIn—Bradley Wheeler

EDITOR'S NOTES: Dr. Wheeler enjoys keeping his home updated with the latest and best technology on the market. He spends his time traveling as a guest speaker and is an avid tennis player. Dr. Wheeler has been published many times and has received numerous grants, many of which have funded his work in open source software. His work directly led to IU being named "One of the best places to work in IT" for 2010 by *Computerworld*.

DISTINGUISHED OKLAHOMA STATE UNIVERSITY ALUMNI 1961-2011

Congratulations to the following individuals who were nominated among the top distinguished MBA alumni over the past 50 years. Each individual was interviewed by a current MBA student whose name appears after the alumnus interviewed. Congratulations, thank you for your time and thank you for representing OSU as an MBA graduate and successful professional.

Alumni		Student	
Last Name	**First Name**	**Last Name**	**First Name**
Alcock	Jim	Cundiff	Sabrina
Antosh	Jim	Eaton	Andrew
Austin	Stephen	Cooper	Matthew
Berney	Rand	Kenslow	Katy
Biggs	Michael	Killion	Grant
Blades	Barry	Knight	Trey
Boesch	Jason	Lackner	Chris
Bowles	Joseph	Eastman	Seth
Boykin	Bill	Lenaburg	Dirk
Bridwell	Gary	Gagliardi	Max
Bridwell	Nita	Summers	Sarah
Brown	Tom	Sparks	Grant
Burch	Frank	Miller	Nick
Burdick	Kevin	Hull	Kevin
Busby	Chris	Greer	Adam
Bussert	Ronald	Parks	Austin
Cagle	Roger	Pham	Phuong
Caldwell	Steve	Nguyen	Gary
Capps	Mike	Deveny	Mark
Carreker	Jim	Hargis	Alison
Carson	Drew	Ullman	Mathew
Caruthers	Kent	Bogle	Ryan
Cash	Dennis	Tebow	Jillianne
Collingsworth	Samantha	Sequera	Axzel
Coonce	Jennifer	Robin	Scott
Coplin	Donald R.	Allred	Mary Elizabeth
Cormany	Bill	Wear	Lorinda

Alumni		Student	
Last Name	**First Name**	**Last Name**	**First Name**
Courtin	Angela	Syme	Matt
Craig	David	Rokkala	Samuel
Crossland	Ronald	Weaver	Jonathan
Cunha	Luciano	Tripp	Holt
Darnaby	Rick	Stutsman	Misty
De La Cerda	Paul	Rogers	Michael
Denoya	Lee	Sangasoongsong	Jarasporn
Dobson	James	Vance	Michael
Dooley	Tim	Kelley	Kip
Dunbar	Wesley	Venamon	Kyle
Dyer	David	Henry	Jason
Eisner	Julian	Schuyler	Lauren
Ferguson	Roy	Whisler	Brian
Ferree	Larry	Hunget	Danny
Fowler	Bob	Cloud	John
Fox	Sentell	Blackburn	John
Fuhrman	Rebecca	Blanc	Beau
Grizell	Paul	Branstetter	Zach
Groom	Randy	Binkley	Nick
Halberstadt	Johnny	Britton	Terry
Hamm	Bob	Makhamreh	Mazen
Hastings	Scott	Fairchild	Emily
Heidebrecht	James	Corrigan	Sean
Hess	Kyle	Prevender	Alexander
Hitch	Chris	Starks	Jared
Holcombe	Scot	Thomas	Todd
Holder	Mike	Davis	Seth

Alumni		Student	
Last Name	**First Name**	**Last Name**	**First Name**
Hollingsworth	Danielle	Williams	Alexander
Householder	Scott	DeWitt	Beth
Hove	Betty	Dobson	Jay
Howard	Daniel	Duran	Noe
Hromas	Jim	Liotta	Lindsay
Hunter	JR	Engel	Eric
Ivy	Lana	Felker	Branden
Jalivand	Abolhassan	Fletcher	George
Johnson	Shane	Wyckoff	Jonathon
Jones	Craig	French	Dennie
Joplin	Toby	Gorsuch	Matthew
Kaiser	Sharon	Graham	Megan
Kaiser	Jane	Groves	Matthew
Killam	John	Hedges	Annie
Kouplen	Sean	Kennedy	Angela
Kovar	Brian	Suellentrop	Jessica
Kreger	Joe	Kolla	Vamsi
Kuehne	Trip	Koppitz	Blake
List	Robert	Lopez	Daniel
Livingstone	Linda	Lusson	Jacob
Lloyd	Sam	Zumwalt	Jason
Long	Michael	Patry	Edwin
Luffman	Herman	Tyson	Patty
Lumley	Roger	Malone	Elissa
Manzer	Lee	Marsh	Brock
Martin	Kenneth	McConnell	Jason
Mayhew	Kevin	Montag	Chris

Alumni		Student	
Last Name	**First Name**	**Last Name**	**First Name**
McCormick	Bob	Nicholas	Katie
McDonald	James	Noel	Burke
McLaughlin	Ross	Nosler	Becca
Merrill	Mark	O'Conner	Chris
Meyer	Dennis	Jamie	Brown
Mezezi	Monica	Pannone	Alexander
Miller	Stephen	Tiedt	Randy
Nahrgang	Jennifer	Barker	Jerry
Naifeh	Sarah	Phillips	Ashley
O'Brien	Matt	Price	Brian
Oswalt	Hal	Thompson	Erica
Palm	James	Bridendolph	Will
Parsons	Darren	Percosky	Kathy
Patimalla	Pallavi	Machani	Aditya
Patterson	Neal	Rider	Blaine
Polk	Julie	Reed	Casey
Poplin	Bob	Daly	Jennifer
Proctor	Thomas	Noordyke	Jennifer
Rahe	Jim	Williams	Rush
Riner	Jody	Pearce	David
Roberts	Stephen	Wohlgemuth	Jonathan
Ronck	Bryan	Rudd	Jeffrey
Sanderlin	Brian	Mauck	Arles
Sellers	Ronald	Sanchez	Rodrigo
Sewell-Howard	Tiffany	Sapp	Aaron
Simkins	Betty	Schneider	Jennifer
Solheim	Andrew	Scribner	Robyn

Alumni		Student	
Last Name	**First Name**	**Last Name**	**First Name**
Stuart	Jerome	Rogers	Bill
Themig	Dan	Swigonski	Scott
Thill	Howard	Sipos	Eric
Trantham	Nichole	Smith	Tiffany
Van	Nhung	Nguyen	Annie
Wantland	Robin	Pietrus	Maciej
Weathers	Julie	Steed	Karen
Weiberg	Chad	Manison	David
Wheeler	Bradley	Zerwig	Anthony
Whitson	Rod	Dunham	Marc
Wiederholt	Jim	Hamblen	Matt
Wilcha	John	Lahn	Kevin
Wood	Kelly	Evans	Jeremy
Wooley	Leslie	Wood	Mark
Wylie	William	Ballos	Greg
Yee	Bruce	Glaser	Graham
Yemenu	Dag	Ralph	Curt

LAWRENCE A. CROSBY, DEAN

Lawrence Crosby, globally recognized expert on the measurement and management of customer relationships, became Dean and Professor of Marketing for the Spears School of Business at Oklahoma State University, effective May, 2010.

First as an academic and then as a consultant and business leader, Crosby has helped evolve the field of customer relationships from satisfaction to loyalty to the branded experience. Crosby's work has been widely published, and his measures, models, and management principles have been adopted by Fortune 500 companies around the world. Most recently, Crosby served as chief loyalty architect of the Customer Experience Practice at global market research company Synovate Ltd. He founded and served as chairman and CEO of Symmetrics Marketing Corporation, a customer loyalty research and consulting business. He sold Symmetrics to Synovate in 2004.

Crosby earned a doctoral degree in business administration, a Master's of Business Administration and a Bachelor's degree in general studies from the University of Michigan. Before founding Symmetrics, he served as CEO and managing director of CSM Worldwide, an affiliate of Walker Information, and served on the faculty at Arizona State University, the University of Michigan, and the University of Nebraska.

Crosby's appointment also carries with it the titles of Norman & Suzanne Myers Chair for Excellence in Business and Richard W. Poole Professor for Excellence.

JERETTA HORN NORD

Jeretta Horn Nord is a professor, an author, and an entrepreneur. Dr. Nord is a professor in the department of Management Science and Information Systems in the Spears School of Business at Oklahoma State University. She is the Founder and CEO of Entrepreneur Enterprises, LLC, and Founder of *A Cup of Cappuccino for the Entrepreneur's Spirit* book series.

Jeretta has appeared on FOX Business and FOX Strategy Room. She has hosted two radio talk shows titled *Empowering Entrepreneurs* on Passionate Internet Voices Talk Radio and *The Entrepreneurial Mind* on Web Talk Radio and has been a guest on numerous radio shows including CBS Radio.

Nord recently served as a Fulbright Specialists Scholar in Europe and has spent time as a visiting scholar at UCLA and the University of Southern Queensland in Australia. Dr. Nord founded the Oklahoma State University chapter of the Collegiate Entrepreneurs' Organization and recently co-founded the Oklahoma State University chapter of the American Association of University Women (AAUW).

Jeretta conducts research in the areas of technology and entrepreneurship. She has served as the associate dean for the Spears School of Business at Oklahoma State University, and is currently executive editor of *The Journal of Computer Information Systems.*

Dr. Nord was honored in 2008 with a Distinguished Alumnus Award at Southeastern Oklahoma State University. In 2009, she was awarded a Fulbright Senior Specialists Grant by the J. William Fulbright Foreign Scholarship Board (FSB), the Bureau of Education and Cultural Affairs of the Department of State (ECA), and the Council for International Exchange of Scholars (CIES).

Jeretta was awarded the Merrick Foundation Teaching Award for bringing free enterprise into the classroom and received the Greiner Undergraduate Teaching Award in 2007 for excellence in instruction.

Dr. Nord has presented papers at international conferences in seventeen countries and is the author of numerous articles and an academic textbook.

Jeretta has provided micro financing to underprivileged entrepreneurs through Kiva.org and donated *A Cup of Cappuccino for the Entrepreneur's Spirit* books to disabled veteran entrepreneurs, women entrepreneurs in Rwanda and Afghanistan (Peace through Business Program), teachers of entrepreneurship and students aspiring to be entrepreneurs.

She enjoys traveling and learning more about the lives of entrepreneurs.